EARLY CHILDHOOD CURRICULA AND THE
DE-PATHOLOGIZING OF CHILDHOOD

RACHEL M. HEYDON AND LUIGI IANNACCI

Early Childhood Curricula and the De-pathologizing of Childhood

UNIVERSITY OF TORONTO PRESS
Toronto Buffalo London

© University of Toronto Press Incorporated 2008
Toronto Buffalo London
Printed in Canada

ISBN 978-0-8020-9768-2

Printed on acid-free paper

Library and Archives Canada Cataloguing in Publication

Heydon, Rachel, 1971–
Early childhood curricula and the de-pathologizing of
childhood / Rachel M. Heydon and Luigi Iannacci.

Includes bibliographical references and index.
ISBN 978-0-8020-9768-2

1. Early childhood education – Curricula.   2. Early childhood special
education.   3. Early childhood education – Moral and ethical aspects.
4. Children with disabilities – Education.   5. Children with social
disabilities – Education.   6. Problem children – Education.   7. Multicultural
education.   I. Iannacci, Luigi, 1970 –   II. Title.

LC4801.5.H49 2008   371.9′0472   C2007-905590-7

This book has been published with the help of a grant from the Canadian
Federation for the Humanities and Social Sciences, through the Aid to
Scholarly Publications Programme, using funds provided by the Social
Sciences and Humanities Research Council of Canada.

University of Toronto Press acknowledges the financial assistance to its
publishing program of the Canada Council for the Arts and the Ontario
Arts Council.

University of Toronto Press acknowledges the financial support for its
publishing activities of the Government of Canada through the Book
Publishing Industry Development Program (BPIDP).

Contents

Preface

Pete was the boy who broke my heart and made me ashamed of being a grown-up. A tall, wiry second-grader with physical strength like none I had ever seen, Pete would choose to spend many of his recesses and lunches with me in my resource room in our 'friendship club.' This was a space where children could take a breather from the stress of the playground or cafeteria and, with adult help, learn how to play cooperative games or have some 'alone time' with a puzzle or building material. Pete usually opted for independent play and we were slowly making strides towards having him interact in positive ways with peers. We were not pushing, though, as Pete was quick to anger and his anger was usually demonstrated by great aggression such as a fist to the nose of the person next to him, a book thrown at a principal, and tidal waves of cursing that left everyone red-faced and exhausted.

You could say I had a soft spot for Pete, but then again, as a special education teacher, I felt it my responsibility to have a soft spot for all the little 'misfits' who came through my door. I saw in Pete an angry young man who missed his mother (she was living in another town) and feared his father. We at the school did all that grown-ups in our situation with a child like Pete were supposed to do. We provided an appropriate curriculum, we built learning opportunities where we could, we monitored the case closely, and we let the requisite 'authorities' know that we had concerns about possible child abuse. We also let Pete know his options if he ever felt unsafe: If he was at school, he could tell a teacher, or if he was at home, he could dial a number.

One day the school social worker and I were called to Pete's classroom. He was being aggressive and we were to implement our safety plan: de-escalate the situation and lead Pete to a quiet room. The plan was working, sort of. We had succeeded in getting Pete to the quiet room; it just wasn't very quiet anymore. The room was stripped bare except for a couch – perfect, we thought, for a little nap (for Pete, not us) once Pete's adrenalin wore off. Today, however, Pete had somehow succeeded in lifting the couch onto its end and threatened to throw it at us. Pete was angrier than I'd ever seen him. Eventually, between the screams and inchoate words, the message came out: 'You told me there were people to keep me safe and you lied. Liars!' Then, from behind the vertical couch, Pete told us about his 'last night'. His dad had been hitting him. Yelling at him. Hurting him. Pete told his dad that he was going to call the police, that the people at school had said it was not okay to hurt people. Pete's dad allegedly told Pete to go ahead, that he hoped the police would take Pete away and lock him up because he was a 'bad seed.' Pete told us that the police did come and when the authorities investigated, it seemed that Pete's dad had the right to do to Pete what he was doing: A parent striking a child on the buttocks with an open hand is legal in Ontario, Canada. The humiliation? The pain? We at the school weren't sure how this did (or didn't) factor into the police's decision to validate Pete's dad in front of Pete or (as we later learned) not provide Pete's dad with any support to parent Pete in positive ways. What we did know was that Pete was now devastated, hopeless, and was not to trust an adult again any time soon. In the face of his narrative that day, the social worker and I hung our heads and couldn't look at each other. How could we when we knew that Pete had every right to rage?

Shortly afterwards, when Pete was diagnosed with Oppositional Defiance Disorder, medicated, sent to a 'behaviour' classroom in a distant school, and identified as pathological, I felt the shame rise up again. For I knew that if pathology existed, it belonged to us adults who failed again in our responsibility to a child.

Early Childhood Curricula is a response to Pete and to other children who have been pathologized. It is an attempt to understand how pathologies get ascribed to young children within educational contexts and to offer alternatives through instances of curricula that strive to preserve children's personhood.

Rachel M. Heydon

Acknowledgments

FROM RACHEL HEYDON

Many people have helped to make this work possible.

Thank you to the brilliant graduate students and friends who were so kind and patient with me during the course of the research, in particular: Magdalena Ciesla, Tara-Lynn Scheffel, Anne VanGilst, and Ping Wang.

Thank you to my colleagues at the Faculty of Education at The University of Western Ontario. I am particularly indebted to the staff of the Education Library who not only gave me fabulous reference assistance and made my job easier by knowing how to build a good collection, but who also helped me when my library books were late, lost, or worse.

Thank you and much love to the people who have been my partners for various parts of the research: Bridget Daly and Luigi Iannacci.

Thank you to my teachers: Sharon Rich, Roger I. Simon, Geoffrey Milburn, Kathryn Hibbert, Roz Stooke, and the educators, children, and families with whom I have had the pleasure to work.

Thank you to the funding sources that have supported the research: The University of Western Ontario, Petro Canada Young Innovators Award, the Social Sciences and Humanities Research Council of Canada Standard Research Grant, and the Canadian Society for the Study of Education New Scholar Award.

Finally, thank you to my family, especially my mother, Betty Ann Heydon.

I dedicate this book to Sean and our boy Oliver.

FROM LUIGI IANNACCI

Foremost I would like to thank my family for a lifetime of encouragement and love.

Sharon Rich's guidance and support informed and furthered my work and I thank her for her mentoring and generosity.

Kathy Hibbert, Rosamund Stooke, Teresa Van Deven, and Rachel Heydon continue to be incredibly committed educators and friends who have tried to help me understand my assets and affirmed the importance of celebrating others. I would especially like to acknowledge Rachel Heydon for her unwavering dedication to this project and to our friendship.

Grants from the Social Sciences and Humanities Research Council of Canada allowed important components of my research to come to fruition. I thank them for their support.

Finally, I would like to thank the Ascension/Malton crew and all my friends who have consistently believed in me for many years.

I dedicate this book to all the teachers, parents, and, most importantly, the children, from whom I have had the privilege of learning throughout my research and teaching career.

Versions or portions of four chapters have been published elsewhere and used here with permission of the publishers:

Heydon, R. (2007). Making meaning together: Multimodal literacy learning opportunities in an intergenerational art program. *Journal of Curriculum Studies. 39*(1), 35–62.

Heydon, R. (2005). The de-pathologizing of childhood, disability and aging in an intergenerational art class: Implications for educators. *Journal of Early Childhood Research, 3*(3), 243–268.

Heydon, R. (2005). The theory and practice of pedagogical ethics: Features for an ethical praxis in/out of special education. *Journal of Curriculum Studies, 37*(4), 381–394.

Heydon, R., & Iannacci, L. (2005). Biomedical literacy: Two curriculum teachers challenge the treatment of dis/ability in contemporary literacy education. *Language & Literacy, 7*(2), Retrieved 21 August 2006, from http://www.langandlit.ualberta.ca/archivesDate.html.

EARLY CHILDHOOD CURRICULA AND THE DE-PATHOLOGIZING OF CHILDHOOD

1
Introduction

Defining Pathologizing

Before we can begin to define and illustrate asset-oriented practices, we must first examine the phenomenon of *pathologizing* – the unfortunate consequence of a number of curricular practices. Most simply, the word pathologizing refers to the processes by which persons belonging to a particular group are seen by a more powerful group as abnormal. This supposed abnormality is perceived to be in need of correction, usually through medical or "scientific" intervention. As we will show, children who are culturally and linguistically diverse (CLD)[1] or disabled most often make up the pathologized groups. In a more comprehensive definition, Shields, Bishop, and Mazawi (2005) explain pathologizing as the processes whereby 'perceived structural-functional, cultural, or epistemological deviation from an assumed normal state is ascribed to another group as a product of power relationships, whereby the less powerful group is deemed to be abnormal in some way' (p. x).

---

1 We have chosen to use the term culturally and linguistically diverse (CLD) (Herrera & Murry, 2005) to refer to children who elsewhere are designated as English as a Second Language (ESL) learners, English Language Learners (ELL), or English as an Additional Language learners (EAL). At the time of the research for the book, ESL was the official designation in Ontario of children for whom English was not their first language. ESL and ELL are problematic since they focus on the language the child is acquiring rather than on the existing funds of knowledge in his or her first language. EAL is also problematic as it puts English at the forefront. Consequently, these labels see low English-language skills as a deficiency. CLD, on the other hand, while not without its own problems, at least has the advantage of making positive use of the dominant language and culture and thus makes explicit a child's resources.

Pathologizing is a recognizable phenomenon within psychology where a less powerful patient is viewed as abnormal and where pathologizing becomes a 'mode of colonization that is used to govern and manage through health measures' (Shields, Bishop, & Mazawi, 2005, p. xix).

In their recent, important book on the issue, *Pathologizing Practices: The Impact of Deficit Thinking on Education*, Shields et al. (2005) document cases in the education of Navajo adolescents in Utah, Maori adolescents in New Zealand, and Bedouin Arab children and adolescents in Israel, where specific forms of curricula, including pedagogy, led to the pathologizing of the social categories to which these youth belong. Through these cases, Shields et al. illustrate how pathologizing within education takes many forms. Most salient is the ascription of 'deficiency' to 'the characteristics of difference' (p. xix), with these deficiencies being seen as located within the 'lived experiences of children (home life, home culture, socioeconomic status)' rather than in 'the education system itself' (p. xx). They also show how pathologizing can result in the regulation and marginalization of a less powerful group and can have devastating effects not only on people's academic achievements, life-course options, or identity options, but also on families and communities. This leads us to ask, what is lost, individually and collectively, when children's diverse 'funds of knowledge' (Moll, 1992) are unrecognized, or worse, seen as impediments to dominant ways of knowing? Funds of knowledge are the resources that children bring to school or other learning situations. These resources can be cultural, intellectual, physical, and the like.

Who We Are, What We Believe, and What We Hope to Accomplish

The problem of pathologizing within early childhood and early childhood education (ECE) is complex and caused by a number of factors. As a result, the development of a theory by which curricula might be created to reverse the pathologizing process requires an interdisciplinary approach. With regard to terminology, we have settled temporarily on the word *de*-pathologizing to describe this process of theory development, because it keeps us within the framework of the work already done by Shields et al. (2005) and allows us to confront the destructive process of pathologizing. We are hesitant about the term, however, as it is phrased in the negative. It thus does not convey the positive approach that we would like to take to early childhood curriculum development. Yet, rather than do away with the term, for the moment we have chosen to supplement it. When we thought about the shift in curricular paradigms we hoped to encourage by our work, we decided to use the phrase *asset-oriented* in conjunction with de-pathologizing. We felt the term asset-oriented suggested a positive approach towards curricula that began from children's knowledge.

Semantics aside, there is much we want to accomplish in this book. We are two curriculum studies and childhood studies researchers whose work is laid on a foundation of experiences as teachers of children who have been pathologized. We therefore have seen first-hand, and sometimes even unwittingly been party to, the processes that take children entering school spaces as people with desires, experiences, world views, and meaning-making abilities, and turn them into 'others' who are seen as deficient and in need of curing. *Early Childhood Curricula* attempts to extend the understanding of the processes of pathologizing as they relate specifically to children pre-school to age 8 and to offer examples of learning spaces within the 'minority world'[2] (Dahlberg, Moss, & Pence, 1999, p. 6) where asset-oriented visions of children and childhood are born and nurtured. From the studies and experiences that inform these chapters, we hope to generate an understanding of the theoretical underpinnings of asset-oriented practices and promote some of what is possible for children when their education begins from their own knowledge.

The beliefs that underpin this book are based on an understanding of childhood that is supported by the field of childhood studies, the theories and practices of critical theory with its goal of emancipation (Habermas, 1972), and theories of the postmodern age with their goal of deconstruction (Lather, 1991). We believe:

- What constitutes childhood is not self-evident; childhood is culturally mediated and therefore dependent upon situation (e.g., time and place) (Gittins, 2004; Jenks, 2004; Rogers, 2004);
- Adult conceptualizations of childhood influence what adults ask of children (David, Raban, Ure, Goouch, Jago, & Barriere, 2000);
- The educational opportunities adults create for children bespeak adult conceptualizations of childhood as well as adult desires;
- Investigating childhood is important for understanding pathologizing from a macro perspective. Still, any understanding of childhood

---

2 Dahlberg et al. (1999) use the term 'minority world' to refer to what is commonly referred to as the 'developed world' (i.e., western nations).

must also be grounded in the actualities of children's lives (Thew, 2000);
- So with the theorizing from early literacy (e.g., Gillen & Hall, 2003), we see children's practices not merely as lesser versions of adult practices, but as valuable in their own right;
- By extension, 'childhood as an important phase in life in its own right' must be preserved (David et al., 2000, p. 21);
- This preservation is part of a package of rights that includes recognition of children's personhood, citizenship, and quality of life; these must be at the forefront of social (including educational) agendas;
- A discourse for this package of rights still needs to be generated that can be interpreted in children's own terms as well as encompass and respect the diversity of children's cultures, languages, and the like (Rogers, 2004);
- Education, as an organizer of childhood in the minority world, is of key importance in the study of pathologizing and de-pathologizing; and
- Education can be an act of hope that expands rather than limits what is possible for children, society, and the world (e.g., Simon, 1992).

Our Readers

Early Childhood Curricula is intended primarily for educators interested in improving the lives of children through interdisciplinary studies. As far as we know, it is one of the first books to look at the processes of pathologizing of childhood and young children in Canada where there is a dearth of literature in childhood studies. Although there have been studies concerning the pathologizing of childhood and children in the United States (e.g., Cannella & Viruru, 2004; Shields et al. 2005), there is ample room for volumes concerning de-pathologizing processes especially as they pertain to young children who live in poverty, are CLD, and/or have disabilities.

While most of the studies in the book are Canadian, the book is intended to be of use both in and outside North America. The book can be of use outside Canada as the trends that it identifies are, sadly, all too common to much of the minority world. As chapter 2 demonstrates, deficit-oriented discourses for minoritized children (and their families) and the process of pathologizing are not new. More recently, however, educational systems in the UK, New Zealand, and Australia have experienced many of the same social, economic, and political pressures (e.g.,

David et al. 2000; Devine, 2003). Chapter 2 expands on some of these pressures in an effort to chart their effects on children and childhood: the other chapters equally attempt to extend the literature by offering new cases that illuminate both the processes of pathologizing and de-pathologizing. Another reason why the Canadian situation may be of considerable concern to a variety of international scholars is that Canada has some challenges (and opportunities) that other countries are beginning to encounter. In particular, because Canada has some of the most culturally and linguistically diverse cities in the world, Canadian public school populations are very diverse. The Greater Toronto Area, for instance, has more foreign-born residents as a percentage of its population (43.7%) than any other city in the world (People for Education, 2005). Thus, this book provides comparative data as well as findings that may be transferable (Donmoyer, 2001) and of interest to other minority world countries experiencing unprecedented global mobility. *Early Childhood Curricula* offers readers:

- A critical look at a range of pathologizing processes in early childhood contexts;
- A window into young children's diverse learning environments and the ways in which children and childhood are positioned within them;
- Detailed illustrations of practices that support de-pathologizing;
- Sustained theoretical engagement with the processes of de-pathologizing; and
- An argument compelling through its use of narrative, vignettes, as well as theoretical rigour.

In the end, what readers may take away from the book are detailed portraits of children and their learning as seen through the eyes of the teacher/researchers who hope their stories can make a difference.

Macro-organizers of Pathologizing: What the Literature Communicates

An emerging body of work has produced a good general understanding of some of the processes of pathologizing and provides the basis for *Early Childhood Curricula*. For example, although Shields et al. (2005) firmly illustrate how particular educational *practices* produce pathologies, pathologizing, they say, is aided by specific, hegemonic discourses.

They define these discourses as 'the meanings we [the minority world] have adopted and that we manifest in positing – thoughts, words and actions that are shaped by power relations and that provide a complex network of images and metaphors that determines, in large part, how we think and act vis-à-vis a given topic.' (p. xvi). Borrowing from Foucault, Shields et al. demonstrate how discourses shape what Smith (1999) calls the 'actualities' of people's 'everyday/everynight lives' (p. 4) in educational settings. Importantly, Smith (1987), who also operates from a Foucauldian notion of discourse, points out that discourses are part of the 'relations of ruling,' 'a complex of organized practices, including government, law, business and financial management, professional organizations, and educational institutions as well as the discourses in texts that interpenetrate the multiple sites of power' (p. 3). Hence, educational discourses affect and are affected by discourses from other institutions. Stooke (2004) emphasizes that discourses of ruling 'consistently privilege the interests of the most powerful groups in a society' (p. 40). Of course, because these discourses are hegemonic, they are difficult, although not impossible to perceive.

Discourses of ruling carry with them particular theoretical frames and ways of knowing that make pathologizing practices possible. For example, a decades-old key discourse of ruling that has made pathologizing possible in education is the technical-rational one. Commonly known through Freire's (1970) critique of the 'banking model' of education, this discourse has had a strong place within education since at least 1949 when Tyler introduced his notion of 'backwards design' (i.e., where the end is determined first, and then a method is selected for achieving that end). The technical-rational discourse is typified in Tyler's reflections on his approach to curriculum planning. For instance, he describes backwards design as 'a practical enterprise, not a theoretical study. It endeavours to design a system to achieve an education and is not primarily attempting to explain an existential phenomenon' (Tyler as cited in Marsh, 2004, p. 202). Marsh reads Tyler's approach as 'primarily a way of simplifying complex situations sufficiently so that plans and procedures can be carried out rationally – that is, in ways that people engaged in the process can understand and, at least potentially, reach agreement about' (p. 203). Many of the cases in the book illustrate how technical-rational discourses and curricula descended from backwards design are manifest in children's lives. It is evident that they all have in common the favouring of practices that reject diversity and complexity for uniformity and efficiency.

Technical-rational discourses and their accompanying practices are today perhaps more dominant and problematic than ever. In an era of unprecedented multiplicity of language, culture, and religion as well as widening class divisions that would seem to demand a firm engagement with diversity and complexity, the trend is instead towards efficiency to such an extreme that it has become a 'cult' (Stein, 2001). Stein explains that a cult of efficiency emerges when efficiency becomes a value or end unto itself rather than a vehicle to other socially important values. This, she says, is currently the situation in public institutions such as education and health care. It could be that one of the reasons for the proliferation of the cult of efficiency is its political expedience. Stein posits: 'Political leaders often prefer to put the debates that engage our most important and contested values into a supposedly neutral measuring cup. They do so to mask the underlying differences in values and purposes, and to dampen political disagreements. They seek the consensus they need and the political protection they want by transforming conflict over purpose into discussion of measures, and in the process they hide and evade differences about values and goals' (p. 198). It is perhaps unproductive to argue about the intent of politicians and other policy makers who maintain the cult of efficiency, since intent is often unknowable. What can be known, however, is effect; focusing on a vacuous value such as efficiency has the effect of obscuring the vital question of what values and knowledge should be promoted in public institutions within pluralistic societies.

Technical-rational discourses allow for an easy acceptance of practices predicated on instrumental theories aimed at offering a degree of predictability and control (Habermas, 1972). For instance, in Ontario, all elementary curricula are, standardized and strictly outcomes-based (see, e.g., Ontario Ministry of Education, 2006a, 2006b). When these curricula are combined with standardized assessments, high-stakes testing, and standardized report cards, the question of methodology (i.e., efficiency) takes precedence over questions of content and what knowledge is of most value, to whom, and with what consequences. This kind of instrumental, outcomes-based efficiency fails to address the questions of who children are as people and what knowledge they possess. This is especially troubling when one considers that Ontario has an area of more than a million km^2 (Government of Ontario, 2005) and is also, as we have mentioned, so culturally and linguistically diverse: Approximately 28% of the population have a mother tongue other than English, and the languages spoken range from Chinese, Punjabi, and Arabic to Inuktitut and Cree (Statistics Canada, 2001).

Practices commensurate with technical-rational discourses, instrumental theories, and the cult of efficiency can all support views of knowledge that foster pathologizing. For instance, standardized curricula establish what is officially condoned as knowledge. Official knowledge is therefore a closed body of knowledge. When taken together with mechanisms such as standardized report cards and standardized assessments, this design limits the degree to which educators in schools can recognize or be responsive to the knowledge children bring to school (Heydon & Wang, 2006). Closed knowledge systems and the practices they allow, or disallow, can predispose educators to see students and children in particular ways. Standardized practices, for example, are predicated upon a notion of a *standard student* and by extension, a *standard child*. As Shields et al. (2005) demonstrate and as we have also argued (Heydon & Iannacci, 2005; Heydon, 2005), germane to the processes of pathologizing is a view of the world that divides the student population into normal and abnormal. Abnormal children do not easily integrate into standard instrumental systems and therefore they begin to cause problems in the system. The processes of pathologizing, however, instead positions children as pathological and in need of fixing. This can protect the system from criticism. Moreover, governments and their institutions (e.g., schools) are working for such high stakes, that they attempt to predict which students will cause them difficulty (see chapter 2). We therefore see the troublesome and ubiquitous category of 'at-risk' student to be an instrumental trope for predicting and controlling the standard.

Who 'Gets' Pathologized?

Although the processes of pathologizing affect individuals, these specific individuals are not necessarily the targets of pathologizing; rather, the targets are the markers (e.g., race, class, language, ethnicity, ability, etc.) that position individuals socially. It is significant that the meaning ascribed to these markers by ruling discourses is never static; it is instead situational (i.e., tied to the specifics of time and place and other markers).

Undoubtedly, as evidenced in Shields et al. (2005) and others (e.g., Iannacci, 2005), the markers 'ethnic minority' and/or 'linguistic minority' have been prime targets for pathologizing practices. This was the case, for example, with the group of Bedouin Arab children in Shields et al.'s (2005) study. Showing the situatedness of markers, however, this group's pathologizing was possible because it was being viewed within Israel through Israeli ruling discourses at a point in history when tensions between the two groups were running high. Thus, such markers in another locale may not have engendered the same response.

Pathologizing is assisted by discourses that minoritize groups of students even when these students are the numerical majority. Shields et al. (2005) explains: 'McCarty (2002) uses the term *minoritized* rather than *minority* to stress the importance of institutional and societal power structures that have marginalized a group that by virtue of sheer numbers alone (one could argue) should have the dominant, legitimate, decision-making voice' (p. 26).

Another example of the situatedness of markers is found in Hicks's (2002) painstaking documentation of the pathologizing of white, poor, and working-class children in the United States. The impetus for her study came from her observation that, because there is limited class-consciousness within the United States, 'white poor and working-class children are viewed negatively but without cultural sensitivity' (p. 4). Hicks's research participants, for instance, were viewed as deficient by their teachers and their knowledge went unrecognized. Hicks constrasts this alleged insensitivity with the situation in Great Britain, where, she claims, researchers and educators are far more attuned to class issues. According to Hicks, this implies that the category of poor and working class in Great Britain is perhaps less likely to be seen as deficient and more likely to be recognized as having a culture and therefore knowledge that is simply *different* from the middle and upper classes.

Gender has also been a situational marker for pathologizing. For instance, boys are more likely to be identified as behaviour-disordered than girls. The ruling discourses (in this case psychology and special education) take such an identification to be pathological and in need of a cure (see, for example, Heydon, 2005; Mickelson, 2000). Behaviour disorders, however, fall within the 'non-normative' category of disability (Rodriguez, 1999). Contrary to 'normative' categories where 'even if the category opened to debate, [there] would [be] some normative agreement between professionals and non-professionals that a disability is present,' non-normative categories are 'open to interpretation in light of their social, historical, and political circumstances' (p. 398). Thus, in the case of behaviour disorders, boys may be identified as behaviourally exceptional at least in part due to the ways in which the ruling discourses construct their sex and the ways in which they practise their gender. In other settings such as sports, this same sex and these same practices could be viewed as normal or even desirable rather than pathological.

Even if one's view of the world did support the notion that behaviour disorders are germane to boys for reasons apart from sociological ones, it is important to note that other markers may also play a role in the pathologizing of the category. For instance in the literature on the aetiology of childhood behaviour disorders, the categories of poverty and 'single-motherhood' are associated with risk (e.g., O'Shea, O'Shea, Algozzine, & Hammitte, 2001). Consequently, a parent's gender, one's family configuration, and one's class all play a role in this form of pathologizing.

Last in our illustrations of the range of situational markers identified as connected to pathologizing is disability. The category of children with disabilities has almost exclusively been the purview of an ableist special education that finds that 'it is most desirable to be physically, psychologically, and cognitively the 'same' as the majority of the population' (Heydon & Iannacci, 2005, p. 4). As such, disability is pathologized and seen as something that needs to be eradicated. Disability, however, may be no more pathological than being poor or male. Instead, we choose to heed the examples from disability studies such as deaf culture's assertion that deafness and hearing are not 'audiological conditions but epistemological constructs' (Baker, 2002, p. 47). Thus disability as a social marker may be pathologized, yet disability to an individual with a disability may instead be another form of knowing and identity.

Our discussion has shown only a glimpse of the complexities that surround pathologizing and some of the social markers and circumstances that can affect its processes. It is noteworthy that, while markers may be situational, all categories of children do not hold the same access to privilege within schools where ruling discourses greatly correspond to white, middle-class ways of knowing and views of the world (e.g., Delpit, 1995; Delpit & Dowdy, 2002; Heath, 1983; McLaren, 1993). As this quick introduction to the processes of pathologizing shows, studies in pathologizing are richer when the markers of race, class, gender, ability, and the like are considered together, within context, and in relation to the ruling discourse(s). This 'intersectionality thesis' (McLaren, 2006, p. 87) is a foundational understanding within the sociology of education and within the book.

Structure of the Book

Early Childhood Curricula highlights some of the trends in the pathologizing and de-pathologizing of children and childhood. The first half of the book addresses pathologizing in particular circumstances and the second half provides examples of practice that build from children's assets: their knowledge and their emerging senses of identity. While we have resisted providing a firm definition of asset-oriented practices in this first chapter, allowing instead the discussion to go on in the last chapter where it can flow from the presentation of the studies, it is critical to state that such practices should not be confused with simplistic 'methods-based' solutions. Murphy (2006), for instance, cautions: 'It is true that in education, we sometimes talk about building on children's strengths, but this demand can lead us into pop psychology fixes and can result in children being given labels like "visual learner" or "right brained." A more interesting challenge, I believe, would be to move away from the idea of strengths and to switch to the idea of children's knowledge' (pp. 9–10). This move to children's knowledge is one that demands that educators consider what forms of knowledge are currently privileged in ECE (e.g., adult knowledge and know-how that comes from dominant racial, socio-economic groups) as opposed to what is often marginalized (e.g., children's knowledge and ways of knowing, particularly if children are minoritized). The move also stresses that educators consider what they take to 'be in the world' and how this compares to what minoritized groups take to be in the world.

The theorizing in *Early Childhood Curricula* is predicated upon our experiences as teachers and qualitative studies we have each conducted over the last seven or so years. Each of the studies adds a new dimension to the questions of pathologizing and de-pathologizing practices. Because the markers of pathologizing are situational, as too are the processes of pathologizing and de-pathologizing, the studies function like those in Shields et al. (2005): They allow for in-depth illustrations of specific contexts and the people who create and inhabit them. This 'learning amid the smallness of lived histories' (Hicks, 2002, p. 14) can be a way of learning 'from' rather than 'about' (Todd, 2003) people and situations. This is an ethical posture towards research participants in that it recognizes that, while individual subjects have much to teach about the larger cognitive and social patterns of teaching and learning, each person has his or her own unique story or set of stories that adds to a particular understanding of the whole. Hence, in the following chapters we move back and forth between the 'small' (the particularities of the cases) and the 'large' (the linking up with sociological trends and the call for transferability). Through this process we equally attempt to ensure that our positions in the research and writing are as evident as possible. This emphasis on the particular and on research knowledge as only ever partial, Hicks (2002) warns, is in direct conflict with the discourses that have traditionally dominated educational theory and practice, namely, those of developmental psychology. As many of the following chapters demonstrate, instrumental forms of psychology (of which developmental psychology is one), with their goals of predictability and control (Habermas, 1972) aim to universalize experience. Spotlighting universality and generalization can result in theories that violate the view of children as unique individuals. Developmentalism, for example, as the 'construction of a linear, sequential and normalized process by which children become adults' (Alldred, 1998, p. 150), belies children's agency in the creation of their own ongoing subject formation.

Hicks (2002) responds to the problem of the hegemony of instrumental psychology in education by evoking what she terms 'hybrid languages of inquiry' (p. 37): theories, methodologies, and prose that 'cut across boundaries of psychology, feminist theory, literacy research, and philosophy' (p. 14). While *Early Childhood Curricula* certainly works in this same vein, we prefer to call its form 'syncretic' (Gregory, Long, and Volk, 2004) to signal that our work draws on known methodologies (e.g., ethnography, narrative, and case study), theories (critical and postmodern), and forms (e.g., prose narratives and essays) but does so in a way that creates something new rather than a mere amalgam of the old. Our syncretism is a reflection of our ethical desire to depict smallness and its various relations to largeness, to make prominent our investments in the process, and to gesture towards the limits of knowledge.

Each chapter contributes to the recursive small and large views that build to a synthesis of ideas (although not a conflation of the distinctive aspects of the studies) in chapter 8. At the same time, some chapters focus more heavily on one or the other view.

Chapter 2 provides a wide-angle shot of the context in which children are trying to learn and teachers to teach. It is an overview of some minority countries' policies and programs for young children that focus on childhood as a time to 'get it right,' that is, to create children who are free of disability and able to be good workers. It draws on literature that argues that this construction of childhood as mainly a time of preparation for the workforce is related to governments' anxieties over contemporary socio-economic woes. Moreover, the chapter demonstrates how the creation of the category 'at-risk' launches a war on what it sees as child pathology, when what might be more helpful to children is to look at how contexts themselves (e.g, underfunded public schooling and governments that allow child poverty to go unaddressed) *put* children at risk. This chapter also foreshadows some of the devastating effects described in subsequent chapters of the marriage between economic discourses and the promise of science to cure or prevent pathologies.

Chapter 3 illustrates one instance of a scientific cure. It is based on a study of the early literacy curricula of Elmwood[3] school, a school deemed by the school district to be 'compensatory' due to its high proportion of children designated as poor and CLD. When he was looking for appropriate sites in which to conduct research into early years programs for CLD students, Luigi's research design called for sites in neighbourhoods with differing socio-economic statuses (SES) and high CLD populations. Elmwood was one of the schools the school district identified as meeting his research design criteria. Rachel was a teacher at this school. This chapter provides a portrait of a particular brand of deficit-oriented discourse and curriculum that lays the foundation for the following two chapters.

Chapter 4 sharpens the lens to two early-years classrooms at Elmwood and their counterparts at a school with a higher SES. Through the 'complex particularit[ies]' (Hicks, 2002, p. 12) of these classrooms, the chapter details the assessment practices and literacy curricula these groups of young CLD children were offered and the subsequent 'identity options' (Cummins, 2005) made available to them.

Chapter 5 rounds out the exploration of the processes of pathologizing and the intersections between social markers and identity options (e.g., normal or abnormal) by drawing on a narrative inquiry of Rachel's memories as a teacher of a young child identified as behaviourally disordered. Using a teacher's analytic lens, the chapter sketches how class, gender, and ability were taken up within the circumstance of special education.

Chapter 6 signals a shift in *Early Childhood Curricula*. In our effort to advance theoretical and practical emancipation, the remainder of the book is committed to providing cases that highlight situations and

---

3 Names of schools, students, and staff discussed in this book are pseudonyms.

practices that are based on children's assets. Chapter 6 examines an innovative, intergenerational, shared-site learning centre where elders and children share space and programming. The chapter looks at the way the centre's curriculum positions childhood as a time when quality of life is a significant concern and children have the opportunity to be seen as fully contributing members of learning communities.

Chapter 7 returns to some of the CLD children in chapters 3 and 4 to illustrate a variety of de-pathologizing practices that derive from the children's own languages, ways of knowing, and views of the world.

All of the studies in the book coalesce in chapter 8, which moves towards theorizing de-pathologizing and asset-oriented practices in ECE. This chapter provides talking-points for educators to consider how de-pathologizing and asset-oriented practices can be developed within their own unique contexts. As such, the chapter attempts to avoid authoritative theories or practices.

Our Investment

Both of us were school teachers who became educational researchers to try to understand why aspects of our practice and the structures in which we taught felt so painful at times for ourselves and, more importantly, for our students. Having been pathologized as children because of our SES (Rachel) and cultural and linguistic diversity (Luigi), we brought to our teaching a sensitivity, although not necessarily a theoretical understanding, of how the social categories to which our students belonged colluded with powerful discourses of ruling to render them abnormal and in need of curing. As researchers, we have been drawn to critical theory with its goal of emancipation and to postmodern theories with their goal of deconstruction. We see emancipation in Habermas' (1972) terms, which ask that we attempt to make sense of the world by 'determin[ing] when theoretical statements grasp invariant regularities of social action as such and when they express ideologically frozen relations of dependence that can in principle be transformed' (p. 310). This means that one must uncover what presents itself as 'natural' or given and then make apparent the points of view from which such versions of 'reality' are constructed (p. 311). Once emancipated from what is taken-for-granted, one can begin to consider the various ways of seeing and being in a situation. This is where newness and possibility might enter. One must also be prepared to 'deconstruct' what one takes for granted, particularly in reference to one's own visions of the world. In this way, to deconstruct is to grapple with the 'limits' (Cornell, 1992) of one's own understandings. This can be an ethical invitation to learn from the other (Todd, 2003). By using the sociological understanding of identity that has come from childhood and disability studies, we have been able to begin to make sense of the origins of some pathologizing practices. Now we are able to turn our attention to curricula that show the potential beauty of early childhood learning.

Authorial Voice

We are closely affiliated colleagues who have known each other for many years. As a result we have collaborated on some of the studies in this book, and in others have lived *alongside* each other's work, offering support through encouragement and critique. We have come together here with the common investment we described above. We are, however, individuals who have different insights to share and lessons to learn. Although we understand that it is often pleasing to readers to deal with one voice in a text since this can create an even, relatively seamless read, we cannot pretend we are always one voice. Insofar as possible we have tried to create a common tone in the book by using similar language and by drawing on the same theoretical framework. There are moments, however, when we assert our individuality, such as in the chapters we identify as individually authored. As in the lesson that Brookes & Kelly (1989) teach in their collaborative writing on critical pedagogy where they retain their individual voices, we would like the moments of transition in the book to be read not as failures of the text, but rather as reminders that texts are never innocent: They are always created by embodied authors who have their own desires and agendas and who are rooted within particular times and places. In choosing to write the book in the way we have, we are also heeding Levinas's (1991) ethic of 'unsaying the said,' that is, of refusing to allow the text to become too smooth, too authoritative, as though it were unauthored. What is perhaps most unifying about *Early Childhood Curricula* is the spirit in which it is written. We have composed this book to share with other educators what we have learned from children, and we offer it with humility and gratitude.

2
Discourses of Risk

RACHEL M. HEYDON

Until recently, I worked as a special education teacher in Ontario, Canada. In that role I often helped families (usually mothers) procure auxiliary services (e.g., mental health support, psychiatric treatment, etc.) for their children. I witnessed much suffering and learned that asking for help takes courage. It therefore struck me as unethical that in the waiting room of one of the main child-services buildings in my area, there hung a sign that compared the 'low' dollar cost of helping children 'now' to the dollar cost of helping them 'later' (i.e., for incarceration, social assistance, etc.). While the sign offended me (I cannot imagine what families in need must have thought of it), in retrospect it did not surprise me. Approaches to childhood, especially in education, have increasingly become part of Stein's (2001) cult of efficiency where standardization, narrow curricula, and high surveillance are the drivers of cost efficiency; children are seen as just another form of capital. We, the public, are told that institutions such as schools need to prepare children to become workers and that to survive in the new economy certain kinds of knowledge and skills will be required 'or else.' Of course this type of discourse has many problematic aspects, not the least of which is that of putting a dollar amount on what children deserve and measuring value by what will fuel the economy. At the very least, such an approach ignores children's lives as significant in their own right. Unfortunately, this trend extends beyond my experiences, Canada's borders, or even children's lives.

Today, every person is judged in these economic terms; people are seen as capital and 'human worth' is evaluated 'against the value of humans as a 'source of wealth,' like natural resources' (Weiner, 2005, p. 5). How people fare within this evaluation is influenced to some degree, as discussed in chapter 1, by the particularities that mark them socially (e.g., gender, class, race, age, ability, etc.). Through an examination of the minority world's current preoccupation with the identification of children 'at-risk' for disability, this chapter explores some contemporary discourses that create and reflect conditions that enable pathologizing.

Children at Risk? Children at Promise?

Just over a decade ago, Swadener and Lubeck (1995a), recognizing the ubiquity of the term 'at-risk' and its pernicious nature within educational policy, produced the important, *Children and Families 'At Promise': Deconstructing the Discourse of Risk*. This volume unearths and challenges the assumptions that underlie the discourse of risk such as its use of 'a medical *language of pathology* [italics in original] to label persons based on their race, first language, class, family structure, geographic location, and gender as 'at risk for failure" (Swadener & Lubeck, 1995b, p. 2.). As with the processes of pathologizing described in chapter 1, Swadener and Lubeck pinpoint how an at-risk, deficit-driven discourse perpetuates the 'myth of the meritocracy' by placing blame for 'problems' or 'pathologies' (including poverty) within children (and/or families) themselves (p. 3). Swadener (1995) demonstrates how the identification of individuals as at-risk is at least a couple of hundred years old; however, more recently, 'children belonging to specified ethnic and language groups [have] been added as major 'risk' categories and thus become a major focus of social concern and public responsibility" (Laosa as cited in Swadener, 1995, pp. 26–27). In further tracing the development of the at-risk discourse, Swadener (1995) found that it was born of and perpetuated through a number of intersecting disciplines 'including medicine and public health, sociology, child welfare and social work, developmental psychology, early childhood education, special education, public policy, economics, and demography' (p. 21). Reinforcing the at-risk discourse's pervasiveness is Fine's (1995) observation that it is compatible with agendas from both sides of the political spectrum: 'The desire to isolate these people [i.e., people seen to be at risk], by the Right, and to display them, by the Left' (p. 76). Regardless of the agenda, the outcome of evoking the discourse is the same: segregation that creates and perpetuates a lampoon of atrisk children and their families. In Fine's words, the discourse creates a 'shaved and quite partial image' of an objectified other, which 'strengthens those institutions and groups which have carved out, severed, denied connection, and then promised to 'save' those who will undoubtedly remain 'at risk" (p. 76). Thus, curricula and policies for at-risk children proceed from a deficit-oriented view where children are seen to exist with a 'lack' (e.g., a lack of skills, knowledge, etc.). Swadener and Lubeck's (1995a) volume asks the important question: If the at-risk discourse were inverted and children seen as 'at-promise,' that is, in ways that recognize what they bring to school, what would curricula and policies look like?

Swadener and Lubeck (1995a) chronicle the various, complex, and self-perpetuating workings of the at-risk discourse. Particularly important is the relationship between the at-risk individual as the site of blame for that risk and the dominant society's attempts to maintain privilege. Swadener and Lubeck show, for instance, that one of the mechanisms supporting this relationship is the omission of 'an interrogation of privilege and the possibility that a more equitable distribution of materials, resources, education, power, and self-sufficiency may' (p. 2) do away with the structural impediments that have been largely responsible for holding back at-risk children's successes. Swadener and Lubeck (1995b) draw on Polakow's (1993) position that the corollary of children at risk is in fact 'privilege [my italics] at risk' (p. 2), a tacit fear that one's own privilege could be taken away if social equity were seriously addressed. A way of retaining one's privilege, Swadener (1995) suggests by again drawing on Polakow (1993), is through the use of cost-benefit accountability, an if-we-don't-get-out-more-than-we-put-in-forget-it mentality that is echoed in the opening of this chapter. This type of accountability figures the at-risk discourse as a circle because it again blames the victim or sees poverty as a private rather than public affair that feeds the economic discourse. As Polakow (1995) in Swadener and Lubeck (1995a) pointedly argues, when 'the education of children' and 'poverty' are configured as private affairs, the following is understood by the architects and users of the discourse: 'First, *if* public money is to be spent, it should always be *less*, rather than *more* – part of the leftovers doled out from otherwise expansive budgets. Second, poor families should have *poor* children, whose lives should be less than those of other children, maintaining their second-class status ... [Children] are deserving of public money only if investment in their lives has clear economic payoffs ... Poor children are cheap. They matter instrumentally, not existentially' (p. 265–266). The instrumental use of children can be observed in Swadener's (1995) analysis of the metaphors used in the at-risk discourse. Expanding the notion of the relationship between privilege, what and who are at-risk, and the economy, Swadener strikes upon Pellicano's (1987) identification of the 'domestic third world' metaphor: an image created by the minority world's fear of 'becoming a "Third World" inhabited by individuals who are dependent, underdeveloped and non-competitive' (as cited in Swadener, 1995, p. 68). Subsumed within the metaphor is the sense that at-risk children and the families said to produce them are the pivotal risk factors in the loss of a privileged world. The at-risk discourse is an apparent means of controlling this risk while not giving up one's privilege; public education then becomes the repository for the anxiety of risk. As Fine (1995) says, 'Perhaps no field surpasses public education as the space into which public anxieties, terrors, and 'pathologies' are so routinely shoved, only to be transformed into public policies of what must be done to save "us" from "them."' (p. 77).

Following the publication of *Children and Families At-Promise,* many researchers continue to note both the presence of the fear that Fine describes and the dominant belief in the minority world that the right kind of education can be a salve for this fear (e.g., David et al. 2000; Giroux, 2006; Segall, 2006). The tenacity of this trend has raised the question of what has happened since Swadener and Lubeck's (1995a) call to see children and their families in asset-oriented ways. The rest of this chapter explores this question. It takes as its starting point Lubeck's (2000) observation that Dahlberg et al. (1999) are correct when they claim that a central contemporary image of the child is 'the child as knowledge, identity, and cultural reproducer' (p. 277). This, Lubeck (2000) says, 'is the child who must be ready to learn and ready to take her place as a future worker in a globalized economy' (p. 277). Although this image of the child was certainly salient when Swadener & Lubeck were writing (1995a), a new branch of the at-risk discourse has since developed that is in-line with the risk of privilege. To illustrate, I draw a connection between two vulnerable social groups: young children and persons with disabilities.

Young Children and Persons with Disabilities: The Ties That Bind

Chapter 1 outlined the notion that what constitutes childhood is context-specific. This form of theorizing can be equally well applied to other socially vulnerable groups such as persons with disabilities. Within education, disability has traditionally been the domain of special education with its emphasis on disability as pathology (Skrtic, 1995), the individual as the site of that pathology (Heydon, 2005), and the perceived need to eradicate disability to achieve homogeneity (Baker, 2002b). The presumption is that it is best to be the same as the dominant, able group. This approach can, therefore, be aptly described as ableist. A critical postmodern theoretical framework described in chapter 1 as seeking the goals of emancipation and deconstruction counters the ableist and special-education approach to disability by finding that disability is not inherently pathological, but is rendered so by its social, historical, and cultural positioning. Disability can therefore be seen as the 'interpretation of a particular person's differences as perceived by others through a normative framework' (Gallagher, 2004, p. 2). This approach is not, however, an erasure of the materiality of disability; it is an assertion that 'disability is a reading of bodily particularities in the context of social power relations' (Thomson, 1997, p. 6) and an acknowledgment that the particularities making a difference are situational.

Although childhood is not the same as disability, the ways in which childhood and disability are taken up socially share commonalities.

These include the ways in which:
- both categories are social constructs that are seen as pathological or potentially pathological states;
- persons within the categories are judged against the image of the 'normate,' that is, 'the constructed identity of those who, by way of the bodily configurations and cultural capital they assume, can step into a position of authority and wield the power it grants them' (Thomson, 1997, p. 8);
- this evaluation affects persons' quality of life;
- persons so categorized are viewed in deficit terms (i.e., what they cannot do, with little acknowledgment of what they can do);
- what persons cannot do may be caused by the environment being set up to service the normate (although the deficit is perceived as being inherent in the person, not the circumstance);
- persons within the categories are perceived by the standards of a post-capitalist economic system as not contributing economically to the health of their country;
- economic contribution is considered fundamental to citizenship; persons seen not to be contributing are thus potential threats to the status quo;
- as such, persons in the categories are seen as in need of control; and

- the dominant means of control involve segregation and scientific technology

These commonalities lay the groundwork for the rest of the chapter, which illustrates how early childhood is currently being pathologized.

The Pathologizing of Young Children

Canada goes with the crowd in its public consideration of early childhood education and care. In the near past, young children have barely begun to register on the radar of many minority world countries, but some countries are now paying increasing attention to the early years (e.g., OECD, 2001; Bertram & Pascal, 2002). Keeping with this trend, Canadian educators are inundated with public rhetoric claiming the early years to be the most critical period of human development (McCain & Mustard, 1999; Government of Canada, 2004). Although this long-awaited interest in early childhood education and care is vital, it is, unsurprisingly, tied to an economic, human-capital discourse. Stooke's (2003) analysis of *Reversing the Real Brain Drain: Early Years Study* (McCain & Mustard, 1999), an influential report commissioned by the Ontario government on the state of early childhood education and care, demonstrates how providing quality education and care to young children is a matter of ensuring the province's economic survival. This echoes the National Children's Agenda which sees improving children's quality of life as an 'investment' (Government of Canada, 2004) that is about 'potential' (Government of Canada, 1999a) and the 'future' (Government of Canada, 1999b). In Canadian early childhood education and care policy, the term 'readiness' is used frequently (Stooke, 2004). One might ask readiness for what? Stooke proposes that 'readiness' is a code word for preparation for the workforce and ultimately for supporting the previous generation – just as Lubeck (2000) states.

The link between children and the workforce is by no means new. In a review of historical views of childhood, David et al. (2000) explain that adult conceptualizations of childhood have always influenced what adults ask of children and that there has always been a link between childhood and the economy. David et al. mention, for example, that numerous children in the UK worked in factories in the eighteenth century. One might also consider the large number of children enslaved in the Americas before abolition. Compulsory schooling changed the way adults viewed childhood, but children's quality of life, in particular for those who did not fit the ideal of the normate, was little considered. The child rights movement of the 1960s and 1970s finally established children as citizens, but, disappointingly, many gains for children's rights made during that hopeful era are now being lost in countries like Canada.[1] David et al. argue that currently 'adult manipulation of the childhood experience has come to the fore with a severity not seen since children's direct involvement in industry in the eighteenth century' (p. 21). What is the source of this manipulation? Akin to Fine (1995) and Lubeck (2000), David et al. (2000) claim the massive social and economic changes around the beginning of the last century have produced anxiety in minority-world governments. Rather than focusing on the complex issues to blame for generally declining standards of living, governments have instead focused on individual workers as sites of deficit; they blame a 'lack of skills within the work-force as the prime reasons for poor economic performance' (p. 21). This is perhaps where governments' interest in childhood and education enters. Following Fine (1995), education is the depository of government anxiety and may be seen as the means of preventing deficient or, one might argue, disabled workers.

The current era is not the only time when there has been anxiety over the economy and when a portion of the population has been targeted as scapegoats for that anxiety. Particularly when technological change in the means of production created changes in the requirement for labour skills, persons with disabilities were understood as potential threats to American capitalist values such as the meritocracy. To allow a moral response to disability while not calling into question the meritocracy, American society turned to science to create fixed categories of disability. Persons with defined disabilities were deemed 'proper paupers' (Thomson, 1997, p. 51) and relieved of the obligation of labour.

The ways in which the minority world currently configures life outside paid labour, however, have some disturbing implications. Dominant discourses today define only certain practices as work or as making a contribution to society. Consequently, 'disabled people are often imagined as unable to be productive, direct their own lives, participate in the community, or establish meaningful personal relations – regardless of their actual capabilities or achievements' (Thomson, 1997,

---

1 It warrants more than a note, but is outside the scope of this chapter to discuss what Rogers (2004) points out: children in the majority world (i.e., developing countries) have borne the brunt of labour exploitation.

p. 46). In Canada, most young children are also removed from vali-
dated labour. Although 'the disabled social category is harder to escape
and far more stigmatizing than youth ... which [is] seen more as [a]
stage[e] in the lives of productive people than as immutable identities'
(p. 51), children's quality of life is also affected by being outside the
labour force. As with disabled persons, children's contributions to society are invisible and their social power is minimized by the limits on
their ac-cess to capital. Through Thomson (1997), it is obvious why
post-capitalist societies eager to participate in the global economy are
loath to accept disability as another form of human diversity or as she
puts it, as a form of 'identity' rather than 'pathology' (p. 137). At this
point an innovation has occurred in the at-risk discourse that reconfig-
ures disability not only in its actual or manifest sense but also in terms
of its *potential*.

The Potential for Pathology: An Innovation in
the At-Risk Discourse.

Numerous governments anxious about social and economic changes
have targeted early childhood as a time to 'inoculate' (Stooke, 2004)
children against potential disability. Practices such as early intervention and developmental screenings, the proverbial 'shot[s] in the arm'
(Swadener, 1995, p. 22) of young children, are a marriage of the medical
model of risk management and deficit-oriented educational policy. In
the province of Ontario, for example, the Ministry of Education calls
for school districts to identify early in children's schooling 'each child's
level of development, learning abilities and needs' (Ministry of Education, 1982, p. 1). This has of late been interpreted to mean screening
children as early as Junior Kindergarten to Grade 3 for deficits (Hunniford, 2004). This emphasis on deficit-identification follows an instrumental trend that tries to locate predictors of future disability (e.g.,
learning disabilities) then control the environment to reduce or elimi-
nate disability. In this approach, disability and potential disability are
seen as physical problems (usually related to brain development) to be
worked out by 'scientists' (often medical doctors). The *Early Years Study*
exemplifies this instrumental approach or rather what in chapter 3 we
term the 'biomedical' approach. Stooke's (2003) analysis of the *Early
Years Study*, for instance, demonstrates that the report uses science as a
trope to convince the public that the study of childhood brain development is the best way to control and predict the kinds of adults needed

by society. The *Early Years Study* intimates that if society does not follow its own guidelines for the stimulation of children's brains, they will not develop to their full potential. Underdeveloped or disabled brains would presumably negatively impact the economy. The selection of Fraser Mustard, a physician and co-author of the *Early Years Study*, reflects this biomedical approach. The proliferation of this form of at-risk discourse has led directly to developments such as *Promoting Early Intervention of Learning Disabilities* (Learning Disabilities Association of Ontario, n.d.), a project again led by a physician, that promotes screening children as young as four years old to diagnose learning disabilities.

Although it might seem commonsensical that if disability can be prevented it should be prevented, this 'biomedical' approach has troubling implications. First is the notion that childhood is solely or mainly a time of preparation and that the future of a nation is borne on the backs of children. Second (and relatedly) is the way these practices fall in with the at-risk discourse, in particular in its omission of discussions of privilege, and by extension, vulnerabilities created by society and the screening procedures. Screening, which has its origins (and overseers) in medicine, intersects with the field of special education. Despite special education's perennial search for valid tools, the overrepresentation of particular groups of children in specific diagnostic categories persists. Especially tenacious is the overrepresentation of cultural and linguistic minority children (CLD) in the learning disabilities (LD) category (see Chamberlain, 2005; Rueda & Windmueller, 2006). This is an important shift from Sleeter's (1987) past observation that the LD category arose from the ruling discourse's (Smith, 1987) desire to distinguish between the school achievement difficulties of white students and students of colour. Specifically, Sleeter (1987) posits that at its inception the diagnostic criteria and protocol for LD allowed white children struggling with achievement to be seen as having an average to above average IQ while struggling children of colour were more apt to be diagnosed with a mild intellectual disability where their IQ was seen to be below average. What both these examples show is how LD is a non-normative category of disability (Rodriguez, 1999), a disability open to social interpretation. Unfortunately, special education does not and has not critically addressed its own paradigmatic foundations that allow for the discrimination of certain socially vulnerable groups of children. Skrtic (1995) says that even while special education has had a number of internal debates, especially around issues of inclusion, as a field it is based in 'naive pragmatism.' Naïve pragmatism sees the recognized problems of, for example, overrepresentation, as a concern that need only be addressed by improvements in method. Special education's efforts to eradicate the problem of overrepresentation, are then, always principally a question of creating a better tool and not of looking at the relationship between method, theory, and the context in which these are being generated.

Another difficulty with the current early identification and intervention thrust is the idea that children who do not perform well on specific screenings or who do not have the kinds of experiences advocated in documents such as the *Early Years Study* (McCain & Mustard, 1999) may become neurologically impaired (i.e., their brains may not develop to their full potential). Thus, all children are seen as potentially disabled and, through the involvement of physicians, as potentially pathological. In identifying the potentially disabled child, one can learn about society's values, and through this, discern the normate. One can see, for instance, that in the ruling discourse a brain that works is a brain that can propel the economy. One can also learn through the discourse's promotion of a particular type of brain that diversity is not valued.

The fourth area of concern relates to government regulation of children's lives earlier and earlier. Whereas in the past governments mainly left children's education and care alone until Kindergarten, the current thrust, as evidenced through documents like the *Early Years Study,* is to intervene earlier. Support for families with young children is, of course, called for, yet my concern is the form of that support. The discourse concerning support in Canadian policy is what Rogers (2004) calls a 'needs' discourse. Related to developmental psychology, this discourse advocates the fulfilment of what it perceives as children's needs based on its own social and cultural understandings of what is valuable, including what kind of adult is valuable. In addition to the notion that this is not a culturally sensitive discourse, the needs discourse is bothersome because it does not respect children's personhood or explicitly address their quality of life. The needs discourse, for example, advocates 'doing things for children simply because they are 'good for them ...' For example: if we accept that children cannot thrive and flourish unless they have warm and caring relationships – this is not all that intimate relationships mean to a child. Adults don't regard being loved and cared about as just about having their "needs" met. Neither do children. For a child, being loved is profoundly meaningful and valuable in itself (Rogers, 2004, p. 134). By adopting a needs discourse based on the desire to create future workers, 'childhood as an important phase in life in its own right ... is under threat' (David et al., 2000, p. 21).

Finally, also problematic in this new brand of at-risk discourse are the brains over which studies like the *Early Years Study* (McCain & Mustard, 1999) worry. Stooke (2003) explains, for instance, how the study is mainly concerned with middle-class children and diverts attention from the pressing issues of child poverty. As many of the circumstances in this book demonstrate, I would also add that it diverts attention away from the social problems that plague CLD children and their families such as racism and the lack of support such as settlement services for new immigrants. The change to the at-risk discourse identified by Swadener and Lubeck (1995a) as most troubling is the downplaying of the particular vulnerabilities of CLD children and children living in poverty. McCain and Mustard (1999), for example, argue for a move away from targeted early years programs to universal programs, saying that middle-class children are mainly in need of help because their numbers make up the greatest proportion of the population and will make up the bulk of the future workforce. This rhetoric is suggestive of the privileging of equality over equity. McCain and Mustard (1998) point out, for example, that targeted programs have dominated the early years landscape and this now needs to be corrected. 'Ontario spends a considerable amount on children ... Less than a third of the expenditure on the younger age group is for programs that can be considered 'universal' in terms of support for early child development ... Since all families and children, in all socio-economic circumstances, can benefit from early child development and parenting programs it is important that programs evolve to be available and accessible to all families in all socio-economic groups' (p. 13).

Three years after publishing their *Early Years Study*, (McCain and & Mustard (1999) produced a follow-up report (McCain & Mustard, 2002) that expressed their disappointment that the early years centres, which the first report had helped to establish, had a 'tendency to focus on at-risk children and targeted services' and had failed to achieve the 'universal focus' (p. 33) called for in the first report. Although few would dispute that social supports should be inclusive, what is disquieting is the omission of the discussion of privilege, particularly the privilege to which middle-class children are born. Sadly, the effect of this new branch of at-risk discourse, which potentially configures all children as at-risk, is to pathologize all children and provide a rationale for abandoning children who have the least amount of privilege while diverting resources to children who already have the most.

Conclusion

Targeted programs? Universal programs? Neither is a panacea, not when both are built on an at-risk discourse. In the case of a targeted approach, Polakow (1995) says 'the armory of at-risk labels, which ironically gain many poor children access to early childhood preschool programs from which they would otherwise be excluded, also contains proliferating weapons of future educational exclusion' (p. 269). There is a fine balance we educators must attempt to identify: How do we acknowledge particular groups in society are less privileged than others and at the same time refuse to take a deficit orientation towards the people who make up these groups? How too do we avoid essentializing people and groups, that is, seeing them as having an unchanging essence (e.g., race) that defines them? Spivak's (1993) notion of strategic essentialism may be helpful in understanding how we could negotiate this terrain. She explains that at moments, to promote what she calls a 'scrupulously visible political interest' (p. 3), that is, a clearly defined material goal, it may be necessary or desirable to band people together using a particular social marker (e.g., race, class, or gender). To be strategic, Spivak explains, one must make a conscious decision at the outset of a project to mobilize in a way that is 'designed to outwit or surprise the enemy' (Oxford English Dictionary as cited in Spivak, 1993, p. 3). She makes a crucial distinction between strategy and theory by finding that strategies must be developed for a particular context and cannot be generalized. Therefore, being strategic means knowing what one wants to accomplish and what or whom one is working against, and then developing *in place* a way of proceeding.

In an attempt to avoid mere essentialism when being strategic, Spivak teaches that one must vigilantly critique one's own operating theory. To do this, she advocates a deconstruction that entails investigating the roots (historical, social and linguistic) of one's theory as well as one's beliefs and practices. Despite its reductive ring, deconstruction to Spivak is paradoxically quite constructive. In a context of strategic essentialism, deconstruction involves recognizing as necessary what people use to get by in their everyday and every-night lives however much problematic it may be. Using deconstruction to create an essentialist strategy is thus 'understood not as an exposure of error, our own or others,' but as an acknowledgment of the dangerousness of something one cannot not use' (Spivak, 1993, p. 5).

When applied to curricula for young children, this approach could ask whether looking at children as socially marked groups might be necessary when the situation requires political expedience. Yet we educators must closely monitor the dangers of this process. We must reject those practices and policies that are predicated on discourses that presuppose knowing the complete experiences and knowledges of others and pathologize those we do not understand. This requires a humility that allows each of us to enter into a relationship with the other believing that that other has something to teach us. In this way the other is seen as 'more than I contain' (Todd, 2003), and the relationships enables us to learn and see the limits of our own knowledge. Such a 'philosophy of the limit' as Cornell (1992) calls deconstruction, is itself an ethic, a way to develop a relationship with the other where we do no violence to that other. As such, when we make decisions for children, when we structure their curricula, when we construct policy that affects their lives, we must fight the urge to colonize them, to see them as empty or deficient, or without knowledge. Rather, we must respect where they have come from, listen to them, and attempt to develop strategies for establishing their rights in terms that protect their personhood and recognize their knowledge.

At the end of this chapter I ask again, as Swadener and Lubeck (1995a) did so eloquently more than a decade ago, for a fundamental shift in values and paradigms. I ask that as communities within the minority world, we open discussions about what is really of value to us all as citizens. This discussion is long overdue and of critical importance, for it is one more thing that the cult of efficiency (Stein, 2001) has stolen. When the bottom-line is the bottom-line, one of the supposed ideals of the minority world, democracy, gets left by the way-side. Consider, for instance, Arnove's (2005) lament that today 'chief among the concerns of national decision-makers is the international competitiveness of their economies and the products (the graduates) of their educational systems (as measured by standardized tests) ... The previous dominant themes of education for the formation of participatory citizens and national unity, as well as international solidarity and individual fulfilment, are barely mentioned or given secondary consideration in policy reforms/deforms which have tended to focus on the excellence or quality of an education system, rather than its provisions of equitable access, participation, and attainment' (p. 81).

Recall from chapter 1 Stein's (2001) notion that politicians have used the cult of efficiency to distract constituents from the significant questions that should be addressed in pluralistic societies, such as, What are 'our' collective ideals? What should we be working towards? What is of most worth? I would answer that the bottom line is a false economy in this cult; for the bottom line has become an end unto itself and has omitted what is humane. The next three chapters in *Early Childhood Curricula* illustrate some of the suffering and lost opportunities that accompany this false economy. This chapter can be used as a primer for the analysis of these cases. Hopefully this analysis can be a form of 'naming' which for Freire is a step towards emancipation (Wink, 2005).

3
The Biomedical Approach to Literacy: Pathologizing Practices within Early Literacy

RACHEL HEYDON AND LUIGI IANNACCI

We find ourselves on a threshold. We are literacy educators and researchers who choose to operate from the field of curriculum studies,[1] because, like Egan (2003), we appreciate being able to answer teaching and learning questions through the methodologies derived from the immediate educational circumstances and not imported from 'psychology or philosophy or sociology or whatever' (p. 18). We accept the confusion that can arise from working within a 'syncretic' (Gregory et al. 2004) model of methodology,[2] but we see it as the necessary by-product of responding to problems-at-hand and keeping open our ways of being, seeing, and doing. Also, because we take literacy as situational and the practices of literacy as dependent upon a sophisticated combination of physical, cognitive, affective, and discursive factors, a syncretic approach can respect the complexity and indeterminacy of literacy teaching and learning. We do not, however, solely belong to curriculum studies; the children who most intrigue us are those who struggle with their school literacy because of a real or perceived disability. Curriculum studies does not typically address the issues of these children. Instead, such children are frequently identified as 'disabled students' and in need of special education services (Lipson & Wixson,

---

1 We understand there is no universal definition of curriculum studies. We use the term to refer to the body of scholarship that predominantly interrogates issues of what to teach and how to teach (Egan, 1978) from socio-cultural and historical perspectives. Throughout the paper, when we refer to curriculum, we are therefore referring to what is being taught as well as how it is being taught (what is often referred to as 'pedagogy').

2 As Egan (2003) identifies, the specific methodologies used within curriculum studies are still being created as the field is not yet even fifty years old.

2003). We are therefore caught with one foot in curriculum studies and the other in special education. It is from this location that we use a case study of the early years (Junior Kindergarten to Grade 3) division of one school to understand a specific circumstance in the pathologizing of children.

Our purpose in this chapter is to understand pathologizing better by first presenting a critical appraisal of the ways disability is produced and practised in early school literacy curricula. To that end, we briefly show the state of dis/ability in curriculum studies and then present two approaches to literacy curricula. The *psychological approach to reading* and the *socio-cultural approach to literacies,* have until very recently been dominant, cleanly splitting school children and their curricula along the lines of dis/ability. Next, we illustrate and analyse what we term, the *biomedical approach,* a hegemonic innovation in literacy education and research already hinted at in chapter 2. We demonstrate how the biomedical approach, when combined with particular educational policies, disables entire school populations and inflicts upon them reductive literacy curricula. Finally, we argue for theory-rich literacy curricula with an asset-oriented definition of literacy.

Dis/ability

As Chapters 1 and 2 have already asserted, disability is not a self-evident term or phenomenon. By extension, disability's counterpart, ability, also needs to be scrutinized. It is frustrating, then, that the curriculum studies literature has been almost silent on special education's claim on disabled students, their curricula, and issues of what constitutes ability and disability. Although Baker (2002a) says disability studies literature has made inroads into curriculum studies, our experience suggests she was being overly optimistic. We conducted a content analysis of ten years of issues of four prominent, peer-reviewed, international curriculum studies journals. After examining all articles to determine whether they considered the relationship between special education and curriculum, examined the ways in which ability and disability are constructed, or dealt with children who had been deemed disabled students we found no journal contained more than five articles referring to issues of dis/ability or curriculum for disabled students.

The lack of dis/ability articles in curriculum journals indicates that educators are little troubled by what it means to be able or disabled and do not question the curricula of disabled students. Yes, curriculum studies literature, with its attention to reconceptualist theorizing, has a fairly strong record of considering educational equity, but primarily only in reference to race, class, and gender. Baker (2002a), posits that disability studies literature challenges this attention to race, class, and gender by arguing that its emphasis on reconceptualist theorizing 'has been part of the blockage to considering the fundamentality of dis/ability to stratification, to even recognizing what or who is a 'human' who can be referred to as raced, gendered, sexed and so on' (p. 49). Although we are not sure that the emphasis on race, class, and gender has been *the* impediment to considerations of dis/ability we do not believe that this line of theorizing can get very far without the inclusion of dis/ability. How can one discuss what to teach or how to teach it, if the question of how students are defined has not been openly addressed? Consequently, questions of dis/ability are prerequisites for all educational conversations.

As with all of *Early Childhood Curricula*, this chapter is informed by a postmodern, critical perspective on dis/ability and literacy. We use dis/ability in Baker's (2002a) sense where the "dis' cannot be separated from assertions of what counts as 'able" (p. 48) and where, before dis/ability can be an educational issue, it must first be an 'ontological' one (Baker, 2002b, p. 663). Ontology here refers to what one takes to be 'in' the world. In our use of the term disabled, we are aware that what constitutes disability is context-specific, but the degree to which is difficult to ascertain.

Rodriguez's (1999) distinction between 'normative' and 'non-normative' categories of disabilities (p. 398) to which chapter 2 alludes and upon which subsequent chapters expand, is a way of thinking about how such a distinction is possible. Rodriguez says normative disabilities are those that, 'even if the category opened to debate, would bring some normative agreement between professionals and non-professionals' that a disability is present (p. 398). Examples include 'deafness, blindness, or severe mental disabilities' (p. 398). In contrast, non-normative disabilities, are 'those that are open to interpretation in light of their social, historical, and political circumstances' (p. 398). Examples include 'feeble-mindedness, maladjustment, and learning disabilities' (p. 398). As we noted in chapter 1, Baker (2002a) makes even normative categories of disability problematic by citing the case of deaf culture where deafness is considered a form of knowledge rather than an 'audiological condition' (p. 47). We therefore acknowledge disability as a signifier whose signification is contingent upon who is using it, the time and place in which it is used, and what is signified. We are careful to note, however, that contextualizing and troubling dis/ability should not be an erasure of disability. Just as in Spivak's (1993) teachings on strategic essentialism, there are social and political circumstances in which the recognition of disability is very important, and disability as it has been constructed within disability studies, as distinct from how it has been constructed in the curriculum studies/special education split, does not denote pathology. Paramount is a consideration of ableism (i.e., the notion that it is most desirable to be physically, psychologically, and cognitively the 'same' as the majority of the population) as it is manifested in education.

Psychological Reading, Socio-cultural Literacies, and the Birth of Biomedical Literacy

Until the advent of the biomedical approach to literacy, two other approaches reigned. Lankshear and Knobel (2003), in their treatment of the rise of the term literacy, explain that prior to about 30 years ago, language education and research was dominated by a well-established field of 'reading' (p. 3) which was the domain of psychology and built on instrumental theories whose goals were to allow for a degree of control and predictability (Habermas, 1972). Reading, seen as 'primarily a perceptual activity centred on sound/symbol relationships' (Gillen & Hall, 2003, p. 4), employed a technology of instruction for decoding and sometimes encoding text. This technology was characterized by a rigid, sequenced, hierarchical presentation of isolated bits of language; mastery of these bits was believed to be necessary *before* students could derive meaning from text. There was an absolute distinction between 'being a reader and not being a reader' (p. 4) and reading could only be taught in schools. Four basic assumptions underlined this behavioural approach to reading:

- children's agency was insignificant
- children could learn nothing for themselves
- children were objects to be manipulated by teachers
- reading and writing were individual acts involving sets of discrete perceptual skills. (p. 4)

The diagnosis and correction of reading difficulties could thus be made by measuring and addressing these discrete perceptual skills.

Lankshear and Knobel (2003) claim there were particular influences that caused the widespread growth of the idea that reading should be conceptualized within a broader notion of literacy. One was the work of Paulo Freire which contributed the notion that to be literate, in addition to decoding words, one needed also to see how these words operated in the world. Being able to read both the word and the world (Lankshear and Knobel, 2003) could lead to emancipation and social transformation. Another influence was a body of work based on the social-science approach to literacy, which argued the necessity of seeing reading and writing as practices within larger socio-cultural frames. This work was aligned with hermeneutic theories developed to interpret specific phenomena (Habermas, 1972). The collective influences of these approaches coalesced in the understanding that:

- children's agency is significant and will affect curriculum,
- children learn amongst themselves and with the support of more knowledgeable others,
- children are subjects with whom teachers need to negotiate,
- reading and writing are situated practices involving a complexity of physical, cognitive, affective, and discursive factors.

These ideas set the groundwork for other theories (e.g., postcolonial, semiotic, and feminist) to enter the field and turn literacy into literacies. The pluralization of literacy comes, in part, from the view that interpreting and/or generating meaning through sign systems, including the analphabetic, are all forms of literacy (Short, Kauffman, & Kahn, 2000). Certain sign systems and languages, however, are privileged within certain contexts; thus, being literate necessitates an awareness of and an ability to negotiate these power dynamics. Literacy difficulties could therefore be perceived as resulting from any or all of a complicated web of factors ranging from the physical to the discursive. An example of a discursive difficulty would be a mismatch between a child's home and school literacies. From this vantage, literacy gains are contingent on the curriculum addressing all relevant factors.

Socio-cultural and pluralized approaches to literacy arose in a time when the literacy demands of most nations had never been greater. Yet, while the use of the term literacy became ubiquitous, it did not, however, always signal a change in practice from what had been done in the name of reading (Lankshear & Knobel, 2003); the reading/literacies approaches to literacy continued to exist along the disabled/abled student divide. Some argue that behaviour models of reading continue even today in special education (Gillen & Hall, 2003), which is itself heavily influenced by psychology and the medical model. Recently, however, a new approach to literacy has emerged.

The biomedical approach to literacy is a reworking of psychological reading with its insistence on behavioural, prescriptive curricula, and literacy as perceptually based decoding, but with two added foci: 1) the 'new phonics,' described as 'a combined emphasis on phonemic awareness, explicit synthetic phonics instruction, and, 2) decodable text' (Pearson, 2001, p. 78), and continuing the trend identified in chapter 2, the brain as an independent entity for scrutiny. In this approach, the shape of early literacy curricula and literacy difficulties are problems to be worked out through biomedical research by 'scientists.' Difficulties in learning to read are seen as most probably the result of a genetic 'brain glitch' which negatively interferes with, for instance, phonemic awareness (Coles, 2003, p. 168); research into reading is conducted through biomedical technology such as MRI scans and audiological and sight measurement. Curricula and interventions designed from this approach focus almost entirely on enhancing brain development and in so doing ignore the affective and discursive elements of literacy. Significantly the biomedical approach not only relegates disabled students to reductive forms of literacy operating from a deficit-perspective, but pathologizes and disables entire schools. The following narrative of a school deemed 'compensatory' demonstrates this phenomenon and its effects on the school's early-years literacy curriculum.

A School's Story

Elmwood Public School is located in Ontario in the centre of one of Canada's largest cities. The building is old and needs repairs and renovations. It is not uncommon to find a maintenance van in the parking lot on a call to 'patch-up' yet another problem. Despite a couple of new teacher-made murals, the cinder-block walls and lack of windows and bulletin boards to display children's work make everything gloomy. The school is surrounded by strip malls, one-storey pre-war homes, and apartment buildings. The socio-economic status of most local families is working-class or working-poor. A couple of years prior to our work at the school, the school district began bussing to the school a substantial number of children from one of the poorest and least-serviced housing complexes in the city. The school district made this change without consulting any of the Elmwood children's families or teachers nor did it transfer the necessary resources with the new children (e.g., furniture, books, educational assistants, ESL support, or funds for translators).

Elmwood had been made up almost exclusively of Canadian-born children, but, at the time of our work, immigrant children (mostly from the Middle East and Eastern Europe) comprised nearly 40 per cent of the school's population. The school population was transient for several reasons. New immigrants initially settled in the bussed area then moved away throughout the year as opportunities for employment of the parents arose. Other families left for economic reasons or the need for a quick change in residence. It was not uncommon for parents to show up at the school and remove their children without warning; likewise, it was not uncommon for children to move into the school. This pattern was true of both immigrant and non-immigrant children.

There was also a high turnover rate among the administrative staff and the teachers. Consequently, many inexperienced and newly qualified staff were placed at the school. In the years we worked at Elmwood, the largely Canadian-born, middle-class teaching staff was already weary of the strain they felt had been placed on them and the school. Teachers attributed their students' 'lack' of early literacy skills (as measured by standardized curricula and assessment) to an absence of at-home 'literacy experiences.' They cited parents' low socio-economic status, low level of English proficiency, and low motivation as reasons why the children were not exposed to literacy in their homes. Teachers did not discuss multiple forms of literacy and generally characterized their students as 'behind.' A series of assessments further confirmed this understanding.

Elmwood's overall achievement on provincial literacy tests designated it a 'compensatory school.' While these poor scores qualified Elmwood for resources it would not otherwise have received, these resources only served to sharpen the focus on the children's weaknesses. For instance, one of these resources was the purchase of speech and language pathologists' time. The time was spent administering phonemic awareness screening to *every* child in Senior Kindergarten and produced *more* poor scores. Also, the 'compensatory' label provided Elmwood with professional in-service on 'teaching with the brain in mind' and a proliferation of literature from the district regarding brain and phonemic awareness development. This reinforced the idea that the children's lack of stimulation at home resulted in a physical delay that showed itself through poor literacy performance. Furthermore, around this time, the district also implemented the Developmental Reading Assessment (DRA) (Beaver, 2001a) in the early years to measure and label students' reading achievement. The DRA places students at a level starting with A as the base then proceeds from level 1 upwards. It then charts what grade and time of year a student should be expected to reach each level; for example, by May to June of Senior Kindergarten, 'normally achieving' students should be at levels 1 or 2 (Beaver, 2001b, p. 41). Many Elmwood early years students were unable to achieve a level A. To define these students, school district personnel thus invented 'level Z,' and claimed it corresponded to a statistical 'ground zero.' No criteria were put in place to measure or account for early or emergent reading behaviours.

Given these deficit-driven forms of data, many teachers felt great pressure to improve their students' performance. Grade 1 teachers, for example, convened several meetings with the Kindergarten teachers and administration to push for instructional remedies. As already noted, Elmwood's labelled status already gave it resources such as speech and language pathology time for phonemic awareness therapy. Educational assistant time was added to administer phonemic awareness programs, resource teacher time to administer a scripted synthetic phonics program, and an early literacy teacher was brought in to work with support personnel to monitor and help deliver the school district's literacy mandates. Regardless of these resources, the meetings headed by the Grade 1 teachers resulted in additional phonemic awareness and phonics-intensive instruction for all children in Junior and Senior Kindergarten in the form of literacy group sessions led by the early literacy teacher. It was believed that the sessions would address the students' deficits so that, by the time they left Kindergarten, they would be better prepared to meet the Grade 1 curricular expectations.

The district's remedies and the literacy group sessions curtailed children's engagement with other types of literacy learning opportunities. This, in addition to the types of assessments and evaluations Kindergarten teachers were now required to complete for their students, frustrated the teachers. One Kindergarten teacher was especially aware of and increasingly vocal about the ways these new steps constrained her program, affected the quality of her interactions with her students, and ultimately the learning that occurred within her classroom. She explained, for example, that the assessment tools measured discrete skills directly related to expectations in the curriculum. Consequently, rather than facilitating and extending other forms of early literacy learning, she now had to determine her students' ability to perform discrete skills almost to the exclusion of everything else. These shifts were even reflected in the physical layout of her classroom. A great deal of space had now to be devoted to pencil and paper tasks, leaving less room for centres. In Grade 1 this approach to literacy continued with increasing urgency, as the received knowledge from the biomedical approach to literacy stressed that early intervention was *the* opportunity to correct literacy disabilities. A consequence of this thinking was that students with scores below the school average were withdrawn for more intensive phonemic awareness and phonics instruction. Those who did not show expected gains (even those who were learning ESL) were referred for psychological testing.

Analysing a School Story

Prior to the biomedical approach to literacy, students were divided between able and disabled along general/special education lines. Now, entire school populations like Elmwood's are perceived as disabled; their treatment has much in common with special education. Skrtic (1995) identifies four tenets of special education that, when modified, equally well address the assumptions of the biomedical approach to literacy:

- [Literacy] disability is a pathological condition
- Differential diagnosis is objective and useful
- [Biomedical literacy] is a rationally conceived and coordinated system of services that benefits diagnosed students
- Progress in [biomedical literacy] is a rational-technical process of incremental improvements in conventional diagnostic and instructional practices. (p. 75)

All of the above can be seen in the Elmwood example. What is most disturbing is how the biomedical approach at Elmwood operated through the at-risk discourse identified in chapter 2 thus pathologizing children. It also shut out other approaches to early literacy curricula and functioned without a critical understanding of its own operations and constructions.

At Elmwood, the biomedical approach was the *only* approach to early literacy curricula. This meant that children were perceived and treated through reductive means. For instance, children were deemed abnormal through their performance on screenings and criterion- and norm-referenced assessments, which did not take into consideration their socio-cultural and linguistic backgrounds. They were subsequently pathologized and seen (for their own good) as in need of labelling (e.g., DRA level Z and psychological diagnoses). This labelling ensured that the children received literacy curricula with origins in clinical biomedical research. For example, the idea that phonological processing is *the* most important element in the process of reading and that phonemic awareness is *the* predictor of literacy achievement, is derived from brain research by the United States National Institute of Child Health and Human Development (NICHD) conducted entirely in a research lab with brain-imaging technology (Coles, 2003). Labs are not classrooms. Classrooms are 'dynamic social space[s]' (Gillen & Hall, 2003, p. 7) where teaching and learning are not simple transfers of knowledge or skills. Gillen and Hall (2003), for instance, have demonstrated that children's perceptions of their roles and identities vis-à-vis the classroom and literacy will greatly affect their achievement and learning. Indeed, learning a new language, as many children at Elmwood were, necessitates coming to see one's self and one's world in different ways. The construction of a new, hybrid self cannot be achieved without loss. This sense of loss will affect curriculum and achievement. Early literacy learning is thus not just about getting the mechanics right, as the biomedical approach proposes. Focus on the individual as a site of pathology and omission of the myriad factors that mediate a child's achievement of literacy are characteristic of psychology (Goodnow, 1995, p. 306), one of the sources of the biomedical approach. Such a focus and the ideologies that underpin it must be interrogated to determine whether the biomedical approach can make any substantive contribution to children's early literacy development.

This interrogation is unlikely to occur without a paradigm shift. As with the trend identified in chapter 2 and to be seen again in the case of special education in chapter 5, the biomedical approach to literacy as implemented at Elmwood was characterized by 'naive pragmatism' (Skrtic, 1995). Recall that this is defined as a willingness to entertain only criticism related to the practical (e.g., debates around 'models, practices, and tools' [p. 76]). The biomedical focus on the individual and how to teach prevented passage beyond the tools to ascertain what was being taught (i.e., what forms of literacy and understandings of children and their families were being perpetuated). For instance, at Elmwood, the blame for literacy disability was directed at children's brains, poor parenting, and the need for specific forms of curricula. There were numerous official steps to monitor students' performance (e.g., provincial assessment, phonemic awareness screenings, and DRA) and curricula (e.g., standardized curricula and an early literacy teacher), but there was little consideration of how these measures as well as other school district decisions created or exacerbated students' difficulties.

Elmwood's early years students' literacy performance would not have been so compromised if the school district had taken responsibility for the difficult position in which they had placed the children and worked from an asset-oriented and theory-rich approach to literacy. This would have entailed addressing the bussed children's feelings of displacement and alienation when they were withdrawn from their home school located across the street from their housing complex and sent kilometres away to a host school not prepared for them; dealing with Elmwood's original population and their feelings of being pushed out of a space that had always been theirs; providing necessary resources for carrying out the work of educating a splintered and challenging population (e.g., culturally sensitive texts, appropriate toys and furniture for young children, ESL support, translators to assist with parent/school communication, and a team to aid with the transition to becoming a new, integrated school population), and implementing a curriculum that included the affective and discursive aspects of literacy learning. If all this had been done, the issues of who the children were, what they knew, as well as their own forms of early literacy, would have been used as resources in the classroom and addressed directly. The children could then have been seen for more than their bodies. To have accomplished this, parents would have had to be seen as curricular informants and invited to join in conceptualizing classroom activity.

Connecting the Elmwood Story to Its Socio-political Context

The Elmwood story is no accident. To say that the history of literacy education has been defined by debates (e.g., whole language, phonics, and the basal reader) (Flippo, 2001a) is perhaps putting it mildly. Smith (2003) contends that 'one has to turn to religious fundamentalism to find another issue that arouses such bitter controversy' (p. viii). While the feuds have been narrowly focussed on method (Luke, 1998), they were at least opportunities for diverse theories, practices, and definitions of literacy to coexist, albeit in tension. Today, it seems that the biomedical approach to literacy is the only voice being heeded by many literacy policy-makers, educators, and those who fund research. This narrow conception of children, literacy, research, and curricula ironically comes at a time when reductionism has been greatly problematized, definitions of literacy have expanded to highlight the social and cultural, and the need for complex literacies is unprecedented. Disappointingly, now any position that does not stem from instrumental science is disregarded by the establishment as baseless (see Garan, 2002; Taylor, 1998).

One way those who tout the biomedical approach silence dissent is by asserting that the theory upon which it is based, is the *only* means of coming to know anything. McGuinness's (1999) work is a prime example. She claims that discussions of best practices in reading instruction could only have gone on prior to the recent 'scientific revolution' (p. xiii) and, consequently, anything outside of this version of science should be disregarded outright. On this point she says, 'True scientific research on literacy only began about twenty-five years ago. What this means is that every 'theory' or 'model' or 'method' of teaching reading, past or present, has been based either on human reason alone, or on empty theorizing or 'fads,' rather than on solid scientific research' (p. xiii). Unfortunately, McGuinness is not a lone voice. The biomedical approach is prevalent and has massive implications for early literacy education and research.

One consequence of the dominance of the biomedical approach is the proliferation of new phonics in public educational policy. Educators and researchers in Canada are watching the United States' example closely for its influence. Following the NICHD's establishment of the National Reading Panel, the U.S. federal government jumped on the new phonics bandwagon and enacted The Reading Excellence Act. The Act became law in 1998 and restricts local decision making by offering federal funding only to institutions whose instructional practices are backed by 'scientifically based reading research' (Allington, 2001, p. 12). Rather than fighting this loss of autonomy, some U.S. state governments (e.g., North Carolina, Ohio, California, and Texas) have actually-created their own laws requiring the of new phonics. They have then enforced these laws through the use high-stakes standardized testing and punitive funding policies (Flippo, 2001b, p. 182–183; Garan, Shanahan, & Henkin, 2001; Lemann, 2002; Lipson & Wixson, 2003; Meyer, 2002; Ogle & Farstrup, 2002).

A second consequence is the stress on instrumental science and the exclusion of voices from other paradigms in literacy research and curriculum (e.g., curriculum studies). This is demonstrated, for example, in the Ontario case, where as chapter 2 has shown, the most influential and large-scale studies and projects are headed by medical doctors; these include the *Ontario Early Years Study* (McCain & Mustard, 1999) and the *Promoting Early Intervention of Learning Disabilities* project (Learning Disabilities Association of Ontario, n.d.).

Biomedical research *is* a component in understanding literacies, and our descriptions of the factors that must be considered in literacy development *do* include the physical and cognitive. What is problematic is that the biomedical approach favours the physical and cognitive to the extent that other factors that influence literary practices are absent or marginalized. In our definition of literacy, reading (only one aspect of literacy) is not just about unlocking a code, but about making meaning from a printed text. This is a situated practice that can evoke emotion, memory, and evaluations that affect the reader's sense of self, others, and the world. Thus reading 'is best regarded as something done by people rather than by brains. To say the brain 'looks,' 'thinks,' or 'remembers' is about as appropriate as saying that the stomach enjoys a good meal' (Smith, 2003, p. 11). To consider reading and by extension, literacy fully, researchers and educators must juxtapose findings from socio-cultural, psychological, and biomedical research. Juxtaposition is not a conflation of approaches, but an examination of what each has to offer (see, for example, chapter 5). This entails a critical appraisal of each approach's theoretical underpinnings and the ways in which each approach constructs ability and disability. In this juxtaposition, attention must also be given to the power differentials between approaches and active resistance made to any form of hegemony.

Any hierarchical approach to literacy policy and research that shuts out other paradigms from *decision making* as well as *knowledge production* as in the biomedical approach in the Elmwood case, has a number of negative results. Chiefly, it de-professionalizes teachers, reduces the potentially helpful contributions to knowledge from research outside instrumentalism, belies the individual strengths and needs of literacy learners, pathologizes these children, and diverts attention from the plethora of linguistic, cultural, social, economic, and political factors that greatly influence students' literacy achievements. This is an impediment to community building and to the generation of new knowledge and practice which could directly benefit children – particularly those who struggle with their in-school literacy.

Conclusion

The children of Elmwood received a literacy curriculum based on a single theory. When one theory is exclusively employed, only the goals of that theory can be achieved. Thus, for Elmwood students there was no potential for emancipation or explanation. Additionally, when only the brain is addressed, other crucial factors in literacy development (e.g., discursive and affective) cannot be acted upon. Despite the bad-news story we have told here, we remain hopeful. Specifically, we believe that positive change in literacy education and research can come through concerted resistance to the single-theory approach. For this to happen, many disciplines must start writing and conducting research into students deemed disabled. There must be a refusal to allow only those who take a medical-model approach to disability to claim responsibility for children who are seen not to be achieving in school. When curriculum studies, for example, begins to take an interest in such students and their literacy development, these children will more likely be de-pathologized. Because pathologizing is so intertwined with instrumentalism and the othering of those who are pathologized (i.e., seeing them as objects to be learned about and done unto), de-pathologizing children could lead to the achievement of more theoretical goals; it also respects their backgrounds, agency, knowledge, and literacies. Some instances of this asset-oriented approach to literacy and children are forthcoming in chapters 6 & 7. Next, chapter 4 provides a greater look at some of the children from Elmwood as well as other CLD children from a contrasting school.

4

A Case Study of the Pathologizing of Culturally and Linguistically Diverse Students in Early Years Classrooms

LUIGI IANNACCI

This chapter takes up and extends understandings of the phenomenon of pathologizing by considering how it relates to culturally and linguistically diverse (CLD) young children. Consistent with the rest of *Early Childhood Curricula*, the research for this chapter takes place in a time when international economic restructuring has ensured increased mobility within labour markets and cross-cultural contact (Burbules & Torres, 2000; Cummins, 2005). Immigration around the world has more than doubled since 1975 (United Nations, 2002); as a result North American elementary school students are more culturally and linguistically diverse than ever before (Obiakor, 2001). Indeed as described in chapter 1, a significant number of children in Canadian urban elementary schools speak a first language (L1) other than English or French (Citizenship & Immigration Canada, 2003; Kilbridge, 1997). Despite these changing demographics, researchers have noted a dearth of research about CLD students in early childhood education (ECE) and a disparity in providing resources for these students (Bernhard et al., 1995; Toohey, 2000; Suárez-Orozco, 2001; Falconer & Byrnes, 2003). Further, the limited scholarship on young children learning English as second language has traditionally been methods-focused with very little produced from socio-cultural and critical perspectives (Toohey, 2000). An overemphasis on micro-level concerns has served to re-assert the depoliticization of ESL teaching and learning (Skutnabb-Kangas, 2000).

In contrast, this study is grounded in socio-cultural theory as it informs understandings of early literacy (Bourne, 2001; Gee, 2001; Boyd & Brock, 2004) described in chapter 3. Coming to literacy is therefore not exclusively about the acquisition of a code, but also, and more importantly, a culture. As such, it is imperative to examine critically what students appropriate as they encounter school literacy as well as the impact of this appropriation on their identities, families, and life-course options. To this end, the study also draws on critical multiculturalism (McLaren, 1994; Kincheloe & Steinburg, 1997; May, 1999; Ladson-Billings, 2004) to further inform an analysis of literacy curricula encountered by CLD students in their early years classrooms.

Critical multiculturalism is based in critical theory whose goal is emancipation (Habermas, 1972). As such, it is 'especially concerned with how domination takes place, the way human relations are shaped in the workplace, the schools and everyday life' (Kincheloe & Steinburg, 1997, p. 23). Translated into education, critical theory can help educators explore 'how pedagogy functions as a cultural practice to produce rather than merely transmit knowledge within asymmetrical relations of power that structure teacher-student relations' (Giroux, 1992 in Sleeter and Bernal, 2004, p. 241). It can also assist educators to link multicultural education with wider socio-economic and political inequalities. This link has traditionally been absent from discussions about and conceptualizations of multiculturalism and multicultural education (May, 1999).

The aforementioned framing informs the ethnography (Iannacci, 2005) on which this chapter and chapter 7 report. The study addresses gaps in the provision of appropriate education for CLD children in two Kindergarten and two Grade 1 classrooms. The ways in which schools pathologized CLD students through various 'dimensions of schooling' (Cummins, 2001 p. viii,), (e.g., assessment, pedagogy, cultural and linguistic incorporation and community participation) was a key issue that emerged in the data.

This chapter examines the processes of pathologizing manifest in assessment practices and the impact of these processes on the literacy curriculum and identity options available to CLD students. The ways schools marginalized the various 'funds of knowledge' (Moll, 1992) possessed by CLD students and their parents while assigning them deficient and pathologized identities is demonstrated through narratives I constructed using multiple forms of data about four early years classrooms. The dominant discourses discussed in chapters 1 and 2 that presently impact ECE are examined in relation to how they privileged and presented forms of literacy curricula as a way of curing students' pathologies. I begin by revisiting the Elmwood case from the last chapter and then provide contextual information about the second site in the study, Norman Bethune Public School. Data are then presented and discussed to highlight the dominant discourses that shaped practices that led to and reinforced deficit and pathologizing constructions of CLD children. Lastly, analyses and conclusions are drawn from the data.

Revisiting Elmwood Public School

As demonstrated in chapter 3, a dominant notion that often informed how teachers thought about and provided for CLD students at Elmwood was that deficiency in school literacy resulted from of a lack of literacy experience at home, their parents' low socio-economic status, low levels of English proficiency, and low motivation. This deficit perspective was further reinforced and confirmed by assessments and evaluations that characterized students as below grade level or behind in meeting developmental norms. Anna-Marie, a teacher new to both teaching and the school suggested the school was considered the 'hood' and 'difficult' because of to the low socio-economic status of the children and their parents. She also described several CLD students as learning disabled and one of them, Janna, as a former 'selective mute,' a term used to describe several students learning ESL in both the schools I studied. Early in the year, Anna-Marie was replaced by Connie who was also new to the public school system and had not previously worked with students learning ESL. She too characterized the school as 'low' since many of the Grade One students did not meet the grade-level expectations outlined in Ontario Ministry of Education Curriculum documents. Cindy, one of Elmwood's more experienced JK/SK teachers, described her students and their situations as follows:

> The children in my class are from a very transient, very poor area. They haven't had the nice things. They haven't been read to. Now whether it's that the parents don't know how, or they haven't been there, or for other social reasons ...
>
> Some children don't even come to JK [junior kindergaten] at all, or if they do, they are so young [in terms of maturation] they come without basic social skills that children in other schools would have. These children have had no nursery rhymes read to them and, you know, they've not had any of the time spent with them that everybody expects that all children would have. It's very sad, but we have to pick that up here and try to give that to them.

Cindy was critical of the term 'selective mute' when applied to students learning ESL and was curious about its origins. She shared insightful discoveries about the designation as applied to a few of her students. May, one of her students involved in my study, for example, had an older brother labelled a 'selective mute.' Cindy was his former Kindergarten teacher and remarked that he demonstrated the same behaviours exhibited by May, behaviours indicative of ESL learners in their silent period. She discovered the origins of his identification and shared this with me during an interview as we discussed the term. Cindy said she had never referred to any child as a 'selective mute' but knew that a doctor had given May's brother that label in a mental health report. Cindy also told me that despite being an ESL learner, May's brother had never received any ESL support. He had instead qualified for speech and language pathology and undergone psychological testing that labelled him learning disabled in addition to his selective mute designation. During an interview with May's father issues concerning May's older brother arose. 'One of the speech pathologists that we've talked to said his tongue is actually far too big; his head has to grow into his tongue.'

Problematic assessment and evaluation practices and procedures were also noted in Anna-Marie/Connie's Grade One class and further contributed to CLD students' pathologizing. Michelle, the ESL teacher, pointed out that as a general rule, teachers did not provide grades for ESL students new to Canada or to school on their first report. After that, D's and A's were discouraged because a D would indicate that the program was too difficult and an A would indicate the student was not ESL. Michelle used either checklists or anecdotes to report to teachers about students. The sheer number of ESL students meant that the teachers rather than Michelle were ultimately responsible for completing report cards. Teachers seemed unaware of documents and frameworks that described alternative expectations based on levels of second language acquisition through listening, speaking, reading, writing and orientation. As a result, the expectations against which the ESL students were evaluated were those of the regular Grade One curriculum. Such assessment of CLD students did not measure their acquisition of English as a second language; instead, it measured their deficiencies. My conversation with Connie documents this approach to ESL assessment.

> Connie: We mark ESL on the report card if it affects that subject and so we can't give them anything lower than a 'C,' but I don't see the long-term expectations for them. Eventually they have to meet the expectations like everyone else. I'm not sure where that's caught up. I guess it's over

the first three years. Maybe the primary grades. But, I don't see the long range plan ... That may be more the ESL teachers ... they may understand that sort of thing.

Luigi: You said you can't give them anything lower than a 'C.' So, when you evaluate them are they [CLD students] being evaluated in comparison to the regular Ministry expectations?

Connie: We still use the Ministry expectations.

Luigi: So, what happens? Do they get administered a 'C.'

Connie: Like, in Language. Most of them got a 'C' because they're at the lowest level.

Luigi: There was a Ministry document that was produced, which I actually have here if you want to take a look at it. It's a purple sort of thick document and it has alternative expectations laid out for levels one through four of ESL learning. Were you aware of the document at all?

Connie: No, I wasn't.

These assessment practices were problematic for both students learning ESL and their parents. CLD students' seeming lack of progress when evaluated without consideration for the fact that they were acquiring a second language and culture signalled a problem to be rectified by psychological assessments and placement in special education. This became especially evident when it came to Nomali (a Grade One student) and her mother.

Nomali: A 'Special Needs' Child

Originally from Zimbabwe, Nomali arrived in Canada in May 2001 and attended Senior Kindergarten at Elmwood. Nomali's first language was Ndebele; her exposure to English in a Kindergarten in Zimbabwe had been limited since Ndebele was an official language of instruction. She lived with her mother and older brother; initially, the family spoke Ndebele at home.

During her first year in a Canadian school, Nomali did not meet grade-level expectations. The school staff considered having the educational psychologist assess her for learning disabilities. The team of administrators and special education resource teachers called in the ESL consultant who advised waiting a few years in order to give Nomali time to acquire English. The ESL consultant stressed that it was too difficult to differentiate between a learning disability and English proficiency issues since Nomali had spent only a short time in a Canadian school. The team took her advice. During the following year, however, (the year of this study), concerns were again raised about Nomali. By December, Nomali's mother had been asked to attend a school team meeting.

Connie, who was part of the team, reported Nomali's mother had phoned two or three times since the team meeting to mention different things. Connie thought that, because Nomali's mother had met face-to-face with the team, she now felt she could speak more freely. Her good command of English enabled her to explain the family background and give Connie a better understanding of Nomali. The mother said the program was far in advance of what Nomali had been receiving in Zimbabwe. She felt that Nomali was having trouble because the Grade 1 program was too difficult and seemed to be preparing Nomali for university. She was not protesting this difficulty, just recognizing it.

A subsequent interview with Nomali's mother also raised the issue of the team meeting and provided a clear but bleak picture of the assessment practices and processes her daughter experienced. According to the assessments, Nomali was not progressing. Nomali's mother had asked at the last team meeting whether they thought the system was succeeding with Nomali. She said the school had recommended Nomali be put in a special class streaming students through to Grades 7 and 8. This is the track to jobs, not university. She felt this was unfair to Nomali and that Nomali should be given another chance before being put in that class. To Nomali's mother, it was too early to be making a final decision about Nomali's future; there was too much emphasis on the negative aspect of her English proficiency. She had noticed at one of the meetings, everybody had been shocked by Nomali's lack of progress and she wondered whether other children were having the same struggle. Nomali's mother questioned the impact of psychological assessments and special education for young children based on her daughter's negative response to these pathologizing processes. She also questioned how appropriate these practices and placements were when directed at young children who were new to a culture and language.

> The special education, as much as I really appreciate it, I just felt that it was the source of intimidation for Nomali, in the first place because there were a lot of people trying to help her and, at that moment, she defined herself as a special needs child, in quotation marks if you want. And that intimidated her. When she started Grade One, she didn't like school. She complained not to like school. And if a child comes everyday from school and says: 'I don't want to go back to school,' it doesn't sound good.

When there was the psychologist who was going to study her at school, I just had to say: 'You know what, I think now this is too much.' Because she [Nomali] told me, I don't like him. And he told me: 'Nomali wouldn't cooperate at one time.'

I think the language barrier, it cannot be over-emphasized because at the end of the day, even though I'm saying that these children have to know a lot – they are prepared for University at grade two – some of it is really not from school, some of it is general knowledge by virtue of the fact that they are growing up here. When you take the two children [referring to her son as well] and make them sit there and compare and do an IQ test, which is based on this type of Western world, obviously you think ok, that child's IQ based on this is low, right? But really the reason is that my son and my daughter they have to learn these things. Just to summarize, a child coming in the country doing ESL has to double perform to be able to be at the same level with the other children who were born here.

As mentioned in chapter 3, Elmwood teachers were under a great deal of pressure to address students' measured deficiencies based on these deficit-driven forms of data. This pressure often forced them to access and privilege forms and understandings of literacy and literacy curricula that curtailed children's engagement with alternative types of literacy learning. They believed that using these privileged forms would remedy CLD students' deficits and prepare them to meet the following year's grade-level expectations. These remedies took the form of scripted synthetic phonics programs delivered through direct instruction. In Kindergarten this was done through literacy group sessions. These sessions required the Kindergarten children to sit for up to 45 minutes while they received their literacy 'shot[s] in the arm' (Swadener, 1995, p. 22). Cindy (the Kindergarten teacher) did not approve of the sessions, did not feel they were effective for students learning ESL (or any of her students), felt she had little choice in implementing them in her classroom, and also felt blamed for her students' poor test results.

We were called to a meeting with the Principal, the literacy teacher, and the Kindergarten teachers. The Grade 1 teachers – because they had results from the phonemic awareness test [administered in September] – said that they were not very pleased with the results and wanted to improve the results of the children.

We had the list of results and when I looked at the list of results, the ESL children were in that list, so they had been tested as well, which is ridiculous, you know, for things being tested, when they can't speak the language anyway or they're just learning it. For them to be able to isolate sounds, and, you know, do all of these other tricky[1] things that are hard enough for anybody to do is ridiculous. So, obviously they scored very low, so their results were part of the overall scores. So, considerations for things like that were not taken in.

We looked at the scores and when we looked at comparisons of other schools or where they should be they might be one percentage off. So, whose fault is that? I just, I don't know. I take it very personally because that's the way that I feel that it's coming. I don't like that feeling because I work very hard and I know that what I'm teaching is very good and very appropriate for them, and I don't like to be made to feel that I'm not.

I heard a lot of: 'They can't do this; they can't even do this; I don't think they know anything, and they come into Grade 1 and they don't know how to do this, they don't know how to do that.' It was almost like the teachers were expecting them to be able to do everything it said in that Grade 1 curriculum when they got to Grade 1.

So, the literacy teacher suggested that we have these literacy groups twice a day with the children and divide them into three groups. So, this was implemented at the beginning of October. So, this happens twice a day for half an hour everyday. The literacy teacher comes in, an EA [educational assistant] comes in, and I am in and have a group of children. Six children in each group, and we are to help them improve in word awareness, phonemic awareness, and reading skills. It's very, very long for the children.

As far as ESL children go, when you sit them down at the tables in large groups or small groups for these structured activities, instead of having them at their play centres, if they don't have the support so they don't really understand what you're saying or what to do, they can be trying to watch the person next to them, but they still don't really know what to do, and I question how much they're learning that way. Whereas if they go to a centre, such as the Building Centre, where I know that you have seen a couple of children interacting, there is so much language use there that they are picking up a lot more learning from the other students. They're learning a lot more there than they are at the table ...

---

1 These are the phonemic awareness screening tools described in Chapter 3. Specifically they contain items that ask children to segment syllables and discriminate sounds within words (e.g., say 'cart,' now say it again without the "/t/"- sound).

When it's time for them to go, especially the ESL children, to the activity centres, they come alive. They talk more to whoever is there, whether it's to me or to the other children. If I'm still at the table working on something with a small group, they'll come to tell me things, whereas they don't always do that when it's just the literacy groups that are going on, or they have to sit down and do their phonics or whatever it is, they're not as open ...

To sit down at the table, I think they worry a little more because they don't know what's coming. So, if they have to feel that way every time they have to sit down in the chair at the table that's not good.

Cindy was not alone in her belief that the sessions were not effective. I observed a number of the phonics and phonemic awareness literacy group sessions that clearly demonstrated students' resistance and displeasure at this form of instruction. Several CLD students sat silently throughout the sessions, did not participate, and were reprimanded for fidgeting. They were disengaged, and completed worksheets as quickly as possible in order to attend preferred centres where they could negotiate their own learning and communication. Cindy's and the students' frustration with this configuration of practice is evident in the following narrative.

'R' Day

The literacy teacher began today's literacy group session by writing 'R' on a big sheet, which she shows to the students. She then showed a small book containing pictures, some of which were things that start with /r/. The students were asked to identify items that began with /r/ and echo what sound /r/ made. A couple of students did so successfully before she called on Amet who sat silently and grinned but did not respond.

Amet, the youngest child in an Albanian speaking family, lives with his parents and older sister, Janna, also a participant in this study. He was born in Canada and began JK shortly after turning four. Although his utterances were often restricted to echoing things his classmates and I said, his oral proficiency in English improved a great deal as the year progressed. Highly communicative, demonstrative, rambunctious, and excitable during play, 'No' was one of the first English words he used independently in January. I observed Amet code switching (switching between languages) into Albanian to himself during individual and parallel play. A common strategy Amet used to finish the mandatory *Jolly Phonics* worksheet quickly was to write a few letters then, using one crayon, furiously colouring the featured picture with a few broad strokes. He would then rush to his preferred sand, water or construction activity. The time spent at these activities was highly productive. On many occasions we discussed and explored concepts such as volume and capacity, colours, directions, and materials as Amet built and experimented. Although other children liked Amet, his proficiency in spoken English meant that he often played by himself. Other boys would join Amet after he initiated his own play.

I usually sat right beside Amet during literacy group sessions because he needed one-on-one assistance. Whenever I moved to sit next to other students, Amet tuned out and fidgeted. The teacher repeatedly had to refocus his and others' attention to keep them on task. At times she left her seat to direct Amet through the task in hand-on-hand fashion.

On this day, the literacy teacher asked Amet a second time for an 'R' word. When I removed my ring and gave it to him, he rolled it around in his hand. I asked him what it was. 'Ring' he replied. After a slight pause, he looked up at the literacy teacher and repeated 'Ring, /rrr/!' The literacy teacher affirmed his answer with praise. She then asked another student to write 'R' on chart paper with a picture of an 'R' item under it. Each student was asked to copy 'R' and draw pictures of 'R' items on individual sheets of paper. The entire session lasted 40 minutes. Towards the end, Amet looked directly at the teacher and said, 'Too long.' The literacy teacher giggled nervously and replied. 'OK' but proceeded despite having to plead for the children's stillness and attention.

At the end of the session the literacy teacher declared: 'Phew, this was a struggle. I think the OT [occupational therapist] has to be called – Do you think? Or is it just they don't get enough practice?' I replied, 'I think they're really young.' She continued, 'Yeah, I'm going to have to check if their brothers [a few of the students' older brothers] had OT [occupational therapy]. They're the same way.' Again, I offered: 'It's hard to sit that long.' She took note: 'Yeah, but I used to do stuff like this all the time with my classes. I mean they couldn't even hold paper. They should know how to do that.'

By this time Cindy had joined our conversation. As the literacy teacher left she looked at me intently and said, 'There will be many changes next year.' I smiled back and said, 'I figured there would be.'

The Grade One teacher used the Grade One version of the same commercially prepared phonics programme (*Jolly Phonics*) found in the Kindergarten classrooms. A great deal of literacy curriculum focused on isolated phonics and phonemic awareness disconnected from other literacy activity and instruction.[2] Conventional literacy was stressed through levelled books, copying of conventional print, and the value attributed to accuracy in the students' journal writing. A parent volunteer came in the mornings to evaluate each student's ability to read the levelled books. Students were called individually from other work to read to the volunteer who then assessed them. These formulaic books contained controlled vocabulary and were levelled according to difficulty. Students who finished their work were permitted self-selected reading and, not surprisingly, the same students read the trade books in the limited class library that contained very few multicultural children's picture books. When the teacher used a trade book during shared reading sessions, ESL and low-achieving students were at times pulled out of class for remedial or ESL support. This denied them an opportunity to hear book language. ESL students rarely experienced a shared reading of literature during ESL sessions.

Phonics and phonemic awareness lessons taught in isolation seemed the mainstay of the ESL support sessions, the regular classroom and the lessons taught by the primary resource special education teacher. Indeed, teachers had at one point agreed to align curriculum so that if a specific letter and sound were taught in the regular classroom, it would be reinforced in the support sessions. Connie even further supplemented the phonics instruction with her own commercially prepared materials. Students who showed no expected gains (even those who were ESL) were referred for psychological testing. Student's cultural and linguistic differences were not recognized as affecting their ability to perform this curriculum. The following narrative crafted from field notes demonstrates difficulties students encountered with this form of literacy instruction.

'F' day

Connie delivered a phonics lesson. Today was 'F' day with a lesson sequence similar to that described in the 'R' Day narrative. After the les-

---

2 The sequence of the *Jolly Phonics* timetable (e.g. week one: s, a, t, i, p, n) is organized so that "letter sounds are introduced at the rate of one letter sound a day" so that "all of the 42 letter sounds are ... covered after about 9 weeks" (Lloyd, 1998, pp. 10–11). Although this sequence was followed, the amount of time spent on each letter was usually much longer than a day (i.e., a week or two).

son, Connie explained that students were to find and circle pictures on a sheet that began with 'F' and ignore pictures of other things. Items included a football, an American flag, and someone playing golf. Before distributing the sheet, she asked questions about the pictures to prepare students for the task. Although she gave clues about the football, no one answered and Ines sat quietly averting her eyes from Connie. She repeated, 'It's an oblong ball – you play a game with it and you kick it with your foot.' Despite Connie's descriptions, both Ines and another ESL student had difficulty determining items that began with 'F.'

Ines attended Senior Kindergarten at Elmwood after arriving in Canada in February from Argentina. She began receiving ESL support at the beginning of her Grade 1 year. She spoke mostly in English but would code switch into Spanish when she could not find the English word (e.g., gélidoo for icy) or to demonstrate her ability to speak her L1. The first time I noticed Ines doing this had been during an ESL session in early October. The ESL teacher's encouragement of first language use fostered a comfort level that allowed the switches. Ines also participated more often in the ESL sessions than during whole-class instruction in the regular Grade 1 class. After the October session, I noticed she began to enjoy teaching her classmates Spanish when the opportunity presented itself in her regular classroom as well. For example, as I read the class two Spanish English bilingual books, *Hairs/Pelitos* by Sandra Cisneros (1994) and *Taking a Walk/Caminando* by Rebecca Emberley (1990), Ines sat in a chair beside me in front of the class and happily translated words and sentences within the book into Spanish as her classmates repeated them (e.g., school/escuela). Throughout the year, some of her classmates would repeat words she taught them. I asked her how she felt about this. She beamed and said, 'It makes me happy.' Ines enjoyed the bilingual books so much she asked me for her very own copies. I provided the books and later, when I asked her if she was enjoying them she said, 'I'm reading with mom. I learn to read in English and Spanish. It's good. I read with my sister first in Spanish, then in English. My mom says it's good.' Ines also asked me for more letters in Spanish similar to the one I had sent home with her asking her parents for permission to include her in my study.

Ines points to the American flag and asks, 'Flag?' while completing the 'F' day worksheet. I assure her that it is a flag, an American one with the same shape but a different look than the Canadian flag hanging in the classroom. I have difficulty explaining the golf picture, since I have never played golf. From time to time, Ines names an item in Spanish 'flores – flowers, dedo – finger.' I listen to her then elicit Spanish responses from her about pictures on the sheet. We compare and contrast them with English words for the same items. Sometimes they both begin with /f/, sometimes they don't. Eventually we complete the worksheet, correctly identifying 'F' items and leaving the others. The class stops at this point for a snack. As Ines gets her snack and prepares to go to recess, she names other items around the room in Spanish.

During an interview with Connie I discussed my observations of some of the difficulties experienced by students learning ESL with the *Jolly Phonics* program. Connie said that some of the actions and pictures were not as meaningful to them as to the other students, but they did not seem to have a problem with pronunciation. There were, however, no ESL accommodations within the program.

Regardless of the teacher's recognition that there were issues with *Jolly Phonics*, there were many incidents at Elmwood and also at Norman Bethune similar to those described during 'F' Day. It must also be noted that non-ESL students' familiarity with some of these items was also occasionally limited.

Norman Bethune Public School

Located in the same city as Elmwood, Norman Bethune Public School is situated near shopping malls and restaurants. What you notice first as you walk through this spacious, well-designed school are the colourful walls and how everything is well maintained. Mostly working – and middle-class families in new semi-detached and detached houses and town houses live in the area. Norman Bethune's students have traditionally come directly from the surrounding community.

Over the past few years an influx of children from a variety of cultural and linguistic backgrounds has changed the unilingual English, native-born Canadian demographic. As with Elmwood, the demographic shift mirrors the increased number of immigrants in the city and the nation. In some classrooms more than a third of the students are immigrants or children of recent immigrants who speak a language other than English. Many young families from various parts of the Middle East have settled in the area. In the early years classrooms a number of children speak Arabic. Eleven of the twenty-four students in the Grade 1 classroom, for example, received ESL support. Despite the growing number of students learning ESL, ESL support had significantly decreased over the years leading up to this study.

The teaching staff at Norman Bethune was mostly white, middle-class Canadians who recognized the socio-economic status of the students. Some teachers lived near the school. Long-time staff members described the recent years as the most difficult because of the changing demographics. They mentioned the increased number of students with familial and economic difficulties that led to behaviour problems as well as the greater number of ESL students. Teachers commonly complained about the lack of resources to cope with the demographic change. Some teachers were sensitive to the wave of immigration into the school community and were beginning to practise culturally sensitive pedagogy; others were committed to the traditional curriculum. Some questioned the teachers who were beginning to change their classroom practice. On one of my first visits to the school I spoke with a teacher about my study.

> Luigi: I'm doing some research on early years ESL students.
> Teacher: Oh, well there are lots of ESL kids here.
> Luigi: Yeah, it's great.
> Teacher: Great for you anyway.

Pat, the experienced JK/SK teacher described her afternoon class (the one I was observing) as the most challenging she had ever encountered at Norman Bethune because of behaviour difficulties. Sarah, the new Grade One teacher in her second year of teaching, also found covering the curriculum and managing students' behaviour to be challenging. The number of ESL students in her class was also a concern:

> Well, just with the curriculum. It's hard to get everything in. You have to, all the other stuff, the discipline and the behavioral side of it. I don't know, I find that tough. I find it tough when you have kids, like a couple of kids that you feel take up ... And how much time they take up saying their name and stuff like that and reminding them ... it takes away from what you could have gotten done. I think the language ... we have a really high ESL population in this school and in this class. I have eleven kids that go out to ESL every other day or so and that's a little bit tough too because you don't want to start something when they're not in the room. And, also, just because ... they don't speak the same languages at home. This is the only time that some of these kids are speaking English and you see that ...

A lack of professional development and consequent awareness of what constitutes ESL development contributed a great deal to the pathologizing of CLD students. This was especially evident in discussions with teachers about 'selective mutism.' The term, used by Sarah to describe a student who was now speaking English at school, continued to puzzle me just as it had at Elmwood and led to the following exchange:

Luigi: I wanted to ask you about the term 'selective mute.' On my first day here you mentioned a student as having been described to you as someone who had been a 'selective mute' last year. Could you tell me where that term came from?

Sarah: Yes. The Kindergarten teacher had her in Kindergarten last year. When I was setting up my class last summer, she approached me and said I was going to have this 'selective mute' in my class. She said the girl was very smart, took everything in, but didn't talk at all. Her family spoke Polish at home. That was all the warning I got. On the first day of school I asked the Kindergarten teacher again which one she was. She pointed her out and I had to tell the Kindergarten teacher she was speaking now. She had obviously built up her confidence over the summer and was now talking. The ESL teacher explained to me that a child learning ESL needs time to learn a second language, to find the right words, and gain confidence. She's not a loud child, but she does speak.

Luigi: Do You think that 'selective mute' is a valid descriptor?

Sarah: Yes, because she's choosing not to talk. The word 'mute' makes it sound as if something's wrong, but it made sense when it was explained to me. She didn't talk at all, not once, whether she was sick or even when she really needed something.

Luigi: But you also said she was learning to speak English at the same time. So, was it entirely a choice?

Sarah: Yes, she was still making a choice. If someone is born mute, there is no choice. But selecting not to talk is a choice. She could have spoken; it might not have been perfect English, but she could have tried. But she chose not to until she felt ready.

Still haunted by the term, I explored it further with Pat, the JK/SK teacher who also described a few students learning English as a second language as 'selective mutes.' Somewhat critical of the term, she nevertheless continued to apply it to Khaled, a JK student whom she initially characterized as an indulged child who experienced very little discipline at home and was immature for his age. She added that he was initially quite frightened of school and had difficulties adjusting. Pat was frustrated by these behaviours and told Khaled's father that he would be kicked out of Kindergarten if they persisted (even though she knew she couldn't do that).

Khaled was born in Canada and is the youngest child in a family consisting of his parents and his older sister and brother, who along with their parents were born in Syria. Arabic was the dominant language spoken at home. Despite Khaled's inexperience with English, he was also subjected to the same assessments as his classmates. His performance on these assessments further reinforced his status as a 'deficient' student. Pat attached a Post-it note that said, 'painful' on one of a series of assessments she administered to Khaled that stressed number, shape and letter/sound recognition. Khaled's paintings, Play-Doh creations and connector set constructions were, however, often vibrant, complex and created with a great deal of vigor that was made obvious by how animated he became as he worked. Despite Khaled's gregarious nature, his father told me that Khaled complained he had no friends and no one would play with him. Khaled's older sister frequently did volunteer work in Pat's classroom at recess, lunch and after school. Pat also referred to Khaled's sister as a 'selective mute' and mentioned that her teachers had deemed her so.

Pat: Khaled's older sister's teachers in Grades Four, Five and Six all labelled her a 'selective mute.'

Luigi: Where do you think the term comes from?

Pat: I'm not entirely sure who made it up. It just sounds like another one of those little labels we throw on people to explain something.

Luigi: You used it as well when I first came.

Pat: Yes.

Luigi: You used it to describe Samina (an SK ESL student).

Pat: I've been hearing the term for a few years now. I may not be applying it in the right way but what 'selective mute' means to me is that the child is stubborn enough not to talk to anyone at any time. It is never a question of ability or physical motor problems. It is simply a matter of will; choosing not to speak.

Luigi: So you think it is a matter of choosing not to speak?

Pat: I think with some kids, yes, definitely. In Khaled's sister's case I do. But if I ask who has done the calendar books and who hasn't, we have extended conversations and I don't know why. I don't think she is doing it out of stubbornness or defiance or anger. I think she's doing it out of a nervous reaction; she has a difficult time speaking in front of her peers. For Zafir (a JK ESL student), for example, standing up in front of the group for his show-and-tell to talk about what he brought is a stressful, stressful, stressful situation. I also think we have gone way too far in using medical terminology in education and society in general with terms like 'learning disabled.'

Luigi: Zafir and Khaled are in their silent period. That's what it looks like.

Pat: Well, yes I would call them silent periods. More so for Zafir but I'm not sure I ever called him a 'selective mute.'

Luigi. When I first came you referred to Samina as a 'selective mute' and said she had come a long way and was speaking frequently now. I thought maybe she had been in her silent period and was coming out of it. The term is used in other classrooms to describe ESL kids who are now speaking a great deal and reading and writing. Teachers will say that last year the kid was a 'selective mute.' Then they describe the transition. You realize what they are talking about is the ...

Luigi and Pat: The silent period.

Pat: With Khaled I would say there are some definite attention-seeking behaviours, but with Zafir I would definitely say not.

Pat's understanding of 'selective mutism' and belief that Khaled was a 'selective mute' had implications for her interactions with him. The following narrative demonstrates the ways Kahled's pathological and deficit-oriented classroom identity shaped how he was taught.

Your Words

A student asked me to work with him at the craft table. We were gluing materials to a paper plate; he said we were building a house. I scanned the room as he tried to get the piece of yellow construction paper he was using as a window to stick. I noticed that Khaled was by himself playing with a bright red car. I heard him making car noises. BRRRRRRRRRRRR. BRRRRRRRRRRRR. RRRRRRRRRRR! The student I was working with successfully applied the construction paper window and asked me to hand him some blue stickers. He told me he wanted me to put a few on the top of the plate to make them look like roof tiles. I complied and focussed on getting them aligned. I suddenly heard a sharp cry and looked up toward Khaled. He no longer had the car. He was distraught. I saw a student heading off with the car. He had grabbed it from Khaled who was now sobbing and pointing toward the culprit while walking toward Pat. She was working with a student at a nearby table when she heard his cries. She stopped what she was doing, walked towards him and asked him what had happened. Khaled was inconsolable and continued to cry and sob. He was still pointing at the other child who was unmoved by his outburst and continued to play with the car. Occasionally Khaled made moaning sounds and heaved as he pointed. Pat continued to ask him what had happened as she comforted him and wiped his tears. This went on for some time. Once Khaled had begun to calm down Pat asked him again what had happened. Khaled continued to moan and point. Pat said she could not understand what he was saying. She tapped her chin with three fingers and said: 'Khaled, you have to use your words to tell me what happened. Use your words.' I had seen this gesture used before by Kindergarten teachers trying to get students to articulate needs or a response. Khaled continued to point, moan and gesture towards the student with the car. Pat continued to tap her chin with her fingers and repeated her command: 'Use your words.' This continued for a while and finally Pat said: 'If you want to tell me what happened you have to use your words.' As she walked back to the student with whom she was working, she noticed me observing. Khaled continued to stand in the same position. He had calmed down and was no longer pointing but now appeared to be confused as he continued to gesture towards the boy with the car. Finally, he sighed and with a posture of defeat, walked over to the connector-set equipment and began a new activity. I felt helpless as I finished off the paper-plate house.

Later, Pat mentioned the incident and I told her what I had observed. She said, 'I'm trying to get him to use his words. It's funny the things he will say, but when you ask him to use words he's such a 'selective mute' that he doesn't want to use his words.'

Much as at Elmwood, ESL students at Norman Bethune were evaluated on their ability to meet regular grade-level expectations. During an interview shortly after first-term report cards had been sent home, Sarah the Grade 1 teacher, and I discussed the nature of assessment as it affected ESL students. Many ESL students were evaluated at a C level. When I asked her whether documents and frameworks that outlined alternative expectations for ESL students were used to formulate evaluations, Sarah said, 'No.' I confirmed: 'You were looking exclusively at the [Ontario Ministry of Education] Grade 1 Language document when you formulated these report cards?' 'Yes. The ESL box was checked off on the report card but there were no comments to go with [it].'

Issues regarding assessment and evaluation were also raised during

an interview with Paula the ESL teacher. She saw the lack of differenti-
ated assessment and evaluation as an important and unresolved issue:

> We have teachers who gave our ESL children Es and Rs on the last report
> card [term one] with no comment to go with it and it's like, 'How can
> you? Don't you know what's going on?' ... One of the women said last
> night [at a primary division meeting Paula attended], 'I don't know what
> to write in the report card for the ESL kids. What are you going to give
> me?' ...

The poor evaluation ESL students received on their first-term report
card because of the undifferentiated expectations was disconcerting to
parents and had negative consequences for the students. This was especially evident in Farah's case.

Farah was a Grade 1 student born in Canada and the older of two
children in her Arabic-speaking family. Farah's parents immigrated to
Canada from Lebanon and had questions and concerns about whether
they should be teaching Farah Arabic or English. They considered
enrolling Farah in Islamic school because of their faith, but decided
against it because they felt that simultaneous formal instruction in both
Arabic and English would confuse Farah. Her success in school was
very important to them and her code switching furthered their concerns about her English proficiency. Farah was proud of her cultural
and linguistic background and demonstrated her developing Arabic
literacy. Throughout the year Farah tried to teach me Arabic words and
would show me her ability to write Arabic.

Farah's parents were troubled by Farah's report card and stated their
concerns on the parent/guardian response form returned to the school.
Sarah showed me the letter; parts of it have been reprinted below.

> I went through Farah's report card. I found that she wasn't having the
> best marks. I try to help her with English spelling, reading, writing, but
> we weren't receiving any of her work in any of the other subjects other
> than her work in English. And I've been waiting to see more comments
> from the teacher about her daily work in the classroom in any subject, and
> I didn't get any to show me where Farah's work level is taking place at
> this time so that we could see things just the way they are and try to par-
> ticipate in helping her where weakness is stated or where help on our
> behalf is needed. I didn't see any comments on the report card from the

teacher which I was pretty much waiting for. I am looking forward to meeting with the teacher very very soon.

Although the school district unknowingly scheduled interviews on a Muslim Holiday, Farah's parents nevertheless came in to speak with Sarah about the report card. After their meeting, I interviewed them and had an opportunity to discuss the letter and their concerns. The picture of Farah's deficiencies presented in the report card caused them a great deal of anxiety which negatively influenced interaction with Farah at home, and their understanding of who she was and what she needed as a learner. Farah's mother explained:

> I just wanted to know if there's any weakness, like that I could be able to make improve or make things better for her. That's the only thing that I was really concerned about ... Because the report card shows in reading and writing, C's. So, I didn't say to myself that was improvement, right? That wasn't improvement, didn't show the improvement. In other subjects, she was having B's. But, in reading and writing in English, it didn't show that excellence ... They're all C's ...
>
> So, I was worried because, oh, she's only having C's maybe she's at one point and that's it ...
>
> Because lately I was telling her [Farah], 'You have to pay attention. Maybe you're not doing well. No, no, you're not reading. Look, read this word and then just all the sudden you don't know the word? Come on. The word 'was' or 'so.' You've read it many times, many times and then you don't know how to read it? No way! Then what are you doing at school then?' Ok, I tell her, 'If they tell you this word and then they come again and tell you, 'Here Farah read this word' and you won't know it, right? Oh, you have to pay attention. You have to be more and more and more with the teacher.' That's what I keep telling her. I said maybe that would help her.

The undifferentiated and problematic assessment of ESL students was further exacerbated through the administration of the DRA (the school district's mandated developmental reading assessment also used at Elmwood and discussed in chapter three) to every student in the primary grades. Sarah, commenting on the validity of DRA, noted how inappropriate it was to administer to students learning ESL. Some of the ESL children, for example, could not use the word 'bus' to identify a bus in a picture in the DRA level A booklet because they did not yet know the word; native speakers all knew the word from their general knowledge. To help me evaluate what Sarah and many other teachers had told me about the problems associated with administering the DRA to students learning ESL, I asked Rika, a school district central-office employee about the assessment. Rika's position put her in direct contact with district-wide DRA results and made her aware of many issues confronting schools.

> There is a difference between a student born in Canada and has gone through our school system and is at a level 'Z' [the board created level signifying below level one performance] and an ESL student who's at a level 'Z' ... So, I need to know that. But, I don't think there's really anything in place to kind of differentiate in terms of the process ...
>
> I don't think anything is specifically done to address their [ESL students] needs in terms of a school-district-wide program or plan.

Since Norman Bethune students performed well enough in provincial testing, it was not designated a compensatory school and therefore did not qualify for resources allocated to Elmwood. Although many ESL students in Sarah's Grade One classroom performed at level Z, the school's overall DRA results were such that an early-years literacy specialist teacher was not assigned, nor was mandatory phonemic awareness screening administered to every Senior Kindergarten student by a speech and language pathologist. However, a teacher who delivered a scripted phonics and phonemic awareness program did visit the school and early-years teachers were made responsible for administering the district-wide DRA to all Grade One, Two and Three students. Kindergarten and Grade One teachers were also using the *Jolly Phonics* programme in their classrooms. There was pressure to ensure that all students were at grade level. Although less alarmist than at Elmwood, this pressure did however impact literacy curriculum in ways Pat found uncomfortable. She was critical of and concerned about district-wide mandates and programs purchased to ensure student improvement. She suggested they were affecting the quality of her interactions with students and altering her pedagogy.

Pat received a survey received from her district that asked her to note the percentage of time her Kindergarten programme allotted to literacy. She felt the type of literacy they were asking her to account for ultimately ensured that children spent more time sitting at a table completing paper and pencil tasks such as phonics worksheets. She therefore answered '100%' and submitted the survey. When asked to change her answer, Pat refused stating that literacy infused everything she did within her classroom.

Pat was also concerned that literacy mandates such as *DRA* and *Jolly Phonics* scripted reading assessment and phonics instruction and compromised her ability to personalize interactions with students to further their literacy development. She had many things to say about these mandates and their narrow construction of curriculum. '*Jolly Phonics* is scripted and a scripted conversation is difficult to use with Kindergarten children; they will want to talk about how their dad travelled to the moon or the stitches some other kid got in his head. There is no 'shhhh, we're going to listen to a story now.' At the end of the day, everybody is still an individual with his or her own unique learning style. One size definitely does not fit all. If the child has some unique way of doing things that cannot be captured by the assessment process and the kid's test score goes down as a result, the system decides nothing can be done. The kids just get shoved through and promoted socially until they are illiterate!'

The school district further extended the administration of the DRA to Senior Kindergarten during the school year in which this study occured. Pat was told she had to test all her Senior Kindergarten students in May or June and give the results to the Grade One teachers in September. The following school year, all Senior Kindergarten teachers in the district would have to test their students and submit results to the district central office. I was present the day the $500 DRA reading assessment kit was delivered to the classroom. When asked about the validity of DRA and ESL students Pat said it was not valid at all; in fact, it was barely valid for children familiar with the context. She grew impatient at in-service meetings and wanted to know why the DRA process was continuing when it was demonstrably so ineffective. To Pat, the DRA template was like SAT or IQ thinking and she felt frustrated having to evaluate ESL children from this mindset.

The speech- and print-focused provincial curriculum and consequent school district mandates were noticeable in Sarah's Grade One classroom, just as they had been at Elmwood. Although Sarah used a variety of commercial and teacher-prepared materials to supplement her phonics program, its sequence and pedagogical orientation was commensurate with and influenced by *Jolly Phonics*. The instructional trajectory of lessons and their outcomes often resembled what I described in the '*R*' *Day* and '*F*' *Day* narratives. Although Sarah explained the pictures featured on the work-sheet much as Connie did, ESL students had difficultly naming and understanding items and needed one-on-one teacher support to guide them. When I asked Sarah how *Jolly Phonics* featured in her phonics programme and how it affected ESL students in her classroom, she had thought it worked well.

> Sarah: I like it *[Jolly Phonics]*. I think it's, I think it works really well. I think it's ...I like anything animated with little kids. I really liked the Animated Alphabet too and I was mixing some of it on my own.
> Luigi: How do you organize what letter gets introduced?
> Sarah: I was told to go in a specific order from ... I think they start off, 's,' 'a,' 't.'
> Luigi: That's the *Jolly Phonics* sequence.
> Sarah: Yeah, the *Jolly Phonics* order.
> Luigi: Do you ever find that they have difficulties understanding what pictorially is on the page?
> Sarah: Well, we go over everything on the carpet, first of all. So, if they're paying attention they'll go through every single picture and what it is. Just, and also for the other ones too, sometimes they're hard to figure out, you've seen the paper- it's kind of hard to ... But, I think that usually once they know what the picture is they can get the sounds just like the other kids if they're listening. But, once they know what the sound is they're looking for it, they can hear the sound to go with it. So, they're good that way ... If we go over the instructions, which you have to do for all of the kids anyway ... then they usually get it, unless they're not paying attention to what ... I think it's an easier way for them to learn it one sound at a time and then put them together. They get the sounds coming from the picture. They do that pretty well.

Shared reading, a regular component of the literacy curriculum within Sarah's classroom included a few multicultural fiction and non-fiction trade books from the school library. Although a remedial pullout model was not regularly used in the primary division at Norman Bethune, an itinerant teacher delivered a scripted synthetic phonics and phonemic awareness *Keys to Literacy* program to students (usually ESL). ESL and low-performing students were at times withdrawn from class during shared reading. The following story demonstrates some of the difficulties this posed for ESL students.

Farah's Shield

Sarah's grade partner came to read stories. The first required the students to find the central character (a ladybug) in each of the illustrations. After reading, the teacher gave the book to Farah who had been sitting at her feet mesmerized and highly motivated to find the ladybug. Farah enjoyed drawing and always became talkative and excited when she discussed her own illustrations. One of her journal entries reads: 'I am an artist.' She was thrilled to receive the ladybug book and carefully and intently flipped through its pages as the teacher began preparing the students for another story.

Just as Sarah's grade partner was about to begin reading, the itinerant teacher entered the classroom. Some of the ESL students sensed her presence, turned, and immediately began walking towards her. Farah remained seated, quickly held both sides of the ladybug book above her head, and made herself as small as possible. The *Keys to Literacy* teacher began calling out the names of students with whom she needed to work. When she came to Farah's name she noticed her makeshift shelter, winced, turned to me and said: 'God, she's hiding behind a book! Maybe I can borrow that and after we are done *Keys*, I could read that to her.' Farah walked over to her without incident and followed her out of the room with her ESL classmates.

By the time they returned, the shared reading session was long over and it was time for lunch. To my knowledge the book was never read to her. Before Farah left for lunch, she drew a picture of herself, wrote her name in Arabic and English underneath, and gave it to me. During the very last conversation I had with Farah in June she asked, 'What did you do with that picture with my name in Arabic and English and my picture?' I replied, 'I still have it. It's in a very special place. It's very special to me and I really appreciate you giving it to me.'

The ESL teacher offered a great deal of instruction that focused on phonics. The limited length of the sessions meant that opportunities for shared reading were few. The commercial phonics program used in the mainstream classroom, however, did not determine the sequence or pedagogical orientation of the instruction. Instead, specific themes and selected literature guided what sounds or blends were examined during the sessions. This meant that ESL students experienced phonics and phonemic awareness instruction in their mainstream classrooms, during sessions with the *Keys to Literacy* teacher, as well as during sessions with the

ESL teacher. Although not as dominant as at Elmwood, this type of instruction was still at the forefront of literacy curriculum offered to CLD students.

Discussion

The influence of developmental discourses was evident in the proliferation of deficit-driven assessment and evaluation practices that measured normal progress as delineated by curriculum expectations and assessments organized by students' ages, grades and developmental norms. The checklists, DRA, phonemic awareness screening, and psychological evaluations all reinforced universal constructions and deficit perspectives of CLD students that advanced their deficient and pathologized school identities. What supported assessment practices such as phonemic awareness screening was the notion of poor phonemic awareness as the predictor of literacy disability; universal, measurable developmental trajectories could then be located within the normal or abnormal range by the student's performance on the assessment (Geva, Yaghoub-Zadeh & Shuster, 2000; Stanovich, 1986, 1994).

Although several researchers (Allington, 2001; Coles, 2003; Cummins, 2001; Smith, 2003; Taylor, 1998) have challenged these claims as well as the types of instruction they have initiated within ECE classrooms across North America, Ontario Ministry of Education reports such as the *Early Reading Strategy (2003)* and large-scale projects such as the *Promoting Early Identification* (PEI) initiative have reinforced dominant discourses in early literacy and fuelled the use of deficit-driven assessment and evaluation practices. These practices constructed CLD students' school identities as pathological despite resistance by students, parents, and, occasionally, some teachers. The social, cultural and linguistic factors that challenged the validity of this assigned identity were not considered. Martin (1988) notes how early intervention strategies have obscured adults' understanding of children's potential. Fedoruk (1989) concurs and argues that Kindergarten screening adheres to a child deficit model that 'attempt[s] to assess specific within-child characteristics without regard for situational variability or ecological factors' and is a 'fatal oversimplification of the nature of learning, the dynamics of classroom interaction and the variables that affect school achievement' (p. 41).

The 'selective mute' (SM) designation assigned to CLD students without consideration of the dynamics of second-language learning is another example of how deficit-driven assessment processes furthered students' pathologizing. SM is a rare condition found in less than one percent of the population and is defined as 'the condition in which children persistently do not speak in select social situations where speaking is expected (e.g., school)' (APA, 1994 in Ford, Sladeczek, Carlson & Kratochwill, 1998, p. 193). In order for SM to be diagnosed, the following communication features described in the *Diagnostic and Statistical Manual of Mental Disorders – Fourth Edition* (APA, 1994) must be observed:

- Persistent refusal to talk in one or more social situations, including school
- Consistent failure to speak in specific social situations in which there is an expectation for speaking (e.g., school), despite speaking in other situations
- Disturbances interfere with educational or occupational achievement or with social communication
- Duration of the disturbance is at least 1 month (not limited to the first month of school)
- Failure to speak is not due to a lack of knowledge of, or comfort with, the spoken language acquired in the social situation
- Disturbance is not better accounted for by a communication disorder (e.g., stuttering) and does not occur exclusively during the course of a pervasive developmental disorder, schizophrenia, or other psychotic disorder

When each of these features is examined in relation to CLD students in my study, the SM misdiagnosis and the lack of knowledge about second-language learners that contributed to this misdiagnosis becomes clear:

- Linguistic constraints experienced by students as they were learning ESL limited their English oral communication. This was not indicative of students refusing to speak but rather an aspect of the silent period in second-language acquisition in which receptive language skills exceed language production (Siraj-Blatchford & Clarke, 2000).
- Ways in which student achievement was measured, assessed and evaluated were not responsive to the silent period or other facets of L2 learning, but to ministry expectations as well as age, grade and norm based criteria. As such, assessment practices created deficits rather than language and literacy capabilities.

- Silent periods are by no means universal and can vary significantly (Granger, 2004). The CLD students in my study demonstrated both quantitative and qualitative differences in the ways in which they experienced a silent period. However, a common characteristic all children shared in their silent period was that it exceeded the one-month SM benchmark, a not atypical experience for second language learners (Siraj-Blatchford & Clarke, 2000).
- CLD students were also to varying degrees unfamiliar, and at times, uncomfortable with English and may have been experiencing English Language Anxiety (ELA) within the school context (Pappamihiel, 2002)
- Silent period and ELA are characteristics of ESL learning, not developmental, communicative or psychotic disorders.

Psychology researchers have pointed out that learning ESL complicates the diagnosis of SM. 'The impact of ESL on SM has not been explored; nor for that matter has the impact of other cultural differences' (Ford et al. 1998, p. 193). Despite these cautions, several CLD students and some of their siblings were described and/or labelled selective mutes. The term stemmed from psychological evaluations circulated among teachers and fuelled misconceptions about CLD students as it pathologized them as learners. My observations regarding the pervasive misuse and misapplication of the SM label on CLD students corroborate the assertion that the silent period is often 'misinterpreted by teachers as an unwillingness to participate' (Krashen, 1992 in Ernst-Slavit, Moore & Maloney, 2002, p. 116). This misinterpretation affected teachers' interactions and relationships with CLD students since the teachers believed the students were capable but unwilling to speak. Standardized curriculum and evaluation practices also fuelled their need to get students to speak English. The SM designation as applied to CLD learners prohibited alternative dialogues about the pathologizing construction of the silent period. These necessary conversations are beginning to occur in SLA research and are expanding understandings about this phase of L2 learning beyond current deficit conceptualizations (see Granger, 2004).

The misidentification minority students experience as a result of deficit-driven assessment has long been recognized (Patton, 1998). A 1994 report by the Ontario Ministry of Education indicated an over-representation of minority students in special education classes (Ontario Ministry of Education, 1994, in Bernard et al., 1995). The problem is evident internationally as well. 'In England and parts of the United States, there is an overrepresentation of children from cultural minorities and working classes in perceived categories of mild disablement relative to population percentages' (Baker, 2002, p. 681). The overrepresentation of Negev Bedouin Arab children in Israel and Roma children in the Czech republic identified as learning disabled has also been documented (Dinero, 2002; European Roma Rights Centre, 2003). Tomlinson (1984) has questioned whether this overrepresentation is not just a matter of a child being labelled, but a culture (in Baker, 2002).

We have known for a long time that CLD students have formed patterns of inferiority because of their placements within special education classes or lower-ability groups (Ashworth, 1975) and that labels have produced negative affects on the labelled and others interacting with the stigmatized individual (Goffman, 1963 in Patton, 1998). This was most apparent at Elmwood as students, parents and teachers were implicated in a chain of blame, where each party was made to feel responsible for perceived deficits, while factors that ensured these dynamics had not yet been identified as contributing to the problem. Markowitz, Garcia, & Eichelberger (1997) additionally argue that segregated special education classes and programming create a 'spiral of lower achievement, decreased likelihood of postsecondary education, and more limited employment' (in Patton, 1998, p. 26). The Association for Childhood Education International (ACEI) summarizes the consequences of standardized approaches to evaluation in early childhood education:

> We know ... that testing results in increased pressure on children, setting too many up for devastating failure and, consequently, lowered self-esteem; does not provide useful information about children, yet often becomes the basis for decisions about ... promotion and retention in grades, and placement in special classes; leads to harmful tracking and labelling; compels teachers to spend time preparing children to take the tests, undermining efforts to provide a ... sound program responsive to children's interests and needs; limits educational possibilities, resulting in distortion of curriculum, teaching and learning, as well as lowered expectations; and fails to set conditions for cooperative learning and problem solving. (in Perrone, 1992, p. 46)

CLD students who have not been provided with adequate ESL support have also fared poorly in schools. A large scale study of immigrant academic achievement completed by Professor Lee Gunderson found that when 'the ESL net disappeared, so did the students' which contributed to 'a disturbingly high 'disappearance rate' of more than 60 per cent among immigrant high school students' (Duffy, 2004a). Strong correlations between socio-economic status and academic achievement were also found within the same study. Similarly, an overall immigrant dropout rate of 31 per cent was found in the Toronto District School Board with rates doubling in poorer neighbourhoods. Roessingh and Watt (2004) tracked 540 ESL students between 1989 and 1997 in a high school in Calgary and found that 74 per cent of them dropped out before finishing and were two and a half times more likely not to complete their secondary education than the general population in the same school (in Duffy, 2004a). Cummins (2001) argues that dropout rates among students learning ESL are not solely about lack of English support but also 'the result of particular kinds of interactions in school that lead culturally diverse students to mentally withdraw from academic effort ... [since] the instructional environment frequently does not facilitate or encourage active participation on their part' (p. 77). All these points are relevant when we consider the misidentification, ineffective instruction and lack of engagement CLD students encountered at Elmwood and Norman Bethune.

A critical multicultural discourse contends that education is grounded in structured power relationships designed to serve the interests of the dominant social, political, and economic classes. Theorists who develop these positions have linked school structures and processes, including those used in special education, with the values, attitudes, and needs of dominant social, economic, and political groups (Patton, 1998). The inequitable and problematic ways in which CLD students in my study were evaluated and provided for reflected structures that both propagated their pathologizing and reinscribed coercive relations of power rooted in macro-interactions between dominant groups and subordinated communities. This is evident from a 2001 census that found 12.7 per cent of immigrants living in Canada for fewer than five years unemployed as compared to 7.4 per cent of the Canadian-born population. Recent studies have also shown that low income rates among immigrants have been rising while falling among populations born in Canada. The symptoms of an immigrant underclass are especially evident in large Canadian cities where most immigrants tend to settle (Duffy, 2004b).

Ley argues that the key to addressing inequity is ironically, education. 'Education is a really important issue because low education levels, specifically high school dropout rates, are a very important cor-relant of the underclass scenario. Education is an absolutely central consideration' (Duffy, 2004b). Despite its importance in ensuring that macro-interactions are not further perpetuated in the ways in which CLD students are provided for in schools, inadequate funding has resulted in a steady decrease of ESL programs in Ontario since 1997 (People for Education, 2005). Within my study, frequent changes to ESL schedules to accommodate increased numbers of ESL students, large ESL classes, the inadequate time allocated for ESL support and the lim-its placed on the types of support offered students learning ESL were examples of the consequences of inadequate and diminished funding. Although a report written by Mordechai Rozanski (2002) that recog-nized the insufficient allocation of funds for ESL support in Ontario schools was released on 10 December 2002, recommendations of the report have yet to be realized. Without proper funding it is difficult to address the lack of support and pathologizing of CLD students.

Arguments against what Cummins (2001) characterizes as 'legitima-tion'-oriented assessment practices that disable students must be exam-ined, but they do not tell the whole story. Baker (2002) contends that eugenics discourse has an impact on education. 'From the outset eugenicists had direct things to say to schools and ... this aspect of eugenic thought has proved to be more pervasive and more enduring than the more spectacular arguments around sterilization' (Lowe 1997 in Baker 2002, p. 665). According to Lowe (1997), several areas of edu-cational policy and practice such as testing, differential treatment of minorities, the questioning of both hereditary and environmental fac-tors in the quality of students' home life and mothering, and the trans-mission of opinions through children's books and school texts have been deeply influenced by eugenic ideas (in Baker 2002). Lowe's frame-work indicates how eugenic discourse is manifest in the ways in which children in my study were assessed, the literacy curriculum made available to them, the ways their home lives were depicted, and finally in the inadequate number of culturally relevant resources provided for them. The various evaluation tools or 'perfecting technologies' (p. 675) that were used to 'hunt for disability' indicate the influence of eugenics as well as the assimilationist orientation these technologies serve. 'The new eugenics is concerned with perfecting technologies to secure qual-ity citizenship through the homogenization of racial/national popula-tions at some level' (p. 676). Baker additionally argues: 'In the often well–intended hunt for disability ... disability becomes reinscribed as an "outlaw ontology" (p. 665) reinvesting eugenic discourse in a new language that maintains an 'ableist normativity' (Campbell, 2000 in Baker, 2002, p. 665). This outlaw ontology is defined as a 'deep seated despise of unevenness, asymmetry, or imbalance that places bodies-minds labelled as disabled at the edge of the abyss, pushing the limits of human subjectivity' (Campbell, 2000 in Baker, 2002, p. 674).

What has therefore been missing from and problematic about arguments against the over-representation of minorities in special education are the ways in which normality and ableism remain privileged and constructed as desirable.

> Critiques of cultural bias in special education can inadvertently recircu-late the forbidden relationship between disability and desire, that is, how desirability, whether it is analyzed as 'biomedical' or 'socially constituted through relationships,' *must not be desired*, how it is used as nomenclature for a negative ontology and posed as a way of being that at all cost ought to be avoided. Where a critique of labeling or overrepresentation turns on the view that 'normal' students are really being mislabelled and made closer on a scale to 'genuinely' 'disabled' students, then it does not under-mine the presumptions that 'it's better to be dead than disabled.' If, as Campbell (2000, p. 307) has argued, the construction/governing of dis-ability and all the compulsion toward an ableist normativity are in fact achieved by the continual reiteration of technologies as 'salvific signifiers' holding out the promise of 'able-bodiedness' then both the hunt to iden-tify disability, and some versions of its critique, leave unproblematized this promise. (Baker, 2002, p. 685)

It is therefore essential to expand arguments against placing CLD students in special education beyond a protest against the construction of difference as abnormal or disabling. To this end, I will examine the dominant pedagogical orientations CLD students encountered and the other ways of knowing marginalized by notions of ableism and a desire for normativity.

Literacy, Identity, and Subjugated Knowledge

To a large extent, the pedagogy and literacy practices and events I observed were linked to and influenced by legitimation-oriented assessments. Instruction was organized in response to pathologized school identities assigned to CLD students as a result of these assessments. Within this context, the psychological model of reading and the biomedical approach to literacy examined in chapter 3 were evident. Literacy was presented as sequential skill attainment through the manipulation of isolated and fragmented parts of language. This was reinforced through pervasive decodable text and compared to normal development that prompted interventions which further emphasized reductive conceptions of literacy. Although there were exceptions, and in some cases, resistances to these dominant orientations, a substantial amount of data revealed the dominance of these understandings of literacy curricula. The policies, procedures and resources provided to teachers had to reconcile privileged and, in many ways, mandated direct and unmodified instruction that focused on the achievement of predetermined institutional goals. Although some teachers negotiated and subverted the constraints, it was clear that surveillance and control of their practice positioned 'pedagogy as a hegemonic technology' (Giroux, 2002b, p. 46) within their classrooms. The hegemony of the backwards design curriculum-planning model furthered these pedagogical restrictions.

Although alternative expectations were provided in the *ESL Resource Guide Grades 1–8* (Ontario Ministry of Education, 2001), there was little awareness or use of the document. More importantly, what remained unquestioned was the impact of a hegemonic approach to curriculum construction, the universal and pathological identities this approach fostered, and the subsequent banking-oriented pedagogy and coercive power relations students encountered as a result of this approach. For instance, when CLD students were assessed as lacking in literacy because they did not meet grade-specific expectations, teachers were pressured to improve their performance in a way that led to particular kinds of approaches to literacy curriculum, namely rote tactics, and intensive instruction in isolated and sequential phonics and phonemic awareness. CLD students' inability to demonstrate proficiency with this type of literacy learning meant that these approaches were also assigned to them during ESL, special education and literacy resource classes, with the result that pedagogical determinism and pathologizing processes were reinforced.

Events such as R Day and F Day demonstrate how CLD students had difficulties negotiating interaction when their reliance on linguistic cues and discourse conventions in English prohibited them from being able to successfully participate in and/or independently complete assigned work. Additionally, some of the items featured in the tasks students were asked to complete were culturally specific and took for granted students' background knowledge. In these worksheet tasks there was minimal external contextual support provided and little regard for students' internal context (life experiences and prior knowledge) (Cummins, 2001). Without contextual support, CLD students found these otherwise undemanding tasks difficult, since the cognitive, culture, language and learning load of the events created barriers to meaningful instruction (Meyer, 2000), thus further contributing to the idea that they were deficient. The ways in which students were positioned by these dominant approaches to literacy and the consequences of this positioning for CLD students' school identities were not considered. As such, these experiences limited their ability to engage with a variety of literacies and subsequently changed their ascribed school identities from that of deficient and passive knowledge recipients to autonomous, able learners in possession of valuable 'funds of knowledge' (Moll, 1992). Ultimately, these dominant assessment and pedagogical orientations privileged certain ways of knowing and marginalized others.

The ways in which CLD students other ways of knowing were marginalized is further demonstrated when we consider that, according to Snow (1983), 'the specific oral discourse style employed by middle-class families at home, which has the characteristic features of being de-contextualized and detached, closely matches school language use, a factor that accounts for the later literacy success of children from these homes' (in Minami & Ovando, 2004, p. 574). Contrary to commonly held beliefs present in the data, this does not therefore mean that school failures are attributable to deficits in children or their parents. Nichols, Rupley, Webb-Johnson, and Tlusty (2000) argue that 'the culture of many students while different from that of school systems is neither inadequate nor deficient; rather, the problem lies in the educational system' (p. 1).

Although CLD students came to school with significant linguistic and cultural resources that comprised what Gee (1990) has termed a 'primary discourse,' legitimation-oriented assessment practices and banking-oriented pedagogy denied them opportunities to both access and alter the secondary or official discourses they were being asked to acquire as they entered the school domain. This exclusion ensured that their ways of knowing or coming to know were undervalued and epistemologically irrelevant in altering the curricular space. As a result, who they were, what they knew, and how they understood the world remained untapped and inconsequential resources for shaping the literacy curriculum they encountered.

Efficiency, Schooling, and Pathologizing

Prevailing economic discourses described in chapter 2 also contributed to the marginalization of knowledge and processes of pathologizing encountered by CLD students. Delpit (2003) has noted how curriculum based on the premise that 'students can only achieve through repetition of small steps that require primarily rote answer and little or no critical thinking' (p. 15) has often been assigned to low-income students within schools. A study of two early years culturally and linguistically diverse classrooms in a school considered at-risk conducted by Barone (2002) mirrored both the observations made throughout my study and the inequity Delpit describes. In the study, students' deficiencies drove literacy curriculum and as a result, a majority of instructional time was focused on letter/sound knowledge disconnected from meaningful text. The researcher noted that, 'although this low level of instruction was frustrating to observe, it is not uncommon in classrooms with children who are not fluent in English (Chamot & O'Malley, 1989; Gersten & Woodward, 1994) [since] a narrow view of instruction is not unusual in schools and classrooms where students are considered at-risk' (p. 435). The links between diversity and the narrowing of curriculum have been propelled by a fear that increased immigration to North America has compromised public schools' ability to produce good workers able to compete in the globalized economy. As described in chapter 2, this anxiety is largely attributable to the notion that not being able to compete globally means having to make do with less. This, in turn, has resulted in reforms that constrain and limit teachers while holding them accountable for measures that prepare students for the global labour market. Apple (2000) articulates these connections plainly: 'Behind the stress on higher standards, more rigorous testing, education for employment, and a much closer relationship between education and the economy in general, is the fear of losing in international competition and the loss of jobs and money' (p. 58). Within this climate of fear other aims and goals of schooling (democracy, critical citizenship) become marginalized or disregarded altogether (Smyth, Dow, Hattman, Reid, & Shacklock 2000; Majhanovich, 2005).

The increased efficiency-orientation of schooling is maintained by an adherence to standardized approaches to curriculum and assessment that govern what and when knowledge must be learned and demonstrated in order to prepare students to become viable producers. These quality control mechanisms have meant that professionals (often woman at the elementary level) responsible for educating children are viewed as accountable to this form of preparation and in need of monitoring. The result is the de-professionalization, de-skilling and silencing of educators noted in research (Apple, 1986, in Easthope & Easthope, 2000; Smyth, Dow, Hattman, Reid & Shacklock, 2000) and evidenced by the diminished professional autonomy experienced by teachers in this study.

In such an orientation, capital is also understood as the solution to human problems (Canella & Viruru, 2004) and the construction of 'child needs' is used to legitimize market-driven 'solutions' (Cannella, 2002, p. 12; Books, 2002). This was apparent through the pervasive use of and reliance on commercial programs purchased to address literacy instruction and assessment under the specious argument that the children needed them to improve their literacy skills. Other commercially prepared products supplemented their use and additionally influenced notions of what constitutes legitimate literacy and literacy instruction. Further, when CLD students did not demonstrate progress as delineated and measured by these products, other learning opportunities (Keys to Literacy sessions, ESL and remedial classes) that were either products designed for remediation, or informed by commercial programs, were assigned to them. CLD students' pathologized school identities advanced a pedagogical determinism that was supported even when some teachers noted a lack of transfer between the use of these products and their students' literacy development. Student needs, informed by essentialized understandings of their social and economic situations, further justified using certain products believed to address what students were lacking at home. Dei and Karumanchery (2001) have documented the ways in which this increased emphasis on efficiency in Ontario education has silenced equity, reinscribed meritocracy and pathologized students and parents while holding them responsible for their pathologized status. Nomali's and her mother's funds of knowledge, for example, were not considered, but, instead, further served to render them deficient. Nomali's inability to demonstrate acceptable progress within the confines of a corporatized curriculum ultimately contributed to her pathologizing.

Elkind (2001) has made links between 'increasingly industrialized and product-oriented' societies, a 'hurried' childhood and the 'progressive downward thrust of the curriculum' (pp. 49–50). He argues, 'When school is looked upon as an assembly line and when there is pressure to increase production, there is a temptation not only to fill the bottles faster but also to fill them earlier' (p. 50). Consequently, schools rely on biomedical conceptualisations of learning and literacy to understand how to detect and diagnose whether students are demonstrating normal learning targets and to determine what kinds of interventions to employ in order to ensure work-force preparation, rather than consider socio-cultural approaches to early literacy that seek to understand children from an ecological perspective and develop literacy curricula accordingly.

Conclusion

The discourses that have been discussed thus far demonstrate how educational settings have been compromised in their ability to create opportunities for educators to access and cultivate children's assets. Within educational settings, CLD children's value is related to norm-based conceptions of what they *should* be able to perform and produce. CLD children are constructed as inadequate and treated as objects to be invested in and monitored to ensure financial return. The state of childhood is generally viewed as an economic impediment in need of pathologizing and clinical intervention. Chapter 5 continues to theorize and document pathologizing practices in preparation for the turn in chapter 6: ways to reconceptualize the present context in order to honour and access children's assets and develop a transformative and depathologizing approach to their literacy and identity in ECE.

5
The Case of Special Education and Pathologizing

RACHEL M. HEYDON

Previous chapters have discussed the minority world's fear of disability and diversity and some of the implications of that fear, namely seeing children as potentially pathological (as evidenced in the cases of the at-risk discourse in chapter 2 and the children at Elmwood in chapters 3 and 4). But what of those children whom educational systems officially, rather than tacitly, name as *disabled*? This chapter considers special education and the management structure for such children. While undoubtedly, special education has led to the amelioration of many disabled children's lives through, for example, its championing of legislation for school inclusion and its development of innovated pedagogies, it also has led to a 'contradictory state' where its collusion with the 'cult of efficiency' (Stein, 2001) has additionally led to 'inappropriate' or, as this chapter demonstrates, even hurtful school experiences for children (Andrews, Carnine, Coutinho, Edgar, et al., 2000, p. 258). Specifically, this chapter foregrounds a narrative developed from my memories as the teacher of Craig, a young child labelled as behaviourally exceptional. Through the analysis of my practice I identify how a special education dependent on instrumentalism (Skrtic, 1995) is a mechanism for pathologizing, and I propose a radical alternative to this hegemonic form of special education. My alternative, which begins to hint at the theorizing that makes possible asset-oriented approaches, is an ethical pedagogical praxis that holds at least five interrelated features:

- It juxtaposes a variety of theories and practices.
- It deconstructs the general, special-education duality while challeng-

ing functionalist approaches to behavioural differences on several fronts.

- It understands its historical context.
- It has a decisive anti-sexist, anti-racist, and anti-classist mandate which constructs the teacher as an action-oriented educational worker who strives to alleviate others' suffering.
- It attempts not to replace one authoritarian discourse with another.

These features and the praxis they form are premised on the ethical orientation of this book (i.e., an ethic that 'focuses ... on the kind of person one must become in order to develop a nonviolative relationship to the Other' (Cornell, 1992, p. 13) and an understanding that this is an educator's first responsibility). Because responding to the question of who we as educators must become is contingent on micro and macro issues (i.e., from the needs of the individual circumstance to the institutional structures that inform these needs), to ground this chapter, I begin with a narrative of Craig. I discuss why this narrative begs for a reconceptualization of special education in general, and then one-by-one I elucidate the five features of the ethical praxis while linking each to my practice when I tried to be a teacher to Craig.

A Narrative of Craig

It was the mid-1990s, and I was a special education resource teacher in a small town in Ontario when my services were requested for Craig, a new second-grader who was described by his classroom teacher as being a behaviour problem. Following this referral, I worked with Craig for 18 months and learned that his case had much to teach about pathologizing and the deficit-oriented discourses that accompany this phenomenon.

By the end of the time I knew Craig, he had eaten his rubber boots, staples, thumb tacks, Lego, pencils, and erasers; he had set fires and hit his mother, peers, me, himself, and the principal. Craig had cried – big, wet torrents that made him choke. He had sworn, hollered, yelled 'You can't make me!' even when he was offered a treat. Craig had cut holes in his clothing, broken toys, computers, windows, at least one tooth, and one urinal.

Craig had beautiful hair and bright, shiny eyes, and, on the rare occasions when he smiled, he could almost convince you that everything was going to be all right. But it was never all right. This is because Craig's smiles came from other people's pain: a leg in the aisle resulting in a trip and fall; a projectile of one kind or another hitting eyes, heads, or torsos; a litany of vicious, racist slurs leading to his classmates' shame. All of these would procure a smile – sometimes closed-mouthed with one corner of the lip turned up with eyes twinkling and, at other times, all toothy-full-apple-cheeked and squinty-eyed.

Despite the seeming pleasure Craig got out of other children's distress, he WANTED a friend. He told me how he longed for someone with whom to play hockey, Nintendo, and soccer; how he wished to be invited for birthday parties, sleep overs, and camp outs; and how he 'never got to do nothing or go nowhere,' because 'it' (the universe I supposed) was never 'fair' But Craig's actions also demonstrated that he desired a friend whom he could boss, bully, and beat at every game; a friend who would be deferential, subservient; and, perhaps most importantly, someone who would play beside, but never *with* him. After school, I often heard Craig yelling down the road to the backs of a troop of children: 'Guys, wait up! Wait for me.' But after the first week of school they never did wait up, perhaps because they were tired of being struck and called a 'titsucker' or a 'motherfucker' the moment something didn't go Craig's way. This, at least, was how many of the community's parents later explained the events to school officials when they asked for Craig to be expelled.

I met with Sarah, Craig's mother, shortly after that first day of school, and we worked closely together for as long as Craig was my student. In our first conference, I listened as Sarah told her story of an adolescent pregnancy, an absence of familial or institutional supports, pre- and post-natal physical trauma at the hands of Craig's father, and the struggle to escape this man and to limit his visitation rights. I listened as Sarah described the early onset of her son's behavioural difficulties, which included violent nightmares and tantrums, and her desperate attempts to find support while having little money.

The received wisdom of the special education literature on behavioural exceptionalities is that Craig's situation is easily described and explained and is pathological in its nature. Craig demonstrated the typical predictors for anti-social behaviour: high impulsivity, attention difficulties, significant academic delays, born to an adolescent mother,[1] a

---

1 According to Fagot and Leve (1998), one of the top three predictors of externalizing behaviour at age 5 is single-mother family status.

single-parent household with minimal resources,[2] a physically abusive father,[3] onset of difficulties at infancy,[4] and male gender.[5] Following the assessment-focus established in the preceding chapters, by October of Grade 3, the school district psychologist had completed behavioural and learning assessments on Craig. In summary, she gave Craig three interrelated diagnoses: a general learning disability, oppositional defiance disorder, and depression. I then sat on the Identification Placement and Review Committee (IPRC) to legally identify Craig as an exceptional student within the category of emotional disturbance and / or social maladjustment. Such assessment, diagnosis, and identification are standard practice in special education.

This identification did little to change Craig's circumstances. True, it legally mandated that an Individual Education Plan guide his programme, but given the realities of Craig's classroom, few manageable and meaningful accommodations or modifications could be made for Craig. The realities of Craig's classroom included a high pupil-teacher ratio, a rigid standardized curriculum monitored through standardized provincial testing, and, because of a punitive provincial granting formula (the Intensive Support Amount), no teaching assistant.[6] Placement in a special classroom was not an option despite the IPRC,

2 Farrington and Loeber's (1999) research on juvenile delinquency concludes that 'several risk factors are replicable predictors of delinquency over time and place, especially impulsivity, poor concentration, low achievement, an antisocial parent, a large family, low family income, a broken family, poor parental supervision, and parental conflict' (p. 5). Except for the large family, Craig had all of these predictors for antisocial behaviour.

3 See, for example, the findings of Fantuzzo et al. (1998), as well as Wolfe et al. (1998), in relation to the behaviour of children who have been maltreated or abused.

4 Lavigne et al. (1998) conclude that a preschool child with a psychiatric disorder, disruptive, or emotional disorder, is two or three times, eight times, or four to six times respectively more likely than a child not diagnosed with a disorder at that age to have a disorder throughout the early school years. Their findings suggest that early onset of problem behaviours is an indicator of later difficulties.

5 84.5 per cent of students in Ontario identified as socially maladjusted / emotionally disturbed are male (Ontario Ministry of Education as cited in Weber and Bennett, 1999, p. 32).

6 The Intensive Support Amount (ISA) is a 'component of Ontario's new student-focused funding model' (Ontario Ministry of Education, 1999, p. 3). Three levels of ISA grants each provide an escalating amount of funding for students with special needs. ISA Level I supports the purchasing of individualized equipment exceeding $800. ISA, Level 2 and 3, 'provides for the intensive staffing supports required by students with very high needs' (p. 3), including teaching assistants. Each year the

because Craig did not meet the school district's strict criteria for special class placement (e.g., his behaviour was deemed too severe, and his IQ too low for the behaviour classroom).[7]

Then in the middle of Grade 3, an inter-agency team that included the school district suggested that Craig be accommodated in a residential school. This created enormous stress for the family. The school was more than 50 kilometres from Craig's home, and transportation for visits would be a burden. Also, because of social assistance rules, with Craig in residence, Sarah would lose his allowance that she needed to pay her rent. Nevertheless, because of the dearth of local services, and the school district's inability to manage Craig in their classrooms, Sarah was offered few alternatives. While the case is severe, the theories and

---

criteria for obtaining ISA grants have changed. What has remained consistent is the onerous, inflexible application procedures and the critical nature of obtaining these funds ensuring adequate levels of support for children with special needs. With Craig, the deadline for ISA grants was in the spring before the school year in which a teaching assistant would be needed, and teaching assistants were directly attached to the students for whom a grant had been procured (with no flexibility to reallocate or share a teaching assistant). Subsequently, for Craig to have a teaching assistant in our school, his previous school would have had to apply for it. Frustratingly, Craig's previous school could not have applied for it, because they did not have the required documentation for the grant. Although the special education resource teachers are responsible for completing the application procedures for ISA, they are excluded from documenting need. Key documentation consists of assessment reports from 'regulated qualified professional[s]' (p. 27) which government auditors inspect for 'objectivity.' This necessitates that the documentation be 'psychological or medical' (p. 19) in nature. The waiting list for the assessments by such professionals (unless parents can pay privately) is very long (Ontario Human Rights Commission, 2003, p. 6).

7 Increasing since the time of Craig's case has been Ontario's tightening of the gatekeeping control for special class placements and services, and an overreliance on instrumentalist-derived data such as IQ tests. This is akin to the funding trends in the United States in the mid-twentieth century which required the 'scientific basis' (MacMillan & Hendrick, 1993, p. 38) of IQ tests for securing differential funding for special education programs. In my former school district (in which Craig was a student), this translated into percentiles obtained from psycho-educational assessments and other norm-referenced tests which were administered and interpreted by persons other than teachers, as *the* deciding factor for students' identification, placement, and other educational programming matters. Consequently, teachers' students' and parents' judgments (except for the minimal amount of quantitative data that teachers could submit as part of an IEP or ISA grant) were deemed non-professional (relative to the status of the psychologist or medical doctor) and held little sway. This bowing to the authority of the expert perpetuates the medical model tradition of perceiving and dealing with difference which is seen throughout *Early Childhood Curricula*.

practices that led to the separation of a family and a child's banishment from his community create the same opportunities for pathologizing for all children in the system. As such, an alternative to the status quo of special education must be found and enacted.

An Ethical Pedagogical Praxis: The Need for a Reconceptualization of Ethics and Praxis within Special Education

Special education as a set of theories, practices and as a field was insufficient and inappropriate for use as an ethical praxis with Craig for several reasons. First, special education is built on instrumental theories (e.g., functionalist psychology) (Skrtic, 1995) whose goals are to predict and control (Habermas, 1972, p. 308). These theories were hurtful to Craig and Sarah, because they attributed the blame and responsibility for behavioural exceptionalities to them alone. This focus on the individual as a site of pathology and the site of 'risk' (Swadener & Lubeck, 1995a) is a feature of special education. Goodnow (1995) maintains that functionalist psychology (which has greatly influenced special education) has myopically placed its 'emphasis upon conditions within the individual.' Instead there needs to be emphasis upon a 'line of theory and research [that] looks to conditions outside the individual' (p. 306). As with deficit discourses, in the studies in the endnotes of Craig's story (Fagot &nd Leve, 1998; Fantuzzo et al., 1998; Farrington & Loeber, 1999, Lavigne et al., 1998; Wolfe et al., 1998) there is no questioning why the 'fault' for procuding children who do not fit the system is attributed to socially and economically disenfranchised women yet there is no consideration of the effects of assigning culpability only to mothers, or automatically pathologizing children's anger. In their etiologies, standard studies do not refer to the complaints proffered by Sarah and mothers like her, such as a 'runaway dad,' 'criminally low social assistance amounts,' 'no local support services,' or 'not enough affordable housing.'

Furthermore, the initial etiological focus and the eventual supposed solutions to Craig's problems (e.g., in-school behaviour modification and later institutionalization) never addressed how the school and its community might have created or exacerbated his pain or itself placed the child at risk. For example, Craig and Sarah's situation was akin to that reported by Harris and Dewdney (1994) in their study of barriers to assistance for battered women. In summary, the principal impediments include:

- The service may not exist (particularly in small towns and rural areas);
- Help-seekers may not know whom to contact;
- Help-seekers may be unable to reach an agency because of 'language difficulties or other forms of social isolation';
- The structure of a service may preclude assistance (e.g., seemingly endless waiting lists, difficult 'bureaucratic complexities,' and narrowly defined criteria for admission);
- The agency itself may be unable to assist for many reasons (e.g., 'inadequately funded or staffed'); and
- Help-seekers may be financially unable to pursue assistance because it would mean incurring costs (e.g., child-care, transportation, and time off work).

All these factors were present in Craig's schooling and in many other aspects of his and Sarah's lives. I witnessed Sarah's struggles with the courts and the police to keep her son and herself safe from Craig's father. These barriers arose again in Sarah's relations with social assistance and in fighting to maintain a healthy living environment, including efforts to be allowed to see a dentist and have all necessary prescriptions covered. Foremost was my horror at the absence of assistance for Sarah when she was a pregnant adolescent with no familial support. The barriers to help in those days are likely what fuelled Craig's later difficulties. Ironically, obstacles to assistance extend to help providers like me, even though our position *within* a helping institution might be expected to give us better access to information and services.

Foucault's (1977) theory of normalization is another way of explaining how the school and its community could be implicated in Craig's behavioural exceptionality. Foucault demonstrates how normality, including what constitutes acceptable behaviour, is situational not absolute, since 'there are no behaviours that exist outside the practices for producing them' (Walkerdine, 1994, p. 61). Disciplinary features lead to the homogenization of norms and standards; if individuals do not adapt to such norms they are deemed deviant (Foucault, 1977). All aspects of the individual are subject to normalization procedures, which by their very nature are difficult to see. These procedures help maintain the status quo: 'Foucault argues that disciplinary techniques are the specific rituals for producing individuals who themselves become instruments for the exercise of power' (Ford-Smith, 1995, p. 60). The discursive régime of an institution produces the parameters for the behaviours that can be enacted as well as the terms by which they are judged. An understanding of such features requires critical practices such as uncovering the invisible, consideration of multiple perspectives, and the placement of an interpretation within its larger sociopolitical context before acting. (For a discussion of critical literacy practices, see Lewison, Seely Flint, & Van Sluys, 2002).

These practices are not characteristic of contemporary special education. In narrative terms, special education is a 'realist tale' (Lather, 1991): positivist, linear, with a clearly demarcated beginning sequence of action directed at closure. The realist tale emphasizes behavioural observations, and privileges what can be quantified. It hides its authorship in a detached omniscience that suggests the text somehow created itself. Without apparent origins, the text conceals an easily identifiable site from which it can be critiqued. Such realist tales, Lather suggests, 'assume a found world, an empirical world knowable through adequate method and theory' (p. 128). The authors of such tales use methods that ensure validity and reliability; in setting up conditions for discovery, they never interfere with the truth, for this truth emerges naturally from the data, untainted by subjectivity.

Skrtic's (1995) analysis points to *omissions* within special education as a realist tale: a discussion of what it takes for granted, and a knowledge of other ways of perceiving and constructing the social world. During the 1980s, after social science had been through its paradigm wars, special education had hardly begun its own. The paradigmatic and theoretical 'diversity' of other fields in the social sciences is thus absent in special education (p. 35). Although there have been debates (e.g., on inclusion) during the history of special education, Skrtic notes that they have been argued on 'practical,' technical grounds and lack criticisms of 'theories and guiding assumptions upon which [the practical debates] are premised' (p. 76). This renders special education (and by extension its workers) ahistorical and acritical, and in many ways anti–intellectual. This returns the situation to the naïve pragmatism already noted throughout this book: it is this naïve pragmatism that upholds the four tenets of special education. Again, they are

- Student disability is a pathological condition.
- Differential diagnosis is objective and useful.
- Special education is a rationally conceived and coordinated system of services that benefits diagnosed students.
- Progress in special education is a rational-technical process of incre-

mental improvements in conventional diagnostic and instructional practices. (p. 75)

Since these tenets are integral to the structure of special education, their instrumentalist origins disappear, and they become accepted as commonsensical. Unfortunately, what passes as commonsense may not be in the best interest of young children and their families (or teachers); certainly the version of special education that I have just described was hurtful to Craig and Sarah. In place of this special education I now submit a five-feature version of an ethical pedagogical praxis.

Praxis

The praxis that I forward is a work in progress. It was created from my analysis of my lived experience as a special education teacher. This praxis recognizes that young children in need, such as Craig, demand action and a thoughtful appraisal of that action on the basis of Cornell's (1992) ethics: an understanding of the kind of people we must become as educators so that we do no harm to others which includes a recognition of the limits of our knowledge and understandings of those others. A number of praxis-oriented philosophies have been developed to deal with 'the theory and practice dualism that has plagued Western intellectual thought' (Quantz, 1992, p. 463). The praxis that underlies the ethical praxis is consistent with the theorizing of *Early Childhood Curricula*, that is, the goals of critical and postmodern theories. Respectively, these goals are to emancipate (Habermas, 1972) and to 'deconstruct' (Lather, 1991, p. 8).

Negotiating critical and emancipatory boundaries is inherent in the five goals of the ethical praxis: it juxtaposes a variety of theories and practices; deconstructs the general, special education duality while challenging functionalist approaches to behavioural differences on several fronts; understands its historical context; has a decisive anti-sexist, anti-racist, and anti-classist mandate that constructs the teacher as an action-oriented educational worker who strives to alleviate others' suffering; and attempts not to replace one authoritarian discourse with another. To elucidate the theorizing of my practice that led me to these goals, and to illustrate their potential, I will now examine each feature in turn.

1. The Juxtaposition of Differing Theories and Practices

In general, it is an egregious error for special education to support and be supported by the hegemony of instrumentalist theories and realist texts. This sealed 'hierarchy of ideologies' (Coppock & Hopton, 2000, p. 65) curtailed the benefits that Craig might have received, if his case could have been considered through other theories and practices including, perhaps most importantly, his mother's perspectives.

Despite their position of closure, however, realist texts can be part of a generative process. Bhabba (1994), in his discussion of how newness enters the world, explains that when different entities are juxtaposed, change may emerge from the crevasses between them. In special education, therefore, the more its realist texts are rubbed against alternate theories and practices, the greater chance there is for newness. In analysing my attempts to help Craig, for example, I juxtapose instrumentalist theories and practices against postmodern and critical theories as well as narratives of practice. The comparisons, contrasts, and spaces between these entities allow entrée into each theory and practice's constitution, limitations, and possible contributions to the case. It is through this opening that I am able to conceptualize an ethical praxis.

Integral to the creation of the new is recognition that each theory and practice has something to teach, although not all should necessarily be employed. With regard to the dominant forms of functionalist psychology that informed the special education driving Craig's circumstances, the contribution of these theories and practices was often obscured by the political necessity of working outside them in order to challenge their power. Still, functionalist psychology has something to say about Craig's situation and the situation of children with whom he has much in common. Craig's case, as with the discussion of disability in this book, demonstrates that it is not simply that madness is discursive; it can be material. No praxis-oriented person who wants to diminish suffering would deny this. Even the operating principle of those sympathetic to the radical anti-psychiatry movement of the 1960s was neither a denial of madness nor a wish to abolish psychiatry, but simply the aspiration to '(re)open a dialogue between reason and those whom it considered mad' (Rose, 1992, p. 148). Therefore, any attempt to end suffering relative to behavioural exceptionalities, 'should incorporate biological, psychological and social perspectives so that whatever the views [or circumstances] of any service user, there is a starting point for a dialogue between service user and professional' (Coppock & Hopton, 2000, p. 168). Incorporation should be read as juxtaposition, not conflation, as conflation could miss problems inherent in functionalist psychology. The benefit of juxtaposition is that it invites dialogue between persons, theories, and practices, while remaining aware of the power differentials between them.

2. The Challenge to Functionalist Psychology and the Special/Education Binary

Given that special education is predominantly a monotone of theory and practice, an ethical praxis must be aware of what challenges to functionalist psychology hold in common, and how they relate to education. The most important commonality is how challenges often arise from critical questions that reject exceptionalities as fixed categories. What, for example, is the relationship between institutional norms and procedures, and the definitions of behavioural disorders? How have notions of un/acceptable behaviour changed over time and in relation to definitions of education, training, teacher, and student? How might school districts, schools, children's aid societies, paediatric psychiatric facilities, ministries of health and education, and community and social services actually be impotent to assist children and their families or, worse, even exacerbate their difficulties? What are the institutions' and help providers' (specifically here, teachers') responsibilities towards students identified as behaviourally exceptional?

One responsibility is to recognize Habermas's (1972) lesson that theories have goals connected to particular understandings of the social good, education, schools, teachers, students, and more generally, knowledge, views of what is in the world, pedagogy, politics, and ethics. Another responsibility is the acknowledgement that the dyad of special education, to 'label' and 'place' (Rodriguez, 1999, p. 395), belies the discursive, social, cultural, institutional, and historical aspects of theories and practices. Moreover, special education's insistence that functionalist psychology be the science that propels this labelling, placing, and attempting to cure adds to these fatal omissions. Because the etiological literature predicted Craig's behavioural difficulties on the basis of his experiences of poverty, social marginalization, and violence, he, and to a lesser extent his mother, became the targets of pathologizing, blame, and intervention. The educational and social services communities did not try to change themselves.

The second feature of an ethical praxis also requires accepting the special/general education duality as a discriminatory structure, since, by virtue of being special and not for all, special education divides the school population and the school itself, regardless of arguments for or against inclusion. This bifurcation ideologically defines normal or abnormal in practical terms. It happens through curriculum: Craig's curriculum was individualized, whereas unexceptional students had a standardized or normalized provincial curriculum. It happens through standardized assessment: Craig's classmates were required to partake in a general standardized assessment from which Craig was excluded because of his exceptional status. It happens through 'classroom geography' (Sandow, 1994, p. 157). Classrooms are usually conceived as for all, yet because Craig was deemed exceptional, he was physically isolated from other children and relegated to the resource room, to his home, and later to residential school). It happens through occupational roles and human resource allocation: my role as special educator named me a teacher for only some; once Craig became my responsibility, his classroom teacher was no longer obligated to him. It happens through the configuration of resource materials: the provincially-approved textbooks were for the classroom, yet because they were not suitable for Craig, they were thus inaccessible to exceptional students. These examples show how most school practices are directed towards a supposed normal student. To deal with its own failure to educate *individuals* instead of *a standard*, the system makes exceptions of a few and relegates them to special education. This standardized approach has implications for Sandow's (1994) question of whose special needs are met through special education. In Craig's case, special education was primarily in the service of the government, the school district, the school, and special education itself as a field. This connects to Polakow's (1993) view discussed in chapter 2 regarding how the privileged, in this case the privileged institution of special education, retain their privilege.

Despite its discriminatory structure, the current configuration of public education prevents special education from being abolished. Some children require services beyond what is presently available in general classrooms from generalist teachers. To do away with special education would be to abandon children in need. Instead, a reconsideration of general education must first occur. 'Because special education,' Skrtic (1995) contends, 'is a structural and cultural artefact of twentieth-century schooling ... deconstructing and reconstructing it necessarily requires deconstructing and reconstructing public education itself' (p. 233). Indeed, as discussed elsewhere in *Early Childhood Curricula*, education for young children premised on the cult of efficiency and at-risk discourses must be rethought. Persons interested in pursuing this re/deconstruction should begin by considering how special education is, in fact, a means of legitimating an education system that does not know how to respect diversity. As Skrtic (2005) explains: 'As bureaucracies, schools are performance organizations, standardized, non-adaptable structures that must screen out diversity by forcing students with unconventional needs out of the system. And because they are public bureaucracies charged with serving all students, special education emerges as a legitimating device, an institutional practice that, in effect, shifts the blame for school failure to students through medicalizing and objectifying discourses, while reducing the uncertainty of student diversity by containing it through exclusionary practices' (pp. 149–150). Such a consideration also requires thinking and working *historically*, to unearth the ancestries of those theories, practices, and movements that underlie general and special education.

3. Understanding the Historical Context

An ethical praxis demands a critical appraisal of the histories of one's discipline, theories, and practices. There must also be an awareness that histories are always composed, never discovered; thus, even the methodologies of one's history making need to be juxtaposed to others. Understanding the histories of educational movements is critical to an ethical praxis, because that understanding helps to demystify special education and one's place within it. 'To understand what possibilities lie ahead for special education,' Skrtic (1991) suggests, 'special educators must understand and, more important, free themselves from that which has conditioned, limited, and institutionalized their professional thought and action' (pp. 23–24). The excavation of a discipline's history is a critical project, in that it uncovers the buried, and makes apparent its genesis and affinities. This is a process of de-familiarization, of distancing and seeing parts, of making connections, and in seeing how the history of one's own discipline relates to other disciplinary histories. In these ways, history seeking and making broadens the number of possible juxtapositions.

4. The Anti-discrimination Mandate and the Action-Oriented Educational Worker

The ethical praxis must seek to de-pathologize children through an announcement and enactment of its anti-racist, anti-sexist, and anti-classist agenda. Although the argument that an antidiscrimination stance must be part of such a praxis exists independently of Craig's case, my narrative here demonstrates how theory and practice can limit and/or expand people's access to safety, autonomy, dignity, and capital.

For instance, by looking at the connection between identity and the conditions of special education teachers' work, I discovered how my membership in a female-intensive occupation (Harris, 1992) limited my control over *what* I did and *how* I did it. My subordinate position as a servant to the technical masters (i.e., carrying out the orders of the psychologists and bureaucracy), had implications for Craig. My lack of professional authority made me less able to act on his behalf, as my word could not secure him provincial funding for the provision of a teaching assistant, designate him as in need of individualized programming, or place him in a safe environment (i.e., in a small class placement) – only documentation from a psychologist could do that. An examination of the foundations of special education reveals how this could be so: Special education with its roots in 'western rationalism ... values objectivity and professional distance' (Kalyanpur, Harry, & Skrtic, 2000, p. 123). Professional knowledge that is 'scientifically based' is 'assumed to be objective and is ranked higher than knowledge that is anecdotal and therefore subjective' (p. 123), such as that of a teacher's understanding of her student based primarily on qualitative data. This can also be seen in the case of the biomedical approach to literacy where medical doctors with their expertise in objective science are influencing classroom literacy pedagogy. Such a 'hierarchy' of knowledge creates '"contextual barriers" in traditional school organisations, such as hierarchical authority and the isolation of professionals which substantively undermine the collaborative process' (p. 123). Parents like Sarah, who had the least amount of status, were even more completely locked out of collaboration.

In addition to the distress of having a needy child, Sarah carried the weight of being the target of blame for that need. Like the at-risk families in Swadener and Lubeck's (1995a) studies, Sarah, being young, poor, and female became the repository for the culpability of all of the difficulties her son encountered. The comments that Mickelson (2000) heard from teachers, when she studied the experiences of mothers with sons who had been identified as behaviourally exceptional, parallel the staffroom talk to which I was privy: 'Find me a BD [behaviour disordered] kid and I'll find you his BD mom,' and 'The apple doesn't fall far from the tree, you know' (p. 169). These stereotypes are a form of violence, in part, because by ascribing fault to mothers, they distract from other sources of liability. The behaviour exceptionalities literature, for example, identifies teenage motherhood as a category of risk. It articulates this risk as a fact related to deficiencies in the mother; yet when the reasons that underlie this risk are exposed, the sphere of responsibility can widen. Consider O'Shea et al.'s (2001) description of teenage mothers: 'Poverty is a reality for young mothers who have dropped out of school. The [United States] Children's Defense Fund 1998 *Yearbook* reported that almost two-thirds of teenage mothers did not finish their high school education. The combination of lack of economic stability due to inadequate job skills and inadequate parenting skills related to education and supports places the teenage mother and her child at significant risk. In this situation the mother is at risk for stressors associated with poverty and the child for social, physical, and cognitive problems' (p. 84). O'Shea et al. articulate some of the challenges that mothers like Sarah may face. In the following paragraph, using these same factors, I divert the blame from the mother to ask who could and should be helping.

In the quotation, the woman's poverty, lack of education, lack of economic stability, lack of employable skills, lack of approved or dominant parenting knowledge, and subsequent stress are identified as the causes of her and her child's at-risk status. The woman is described as the site of deficits. Yet a variety of systems were inadequate in responding to Craig's and Sarah's needs. The source of at least some risk should be attributed to the deficits of social organizations, including schools. Perhaps these institutions are themselves lacking in skills to eradicate poverty, educate persons outside a narrow definition of student, provide economic stability, broaden the definition of contributing member of society, teach family members to care for each other, and reduce the stress of trying to do too much with too little. In short, where are the communal skills to feed, educate, care for, and protect children and citizens? An ethical praxis requires an examination of the social positioning of children and their parents based on categories of difference such as sex, race, and class. The corollary to this examination is the appraisal of the ways in which these categories mediate people's lives through organizational policy, procedures, and the work of teachers, including how particular categories are more or less pathologized under particular circumstances. Educators in an ethical praxis must then actively challenge what allows discrimination through pathologizing.

5. The Active Refusal of an Authoritarian Discourse

The complexity of the challenges in educating Craig deserves more than a stock pedagogical approach. In fact, as has already been proposed in chapter 3, one could argue that all children deserve more than a one-size-fits-few solution. An ethical praxis does not claim to privilege one theory or practice over another; it asks us educators to assess our ways of knowing, being, and doing in order to reflect upon the assumptions that underpin their structure and then make known the conditions of these structures to oneself and others. Akin to the deconstruction discussed in this way by Spivak (1993), the form determines what is included and excluded and how the subject is configured. This uncovering of the subject positioning is important to the construction of an ethical praxis, given Cornell's (1992) notion of ethics and its connection to identity. The deconstructive goal of an ethical praxis can be realized through several of its features: seeking to make the known unknown through the dissonance and comparison offered by juxtaposition; understanding the histories of theories and practices; and striving to understand one's needs, desires, and identities, and those of whom one is helping. This means that special education with its insistence on standardization must become more of what Skrtic (1991) calls an 'adhocracy.'

An adhocracy is an organizational structure that relies on 'innovation' (Skrtic, 1991, p. 182) not standardization. This dependence is based on the adhocracy's recognition of the mercurial nature of human endeavours such as education. In an adhocracy, labour is shared by professionals making ongoing and reciprocal decisions concerning theory and practice relative to the tasks at hand and the desired goals of the community. Accountability is not derived from, in Craig's example, the Ontario government's determination to tighten and expand bureaucratic procedures and paperwork, rather from a 'presumed community of interests' that Skrtic describes as 'a sense among the workers of a shared interest in a common goal, in the wellbeing of the organization with respect to progress toward its mission' (p. 184). Apart from the adhocracy's compulsory features of 'collaboration,' 'mutual adjustment,' and 'accountability' through common interest, such an organization also requires what Skrtic calls a 'discursive coupling' (p. 184). This is a process of actively forming judgments and reflecting on those judgments in the daily, embodied experiences of its professionals. Thus, practitioners make explicit and binding links between theories and practices in actual educational contexts.

An adhocracy is preferable to the standard bureaucratic system in which I was teaching. By constructing a collegiality in which each member is regarded as a full, professional decision maker, the adhocracy addresses the difficulties I had in educating Craig when my role carried little status. As a special education teacher, I was assigned a set of rigid practices and theories that made me operationally ineffective. I was then expected to carry out policies and programmes with scant room to decide what was in the best interest of my students. The adhocracy, on the other hand, offers its workers power through collaboration, and enough structural flexibility to choose the theories and practices best suited to a problem. An adhocracy defies the routine approach as well as the hierarchical organization of contemporary schooling. Moreover, it counters the dangers of my having to work in relative isolation to secure an education and appropriate services for Craig. It demands that members work closely together to monitor, dialogue, adjust, and reflect upon the group's work. With its adaptability, elasticity, and focus upon cooperatively creating the novel within the context of a given problem, an adhocracy could create a praxis responsive to the needs and desires of an educational situation without merely replacing one authoritarian discourse with another. This continuous deconstruction and reconstruction could also contribute to an ethical praxis by accentuating, through recursive dialogue, the shifting landscape of one's needs, desires, and identities as they are created by and function through said praxis.

Conclusion

All elements of an ethical praxis suggest it is in the interplay between theories and practices of teachers' work that we as educators can best understand how the structures of theories and practices guide our eyes, encourage particular lines of thought, and make possible what can and cannot be expressed and understood. The five features all adhere to an ethic of relationship with the other that does a minimum of harm. It rejects reduction and standardization in favour of investigating the complex nature of educational thought, action, and circumstance, and the persons enmeshed in them. The ethical praxis limits and guards against lapses into complacency or the oversimplification of human experience into something to be controlled or predicted. This is an ethical imperative, for as Derrida (2000) suggests: 'If the whole political project would be the reassuring object or the logical or theoretical consequence of assured knowledge (euphoric, without paradox, without aporia, free of contradiction, without undecidabilities to decide), that would be a machine that runs without us, without responsibility, without decision, at bottom without ethics, nor law, nor politics. There is no decision nor responsibility without the test of aporia or undecidability' (n. p.).

Embedded within the ethical praxis is also the call for continued thought and work on the problems of educational theory and practice, as well as special and general education, and the role of pathologizing within each. Sadly, it is too late to save Craig from the suffering he endured. This analysis of efforts to teach him has, however much to teach us educators about the processes of pathologizing. The ethical praxis hints at some of the requirements that could make up asset-oriented practices. The praxis here signals a transition in *Early Childhood Curricula*. In the remaining chapters we devote ourselves solely to understanding and promoting curricula that see children as 'at-promise' (Swadener & Lubeck, 1995a).

6

Communicating with a Little Help from Friends: Intergenerational Art Class as Radical, Asset-oriented Curriculum

RACHEL M. HEYDON

Chapter 2 drew a parallel between the ways in which the social categories of young children and persons with disabilities are pathologized or seen as potentially pathological. It explained how persons belonging to these categories are evaluated against the image of the 'normate' (Thomson, 1997, p. 8) and that they are viewed in deficit terms and seen as potential threats to economic prosperity. The chapter also laid out how such persons are therefore subject to control measures that primarily involve segregation and management through scientific technology. These forms of control are illustrated again throughout the book in the biomedical approach to literacy that is highlighted in chapter 3, in relation to young culturally and linguistically diverse (CLD) children in chapter 4, and in the case of special education in chapter 5. Related to this, *Early Childhood Curricula* has told the story of children whose opportunities to draw on their funds of knowledge, express themselves, and develop their identities have been limited by curricula that legitimate and encourage a rigid and narrow view of knowledge and communication. Consider, for example, the children at Elmwood who were described through a deficit discourse. They were provided with a curriculum that privileged a version of literacy as reading where the purpose of the act was purely mechanical. Think too of Craig, whose attempts to communicate his experience through his body were shut down at every turn; the school curriculum could only give him more of what he had already been railing against. In every single case thus far we have told tales of children provided with curricula that denied epistemological and semiotic diversity (i.e., different ways of knowing and different ways of expressing that knowledge), and that negated the importance of a curriculum built on, or that could address, children's desires, pleasures, or empowering identities. Akin to the question we ask in chapter 1 about the costs of pathologizing, I ask here, what is lost, personally and socially, when children are limited in terms of what they can or want to signify and how they signify it? Thinking about what it means to be human begins to show some of the loss: 'being human means not only struggling to make sense of our environment and our place in it, but sharing and elaborating on that struggle with others. Human beings strive to make sense of life. We seem to find solace, challenge, pleasure, and sociality in representing our sense-making to others and in considering and interpreting the sense-making of others' (Albers & Murphy, 2000, p. 7). When the cases are thus taken within Albers and Murphy's understanding, it might not be an overstatement to claim that being segregated, being seen as deficient communicators and knowers, and as incomplete brains, as well as being denied the opportunities through rigid curricula and pedagogy to engage semiotically with the world in multiple ways and on one's own terms, is an assault on one's humanity.

In contrast to the notion of what/who matters is the notion of what/who is helpful to the economy. In this theory, because the value of childhood lies in what the child can produce in the future, the child's creation of knowledge and meaning must be tightly regulated. An example of a curriculum that disregards this economic valuation of children and focuses on the positive values of the child in his or her own right is the intergenerational (IG) art class at Providence Mount St. Vincent (PMST).[1] The Mount is a co-located child and long-term care facility for older and younger adults with disabilities located in Seattle, Washington. This chapter explores Art at The Mount, an IG art class, as a radical, asset-oriented curriculum that brings together three groups that share a common social position: young children, persons with disabilities, and elders.[2] The hope of this chapter is that Art at The Mount can be a bright example for curriculum development within a variety of milieux (e.g., inter- and intra-generational).

---

1 All names have been changed with the exception of the art teacher, Bridget Daly, and The Mount, who requested that they be named in all publications.
2 The age at which someone is considered an elder is, of course, context specific. I use the term elder here to indicate the people whom the minority world considers to be senior citizens.

The Study upon Which the Chapter Is Based

My aunt Bridget Daly is the art teacher responsible for Art at The Mount. Years ago, I visited Bridget in her classes and enjoyed observing and sometimes making art with the elders and children. Having spent large portions of my early life with my grandmother and her sisters and loving more than anything to collect their stories and 'be at their knees,' I felt at home with the elders and adored hearing about their past lives and their present perspectives. The vibrancy of the young children provided the perfect counterpoint to the deliberate pace of the elders in the common experience of art. My own early days in the art program were pleasurable, but I was sure this experience was nothing more than an oasis from my hectic life as a teacher. Almost a decade later, when I was feeling depressed about the state of early childhood education in the minority world for the reasons we outline in this book, I began to see Art at The Mount as more than just a personal fancy. I realized that the beauty of the place could be a lesson for all those interested in how to take seriously the quality of life and the meaning making of marginalized people, in particular, young children. As I witnessed people in the last days of their lives choosing to engage in learning and communication, the program reminded me of important lessons I had once learned about education: it is personal while being social; its importance can reside in its ability to improve one's current quality of life, even though learning may be a struggle; and it can help people realize their full potential as humans by supporting them in developing new tools for expression and giving them new knowledge to express. With these realizations, I undertook a formal study of Art at The Mount and now conduct research on IG programming generally. To date I have researched a number of IG programs and have felt heartened by the great work going on in these spaces. Still, I have found nothing as sophisticated and rich in learning opportunities as Art at The Mount.

Setting

The Mount is a space where children, elders and some younger adults live in surroundings that encourage interaction and stimulation. Although a visitor will notice the usual institutional props necessary for daily living by young children and people with disabilities (e.g., grab bars, accessible washrooms, easy to clean furniture and the like), The Mount is also inhabited by art (much of it created by the children, elders, and staff), birds, and small animals. It also includes meeting places such as the children's outdoor play area containing an observation patio for elders built within a courtyard and visible from the windows above. Visitors might also notice another important meeting place: the piano room in the lobby where people of all ages gather for singalongs or for just a casual tinkling of the keys.

Prior to the early 1990s, The Mount was a nursing home with a hospital-like structure. It then adopted a resident-directed format (i.e., residents make the decisions about their daily living and care), by turning wards into neighbourhoods and by facilitating IG contact and learning through the establishment of the Intergenerational Learning Center (ILC), a child care program. In 2004, more than 400 adults between the ages of 29 and 103 (with an average age of 89) resided at The Mount, and the ILC provided care to 125 children between the ages of 6 weeks and 5 years. For about 8 years Art at The Mount has brought residents and ILC pre-schoolers together to view, discuss, and create works of art. Art classes are alternatively offered in a conference room centrally located and in the dining area of the rotating neighbourhoods; the conference room has more amenities for art making (e.g., large work tables, cupboards for storage of supplies, and a large sink). Bringing the class to the neighbourhoods increases inclusiveness as even adult participants whose disabilities prohibit or make it difficult to get to the conference room may attend. Products from the art classes are proudly and publicly displayed year-round throughout The Mount, and participants hold an annual public art show to promote their work and to raise funds for art supplies.

My formal work concerning Art at The Mount began in 2004. The research participants in this chapter include 16 adults (ages 31 to 96; median age 85; 3 males; 13 females), 25 children (all between 4 and 5 years of age except for 2 children who were 3 years of age; 9 males; 16 females), 1 art teacher (i.e., Bridget, who functioned as a collaborator for the study), 2 ILC teachers, 1 ILC supervisor, 2 recreation therapists, 1 volunteer coordinator, and 3 volunteers. I collected data from two different IG art classes: Class 1 consisted of any adult at The Mount who wanted to participate plus ILC teacher Gary's group of children. Class 2 consisted, of any adult who wanted to participate (including those who participated in Class 2) and ILC teacher Linda's group of children. The pool of adult participants was drawn from those relatively self-sufficient and living in The Mount's apartment-style accommodations, those who lived in the neighbourhoods because they required more

intensive support, as well as those who attended adult day programmes.

Theoretical Framework

I use several theories to understand how the curriculum and overall
educational milieu operate at Art at The Mount. First, in keeping with
the rest of *Early Childhood Curricula*, this chapter is informed by a critical, postmodern view of childhood and disability and adds to it the
understanding that the minority world's social category 'senior' (i.e.,
which in my vernacular is elder) is also often pathologized. Second, I
draw on a variety of theories that relate to the curricular questions germane to this research: *What is being taught? How is it being taught? Who is
teaching it? To whom is it being taught?* These are fundamental curricular
questions as they all coalesce in various ways with Schwab's (1973)
'curricular common places' (p. 513) and Egan's (1978) answer to the
question 'What is Curriculum?.' Because the art program's curriculum
centres on meaning making between participants and fosters the use of
a variety of media, I borrow from a social semiotic understanding of literacy as interpreted by multimodal literacy to answer these questions.
As in chapter 3, literacy is thus seen as litera*cies*, which are not simply
the typical foci of reading and writing but also the myriad of ways in
which people make meaning through the creation of signs that are
themselves made through various modes and media (Jewitt & Kress,
2003).
     A multimodal approach to the development of literacy practices that
is built on social semiotics (the study of meaning making in relation to
social agency [Jewitt & Kress, 2003, p. 9]) requires researchers to pay
attention to situational factors (Heydon, Hibbert, & Iannacci, 2004/
2005, p. 10) as well as the physical, cognitive, and affective factors
already recognized. Situation matters because, contrary to traditional
semiotics which sees individuals as mere *users* of pre-made and fixed
sign systems, social semiotics sees people as *producers* of signs (Kress,
1997; Jewitt & Kress, 2003). Jewitt and Kress (2003) explain that production occurs because the signifier and the signified are never a perfect fit.
Signs, therefore, are metaphors that attempt to find the best fit between
signifier and signified at any moment in time; newness might originate
in the crevasse between the signifier and the signified. Novel signs can
also emerge from the reading of signs. Like Rosenblatt's (1978) notion
of reading as a 'transaction' between reader and text, this is a process of

taking an outward sign (e.g., a text) and creating from it, an internal sign: 'A person receives a sign, in the material form of its signifier, in which it was realized. She or he takes the shape of the signifier as an apt indication of what was signified, and forms from that a hypothesis of what the signified is. But the readers' hypothesis about the likely, plausible, apt, signified is based on *their* interest. It too, forms a new sign' (Jewitt & Kress, 2003, p. 13). Signs are therefore not 'arbitrary' (p. 10), rather they are connected to the conditions in which they were created. By extension, individuals do not have unlimited possibilities for the generation of new signs; possibilities are again tied to the situation in which signs are created (Pahl, 1999). Another social dimension enters when one considers Jewitt and Kress's (2003) distinction between the making of signs and the communicating of signs: 'The first is concerned with the sign maker, and with what he or she wants; the second is concerned with the sign maker's perception of the audience and what he or she imagines they want' (p. 12).

Other theories strengthen this emphasis on context. For example, I use Hicks's (2002) 'hybrid' approach when trying to make sense of the asset-oriented climate in Art at The Mount. Hicks's methodology, which could also be termed interdisciplinary as it draws on philosophy, educational studies, and literary studies, suggests that while she might agree with social semiotician Michael Halliday's (1978) contention that 'language is a form of interaction and is learnt through interaction' (p. 18), she might also find that one's identity and emotional connections to others need to be further highlighted. Hicks (2002) argues that 'all knowledge occurs as a social relation between subjects' (p. 138), and her research demonstrates that what one learns, particularly in early childhood, often depends on whom one values and loves. Experiences and contexts all affect the development of signs. It follows then that literacy practices are high-stakes practices in that the moments of sign production are characterized by relationship.

The work of Bakhtin has often been called upon to help researchers interested in the social nature of language, literacy, and thought in general to appreciate the link of social relationships (e.g., Kendrick, 2003). Wertsch (1991), for instance, argues that Bakhtin's brand of semiotics acknowledges 'the most important thing for making sense of meaning is not the sign, but the whole utterance into whose composition the sign enters' (Ivanov cited in Wertsch, p. 49). Bakhtin (1986) coined the term 'utterance' to signify that 'speech can exist in reality only in the form of concrete utterances of individual speaking people, speech subjects.

Speech is always cast in the form of an utterance belonging to a particular speaking subject, and outside this form it cannot exist' (p. 71). The form of the utterance is contingent upon the perspective, disposition, and values of the individuals who produce them; this, Bakhtin calls 'voice.' Although Bakhtin's language is suggestive of oral language, his theory 'applies to written as well as spoken communication, and it is concerned with the broader issues of a speaking subject's perspective, conceptual horizon, intention, and world view' (Wertsch 1991, p. 51). What is crucial is that the utterance is always addressing another who is present or implicit. As Bakhtin (1986) says, 'addressivity, the quality of turning to someone, is a constitutive feature of the utterance; without it the utterance does not and cannot exist' (p. 99). This is where the notion of the dialogic enters: Bakhtin demonstrates that the productivity of signs is based in 'the ways in which one speaker's concrete utterances come into contact with ... the utterances of another' (Wertsch, 1991, p. 54). Thus, the dialogic involves understanding that because reading is productive rather than merely transmissive, one's signs demand an audience and this audience is present throughout every stage of sign-making. Bakhtin (1981) teaches that the presumption of an audience and the yearning to have one's words shown back to one's self through another's reading of those signs, leads every sign maker to include that implied other in his or her meaning making. This is the dialogic which enables every text to be heterogeneous, containing within itself, aspects of the other. Subsequently, the more sign production and meaning making are carried out within a heterogeneous and explicitly social environment where relationship and community are valued and promoted, the greater the learning opportunities may be. This suggests that the sign-making opportunities, and by extension, the learning of child participants in the IG art classes might be positively affected and perhaps augmented because of the IG aspect.

There is one more piece to be added to the hybrid theoretical framework of this study: the nature of early literacy itself. There is no shortage of support for art-making in early childhood curricula. Art-making is seen as a key way of enhancing children's physical, cognitive, sociocultural, and literacy development (e.g., Brynjolson, 1998; Danko-McGhee, & Slutsky, 2003; Richmond, 1998; Wright, 1997). I am interested, however, in how the curriculum in Art at The Mount supported sign production as *itself* a form of physical, cognitive, socio-cultural, and literacy engagement important *in its own terms*. Thus, the theoretical framework of this study is also made up of an early literacy perspective. Such a perspective, rather than seeing children's meaning-making as a lesser version of adult literacy or as preparation for other forms of meaning-making, 'allows early childhood to be seen as a state in which people use literacy as it is appropriate, meaningful and useful to them, rather than a stage on a path to some future literate state' (Gillen & Hall, 2003, p. 10). All persons engaged in meaning making, regardless of age, are thereby seen in an asset-oriented way as literate beings.

Art Class: A Curriculum Built on Community

No single art class was wholly representative of the others. This is because classes were held in different places with different participants. The personalities and pedagogies of the two ILC teachers were very different, and the media and subject matter being explored changed from class to class and always affected the tone of each class. Still, art classes had five identifiable components: orientation, the creation of a catalyst for the project, the teaching of the technical aspects of the project, working on the project, and the completion of the project. The structure of the classes provided opportunities for participants to

- form part of a diverse community
- draw on their knowledge and skills to support each other in the here and now, not in preparation for some distant future
- engage in meaningful, authentic learning where they were respected as people with something to express and contributions to make by reading others' expressions
- develop competence in a variety of modes and media so as to expand their choices in apt signifiers

Next, I address the curricular questions of who, by whom, and what, which help to illustrate the opportunities just listed. Also, the question of how is addressed within my response to the three former questions.

Who Is Being Taught?

The curriculum of Art at The Mount is a uniquely IG curriculum intended to capitalize on the diversity created when different generations are brought together. This section explains how orientation, touch, teachers' modelling of comfort with elders, support for communication

with elders, and elective participation all coalesced to provide participants with optimum learning and opportunities for interaction.

Every class began with Bridget the art teacher leading a formal
period of welcome where participants reminded each other of their
names and became (re)acquainted.[3] If there is such a thing as a typical
beginning to class, the following example of introductions that took
place in the conference room, might be it. This episode reveals the lay-
ers of emotion and the types of interactions germane to the class. Evident are the playfulness of the routine, the slight apprehension on the
part of the children, and the excitement of the adults. Characteristic too
is the way in which Bridget and Gary, an ILC teacher, work together to
facilitate interaction and connection-making between participants.

Foundations for Community: Getting Oriented, Getting Safe

Introductions on a Spring Day

Bridget models for the participants in a big, clear voice, 'Hi, I'm Bridget,
and I'm the art teacher. Who's here today?' Participants say their names
with Bridget and Gary coaching them to look at each other. It is then
Carl's (cp)[4] turn.

'My name's shy boy.' Carl squeaks out these words as he pulls the neck
of his T-shirt up over the bottom of his face.

Gary doesn't push Carl; instead he looks to Carl's friend, Arthur (cp).
'Arthur's been very excited about today. He's been greeting all of his
friends at the door telling them who's going to art studio.' As Gary says
this, he moves behind Arthur and places his hand reassuringly on his
shoulder. Arthur smiles, and I notice Carl peeking out.

Frieda (age 96) calls Gary over. She extends her arm to him and smiles
widely. Gary takes her hand. 'I like your overalls,' Frieda beams.

'You like my overalls?' Gary puts his thumb under his suspenders and
does a little twirl, showing off his outfit. The children giggle.

'Yah!' Frieda reinforces.

Bridget allows this enthusiasm to be a way to bring Carl back into the
introductions. She says to Frieda, 'The boy next to you says he's shy boy.

---

3 Most participants would have met already either through art class, another IG activity,
   or through informal means within the structure of The Mount's physical architecture
   which had been created for formal and informal IG interaction.
4 Child participant.

Do you think so? Do you think he's shy?' Carl covers his eyes, but I can see him smiling between his fingers. Frieda smiles and points at Carl. Bridget eases the interaction further. She moves over to Carl and touches his arm. 'He says he's shy. Do you think he's shy?'

'Are you shy?' Frieda asks as she reaches for Carl.

Gary, too, eases the interaction. He speaks in a booming voice, makes eye contact with most of the participants, and uses inclusive language so that everyone in the room is in on the conversation. 'He's not shy when he visits Frieda on our Grasshopper days.[5] Then he has his hand out for M&Ms! Carl, you like M&Ms?'

'His real name is Carl,' Bridget clarifies for Frieda. She repeats his name clearly and bends down so that she is right at Frieda's ear. Then she spells Carl's name aloud: C-A-R-L.

'His real name is Carl!' Another child in the room repeats.

Frieda looks at Carl and coaxes, 'I can be shy too, but I'm not going to hide my eyes.' Frieda is matter-of-fact.

'Shy boy!' Carl asserts after hearing his 'real' name said aloud.

'Hey, shy boy,' Bridget allows Carl to name himself, 'Do you know who this is? Do you know who's sitting next to you?' Bridget gestures towards Frieda.

'Yes.'

'Who is it?'

'Frieda!'

'See,' Bridget says, 'he knows without even looking.'

Introductions like this one began the art-making that was to come by highlighting the social aspect of the practice. Participants, by engaging in the routine of sharing names, were reminded that their work was not independent but rather grounded in community. The introductions went hand-in-hand with the seating arrangements. Bridget insisted insofar as possible that participants sit in a pattern of adult, child, child and adult. Gary (ILC teacher), Marianne (volunteer), and the two recreation therapists interviewed all commented on the effectiveness of this seating plan. The plan allowed children and adults to access each other, but did not isolate children from each other. It was crucial for all partic-

---

5 In the ILC the children are grouped according to insect names. On Grasshopper days, the children from this particular group go to the neighbourhoods to visit residents and sometimes to participate in pre-planned activities. Note that the real names of the groups have been changed for confidentiality.

ipants to acquire the sense of safety necessary to interact and ultimately to create art together. Orientation allowed this by providing the opportunity for participants to situate themselves in relation to each other. For example, in the vignette, Frieda and Carl, despite Carl's apparent shyness, did connect. In fact, Carl's shyness, when taken in context, may have been a catalyst for the connection-making. Notice that Carl played at his shyness and ironically placed it in the foreground as a means of being at the centre of conversation. In the end, one could see that he knew Frieda all along, and his peeking and smiles tempered his supposed apprehension. This is reminiscent of a young child playing peek-a-boo with a caregiver. Carl created a character of 'shy boy,' and he brought him back out in subsequent classes. Some of the other boys participated in the play, and they eventually began to introduce themselves as 'shy boy number two,' 'shy boy number three,' and so on. Orientation, therefore, became a light-hearted time when participants could play with each other.

Orientation was typically a time of refamiliarization. The art classes are imbedded within a shared-site situation which allows for the establishment of an IG *program* rather than mere IG *activities*. The difference between these approaches is that IG programming 'provide[s] a way for experiences and interactions to take on meaning relevant to one's life' whereas IG activities 'do not allow the level of meaning to exist because they lack depth and long-term significance' (Friedman, 1997).

Within a shared site, art class participants encounter each other in other parts of their day and other spaces of the building. Thus, the class is not a stand-alone. Many children had been at The Mount since infancy and aspects of the facility enhanced natural (i.e., unscheduled) interaction through, for instance, the architecture of the building and the proximity of children's physical space to adult space. There were also scheduled interactions such as singalongs and neighbourhood strolls. Embedded within a co-located facility, the art class could draw on participants' prior experiences with each other. Most had already met or at least seen each other. These connections were chances for stronger connection-making within the art class. For instance, in one class, Mina (age 81) engaged Chloe (cp) in conversation by telling her that she could see her playing from her bedroom window: 'I wave to you, but evidently you can't see me' Mina explained, 'It's way above where you play in those houses. If you look straight up, you'll see my window. There's all kinds of windows in my room and there are flowers. There are lots of flowers and green. I love flowers.' The playground with the 'houses' of which Mina spoke was part of the strategic IG architecture at The Mount. Whether or not Mina had actually seen Chloe from her window is debatable; but Mina had seen children playing in that location and Chloe would have played there. The conditions for connection were therefore met and extended through Mina's orchestration of the conversation.

Touch and leading by example were also significant parts of getting acquainted and gaining a sense of safety, particularly for children new to The Mount. As Gary, told me:

> Well, when they get in here too, it's interesting to see the kids who aren't used to being with residents. They will, when we go and visit, they'll hide behind my legs. They will just peek around. I had one kid tell me he doesn't want to shake the woman's hand because she's going to eat him, 'cause for a lot of kids, the elders, the wrinkles, and the discolouring, it's very intimidating to them. And after a month or two, at first by example, I have them see me touching the residents, hugging them, touching their hands, speaking softly with them, and eventually we get to ... what I really like to do is do the lotion with the hands, with the residents. Take them and put lotions on their hands, and of course at first some of them won't. A lot of them instantly will, and they're loving it. It's fun to see the transition from the beginning of the year where those students who had nothing to do with it, now are the first ones that want to run up and have their favourite residents. And, when I put the lotion out, they're proud to bring their little toys and whatever it is they have. They want to come show the residents. So the circle of life ... is just great here because we have babies to our residents who are on their lasts days. It's a little, little community in the centre here.

Touch, as can be seen in Gary's interview, was also a way of soothing adult participants. This was seen again in the art class through regular practices such as handshakes and the placement of shawls on adult participants' shoulders. Frequently, I observed staff bringing participants together by touch; for example, when Bridget wanted two participants to interact, she would squat down between them and stretch her arms around the participants' shoulders, thus making a physical link between them. Touch was also used as an opportunity to alleviate fear of illness in both children and adults. For instance, Frieda had been absent from class for a few weeks because of illness. When she returned, she was frailer than before, and she had an oxygen tank. During a portion of class when Frieda was working with child participants, she began to cough aggressively. Volunteer Marianne provided an opportunity to calm Frieda and to let the children know that she wasn't frightened. She did this by using a gentle tone of voice, rubbing Frieda's back and engaging Frieda and the children in conversation about the art piece they were creating.

The adult participants also instigated the use of touch as a form of connection between diverse participants. During the orientation portion of one art class, Alma (age 92) was very interested in Clara (cp). As Alma's voice was not sufficiently strong to catch Clara's attention, she reached over and touched Clara's arm. At first Clara recoiled and looked frightened. Her eyes were wide and she stared at Alma. Marianne, however, noticed this and intervened to facilitate positive IG interaction. Marianne put herself between Alma and Clara, squatted down to be at both of their heights and said to Clara: 'It's okay. Say hello to Alma.' Marianne then modelled this for Clara: She allowed Alma to touch her; she touched Alma on the arm in return and said: 'Hi Alma.' Clara then released the tension from her body (her shoulders relaxed and her eyes shrank) and she moved towards Alma and started to talk with her about the impending art project.

Connection-making through touch was something that needed to be fostered. Gary related that some children were hesitant to interact with adults whom they didn't know – particularly when those adults looked different from what they were used to. Consequently, modelling behaviour conducive to connection-making and safety was necessary. Bridget echoed this need to model how to feel safe with disability and aging in addition to the importance of the overall IG structure of The Mount. When I asked her about the possibility of the children being afraid and the changes that occurred in children's attitudes over time she said:

I can address this partly as a parent of a child in [the ILC]. One of the reasons I want[ed] my kids to be there, is because we don't have elderly relatives nearby they would be exposed to regularly, and have interactions with. Just by eating in the cafeteria with them you get used to seeing people in wheelchairs, and, say, being around. If somebody is trying to push the wheelchair through a doorway, and some other adult will come and just help them with it ... it doesn't become something weird. I mean, it becomes part of their regular life, and they start to see the people in the wheelchairs and not the wheelchairs, not the walkers. They also, I think, start to see ... that when you are around somebody who that age, you don't run, so they get to be a little more empathetic. But just even in the course of one class, sometimes frequently, I can see, they come in, they don't want to sit next to a certain resident, maybe that resident has never been there before, or they might be mumbling to themselves, or they might be asleep. And those are things, the kids would think might be odd. But once the class gets going, they might have me or [Gary] or [another] teacher. They see that person being comfortable with this resident, and talking to them, and maybe even encouraging them to talk to the resident. It gets easier and they get more comfortable, and by the end they'll go up to them and maybe shake their hand, or let [Frieda] kiss them.

Bridget used the term comfort, but this comfort may have been a form of safety. Safety requires that all participants learn how to live and work together. As Bridget said, the art class provided children the opportunities to learn how to comport themselves around the adult participants. She used the example of children learning that when they ran around in art class, it felt less safe for adult participants.

As in Introductions on a Spring Day, children were also provided with the opportunity to learn how to communicate with others, which is essential for community building. For instance, the children saw many adult participants had difficulty hearing. Thus in such a situation, if one wanted to be understood, one needed to speak loudly and clearly. Additionally, children were provided with the occasion to learn how to resolve conflict and to talk about their fears. Marianne highlighted such an instance:

These kids, a lot of them, have been with the ILC since they were real tiny ... And [the ILC] take the kids out onto the [neighbourhoods] on a regular basis. They're very comfortable with the adults. They're comfortable with them being in a wheelchair. They're comfortable with their drooling or the fact that they fall asleep ... Sometimes an adult ... We saw it a couple of weeks ago, somebody got angry about a little boy 'cause he kicked her chair ... And he was good about it. I mean she was rude and it was not a good thing ... I think it upset him. He didn't start [to] have a temper tantrum. ... Johnny [the child] was up on the [neighbourhood]. There was no room to really separate the two. And I talked to him about it, and I explained that she may not have understood what she was saying ... And I praised him because I thought he was really ... good about it. I think he understood. He was a little uncomfortable with it, a little scared about it, but he held it all together and he was able to talk about it.

Many of the adult participants, especially when the classes were held in the neighbourhoods, had diseases that affected their behaviour (e.g., Alzheimer's disease). Sometimes these adults had difficulty with impulse control, memory, and the like. Living and working with people who had such illnesses provided opportunities for children to learn about normate behaviour as well as how to resolve conflict and to understand one's fears. A number of times I observed the children responding in positive ways to adult participant behaviour incommensurate with the norm. Often, for example, Frieda would forget she had just introduced herself to the class, and so she would repeat, 'Hello, I'm Frieda!.' Without missing a beat, the children's response would simply be to return the good humour with an equally gleeful, 'Hello, Frieda!'

During no part of the art class were participants put in danger. While some adult and even child behaviour was unpredictable, all participants had chosen to participate. Moreover, participants could leave at any time as Marianne made clear:

> We have to make sure that the adults we bring down want to be there because the kids are there. You have to have adults who are interested in children. And a lot of adults, you know, they find the kids too loud or too noisy, or sometimes the kids will kick them by mistake and they get very upset at that. And sometimes they just don't really want to be around children. So we have to make sure that the adults know that this is one with the kids, and do they want to come down and visit and watch and work. And even if they don't want to do anything, I'll ask them to come down anyway: 'you know, if you don't want to stay, I'll take you right back,' so they don't feel that there's any pressure to go down and do artwork.

Children too had the choice of where and when to participate and for how long. In my observations, however, it was usually adults who left class early (for such things as checking insulin levels and using the toilet). The children did not ask to leave early, and on several occasions, the children asked to stay longer. Community in this sense meant that all participants in the class were viewed as full persons with decision-making capacity[6] and the right to exercise that capacity.

---

6 Legally, not all adult participants had decision-making capacity, yet this did not interfere with their right to make choices within the art class.

Who Is Teaching?

As Hicks (2002) teaches, children learn best from those whom they value and love. The child participants were most bonded to their own teachers. For this reason, for children to feel safe with people who were different from them, teachers themselves needed to model feeling safe. As formal preparation to become an ECE teacher in an IG setting is rare, most teachers had to learn on the job. A willingness to take on this challenge is something the IG administrators I have interviewed over the years look for when they are hiring. Working through this challenge is evident in the case of ILC teacher, Gary.

Feeling safe with people whom he saw as old and/or disabled was not automatic for Gary; it was a gradual process that required him to face his own mortality. In our first interview, Gary confessed his fears after just starting at The Mount. He spoke about not having prior experience with older adults or with people with disabilities. Gary explained that his first performance appraisal at the ILC suggested that he improve his interaction with the adult participants in art class. Gary said that suggestion 'was really good for me 'cause it really brought out more of what you see now.' I asked him whether he meant the various forms of interaction with the adult participants that he modelled for the children. He answered: 'Yeah, that's a big thing at first I wasn't doing enough of. I was interacting with my kids, trying to make them do the art, and I would a little bit talk to the elders, but I didn't know the residents that good. I was still a little bit uncomfortable. I didn't want to offend people. I was trying to be, you know, too politically correct.' Gary signalled that rather than interacting with adult participants as peers or on an individual basis, he perceived them as a homogenous group that was other. This distancing of himself from the group hampered Gary's interaction and communication with the participants.

A couple of months after our first interview Gary talked about his recent bout with cancer and the effect it had had on his relationship with the adult participants. He then said,

> To tell you the truth, when I first started interacting with residents, at first I wasn't comfortable with the touching and everything. My fears of being old and at the same time going through cancer. Now, when cancer came I felt more on par with the residents all of a sudden, you know, because I was walking around with radiation in my body, going slow, so I got this whole new love for the residents too, realizing I'm closer there than I am

with ... In my head, my mind, my heart, it's closer to the kids, 'cause I feel like I'm a big, goofy kid. But the body, I have to remember, is closer to this side.

Gary attributed his increased sense of safety, interaction, and effectiveness as an ILC teacher, particularly within the art class, to his illness, and to the realization that the other is in fact 'us.' He recognized that his fears were getting in the way of his development as a teacher. Gary stated,

In America we joke, you know, when you're 18, you're American, you think you own the world type attitude. That's where a lot of Americans are anyway. When you're 18 you think you have the right to totally own the world. So I think any time we are faced with those things, we realize [our] mortality. [It's like the album by] Sting, *Nothing Like the Sun* ... and he had a song there called 'Fragile,' how fragile we are, and that song just stuck with me 'cause it's so true. We walk around with an invincible attitude. But there's a fine line between an attitude and the vulnerability we all face every day. A lot of us just don't admit it because part of that is the ego that keeps you going.

In the former interview clip, Gary still distanced himself from the other adult participants. This was communicated in the distinction he made between his mind, which he aligned with youth, and his body, which he aligned with old age. Yet Gary's talk and actions in the classroom demonstrated that he had been consciously working on feeling safe with himself in relation to the adult participants. Moreover, through his descriptions of how to foster a sense of safety in the children, Gary noted that this sense was fundamental to the children's own relationship-building with the adult participants.

In sum, despite moments of fear, overall the children demonstrated behaviour consistent with feeling safe in the classes. From this I inferred that they also felt safe in the face of disability. An instance of this was when Mark (age 31), one of the younger persons living in The Mount, was invited to an art class. Mark had never before participated, and his physical disabilities were very pronounced. Like many of the adults at The Mount, Mark used a wheelchair, but his wheelchair was much larger, as it needed to support his upper torso and head. The shape of Mark's body set him further apart since it did not look like that of most others. His arms were smaller than average and were twisted up by his head. His fingers were splayed and he seemed to have little control over his limbs. When Mark approached the table, Kevin (cp) stared with wide eyes. His staring, however, was not due to Mark's disability. Instead, Kevin exclaimed, 'Whoa, he's got a Hooters shirt!' Kevin's interest in Mark was because Mark was wearing a shirt from the chain of restaurants famous for its scantily clad female servers. Evidently stereotypical gender practices can surmount the gulf between generations and abilities!

What to Teach?: Art as a Shared Focus for Community-Building

Opportunities for the de-pathologizing of childhood, aging, and disability and the IG interactions that enhanced them were created by more than bringing different people together or by having teachers who were comfortable with aging. The data suggest that because participants in Art at The Mount gathered around a meaningful, authentic purpose that insisted on community and that built on participants' strengths, their learning and interactional opportunities were strengthened and widened.

All aspects of the art classes supported participants in making the semiotic decisions Jewitt and Kress (2003) list as significant: (1)'decide what is to be signified,' (2)'decide what is the apt signifier,' and (3) 'decide how the sign is made most suitable for the occasion of its communication' (p. 11). No doubt these decisions are interrelated and do not necessarily occur in lock-step; however, the data suggest that different components of the class emphasized different decisions. The introduction to the project component of the class illuminated decision three, while the catalyst component emphasized decision one.

Following orientation, Bridget introduced the project. Because of the changing participants in the class and the memory difficulties of many, Bridget tried to make sure the projects could be completed in one period. Participants were usually invited to think about a problem or theme and then asked to interact with each other to generate ideas. This again highlighted the social component of the class and encouraged participants to create signs they would not have if they had simply worked independently. In a textile project on the subject of summer, Bridget started the class by reminding participants of a special family quilt hanging in Frieda's room, which most participants would have seen. She used this to begin a discussion of how quilts can tell stories and connected it to some outside texts such as *Dancing at the Louvre:*

Faith Ringgold's French Collection and Other Story Quilts (Cameron, 1998). Ringgold is known for her beautiful painting on fabric to create story quilts; her book showed many images of quilts depicting aspects of summer. After the picture walk, Bridget asked the participants: 'What do you do in the summer? Tell the person beside you what you do in summer.' Conversations then ensued, allowing for the generation of ideas for art-making. Sometimes these conversations needed to be supported and would persist throughout the whole art period as happened in the following vignette:

Summertime

It's that time in the class when the introductions have been made, the motivating activity is over, the instructions for the project have been laid out, and participants begin their work. Today's project involves the theme of summertime. Participants are to paint milk onto a piece of canvas then draw on it with chalk pastels. Finally, the canvas is ironed to give the look of batik.

Carl is sitting on one side of Annie (age 84), and Marianne, who knows that Annie usually needs a push to begin, is sitting on the other. Annie rarely uses words to communicate, but now she is expressing some difficulty in knowing what image to create. She does this by staring at her cloth and keeping her hands on the arms of her wheelchair rather than at the ready with a pastel. Marianne is crouched down beside Annie, and the two seem to be having a good time. Marianne is doing lots of talking, and Annie laughs and laughs. Marianne asks, 'Is there anything special you do [in summer]? Or do you just sit in the sun and go ah! I'm so glad it's finally sunny!' Annie giggles and Carl turns to face her. While he watches the interaction between Annie and Marianne, Carl continues painting and has a pleasant look on his face. Marianne continues the conversation, this time looking at Carl too to draw him in, 'That's what I do. I say, thank God it's warm!'

Carl gives a slight smile. 'It's true!' Marianne exclaims, and then turns back to business. 'But we have to think of something that you do in the summer. What would that be?' As Marianne talks, Annie turns and looks at Carl.

Marianne begins to sing 'Summertime' from *Porgy and Bess*. 'Summertime, and the livin' is easy. Fish are jumpin' ... 'Do you like to go fishing?' As she says this, Marianne joins Annie in looking at Carl. Both watch him and notice that the cup of milk from which he's painting is getting dangerously close to the edge of the table. Annie reaches out and moves it closer to Carl. She holds the cup up to him and continues to hold it as he uses it; Carl simply continues to paint.

Marianne acknowledges the connection between the two through a pause, but then attempts to bring Annie back to the task: 'Annie, I'm struggling here!' Marianne continues to sing and looks Annie right in the face: 'Oh your daddy's rich ... Is your daddy rich?' Annie laughs. 'And your ma is good lookin.' So come on, let's think of something you like to do in summertime.'

Annie smiles, laughs, and then utters her first word of the day: 'Okay!'

'OK Annie, put your thinking cap on!' Marianne now forms a bridge. 'Carl, could you help us please?' Carl smiles that slight smile again and looks at them. 'What do you think would be a fun thing for Annie to do in the summertime?'

'Go on picnics.' Carl answers.

Marianne ensures Annie has heard, 'He says go on picnics. What do you think of that?'

In a small voice Annie says, 'In the summertime.'

Marianne takes it as a question, 'Yes. Go on picnics.' All three people look at each other. Marianne, noticing she's garnered the greatest response from Annie through Carl, pushes further: 'What else can Annie do in the summer?'

With pastel in hand now, Carl pauses and answers, 'Go swimming.'

Marianne makes an excited hand gesture, 'Go swimming! That's a good one.'

Annie agrees, 'I like that.'

'We both like that one,' Marianne offers.

Annie now turns right around to look at Carl. She focuses on his pastel drawing. 'Oooo!' she enthuses.

After a little more discussion and a lot more drawing on Carl's part, Annie is in good humour, but has yet to make a mark with a pastel. Marianne tries a new tactic. 'So Annie, I'm going to make us a border and that will help us focus on where we're going to draw. You won't feel like you have a great big space to fill in. Now you'll have a little space.' Carl watches as Marianne does this. 'Now look at Carl's.' Annie looks. 'It's beautiful! The colours are so rich! Wow! I'm going to go talk to Frieda for a while, and then I'll come back and help you, because that's my job.' Marianne has had her arm around Annie for the last few minutes. She pats her shoulder and leaves. Annie watches Carl intently. Carl continues drawing, nonplussed. A short time later, Annie has drawn water on her cloth just like Carl.

In this vignette Carl is drawn on as a resource to stimulate Annie and she receives his contribution as an asset. Although interactions like this certainly create opportunities for child participants to make a contribution, notice now how in the following interaction, it is the child who explicitly benefits from the interaction in terms of her art-making:

From Oral Story to Visual Story

The participants are all working on their projects; Frieda is sitting but not working. Frieda is going to make a drawing that will illustrate a story she has told the class about her memory of falling into a flour bin in her father's bakery. She calls Bridget over and motions towards the children: 'Their drawings are better than mine.'
'Kids have good imaginations.'
'Ah, ha.' Frieda agrees.
'But I think we could draw a picture of you falling into the flour bin.'
'Okay.'
'Let's think about how we could draw it.' Bridget gets the thinking going, and catches Sophia's (cp) attention. She stops working on her own image and joins the two women in their problem solving.
Frieda contemplates her paper.
Placed between Frieda and Sophia, Bridget herself begins to sketch on a scrap paper. The sketch shows the position of Frieda's body and her dress as she flies into the barrel. Sophia looks on intently as she clutches her own pencil. She switches her gaze back and forth between her own drawing and Bridget's scrap paper. 'So Frieda, the shape of your body, I thought you might have your arms up in the air,' Bridget explains as she sketches.
'Oh yah!' encourages Frieda.
'And your dress would be flying up in the air, and your hair would be sticking out and you might be screaming. What do you think, Frieda?'
'We'll put some bows in her hair too!' Frieda sounds encouraged. She also, through the use of 'her' instead of 'my,' distinguishes herself from this emerging metaphor. Bridget obliges Frieda's request and sketches in some bows.
Sophia is now hooked. She is no longer looking at her own image.

Instead, she studies Frieda's and then states, using Frieda's pronoun, 'She looks funny!'

'Sophia says you look funny falling into the bin.' Bridget makes the link between Frieda and Sophia, the image and Frieda's story. 'Here's your dress flying up.'

Frieda points to the dress, 'Oh, I see!'

With Frieda now able to proceed independently, Bridget moves on to other participants, and I observe Sophia drawing with a fervour she hadn't previously shown.

Just as Carl got Annie going, Frieda was able to be a catalyst for Sophia. By witnessing adults, particularly those in the last days of their lives, struggling over and making progress in learning and communication, children got the opportunity to see learning and communication as relevant to the here and now as well as the process of sign-making.

Technical Aspects

While encouraging sharing with others, the curriculum also allowed child participants opportunities to recognize and use an increased number of signifiers to communicate their schemata. After the period of conversation that allowed the children to conceptualize the topic and for the adults to generate memories, Bridget demonstrated the necessary techniques for completing the projects. I observed projects that involved multiple modes such as printmaking, painting, drawing, collage, and cut-outs in media such as rag paper, cloth, kraft paper, ink, chalk and oil pastel, and acrylic paint. The technical aspects of sign making are critical problem solving occasions for children. When creating art, children are confronted with 'problems ... related to materials and their physical properties' that arise from their 'initial difficulty in using the materials due to undeveloped sensory/motor skills or unfamiliarity with new objects and situations' (Pitri, 2001, p. 50). Teaching the 'how' as in 'how to create a sign' allows children to develop the necessary motor skills for diverse sign making. It also offers children the opportunity to develop an awareness of the possibilities of mode and media. This can expand their sign making options so that children might select the mode and media that best suit their communication needs/desires. In all aspects of the IG art classes, participants were given opportunities to view and create images and to interrogate critically what affects images (e.g., media and composition) and with what effects (i.e., how the media and composition of an image affect the way the image communicates its subject and is read or viewed).

What perhaps made the technical directions so effective was that they were contained within a meaningful whole rather than the fragmented and decontextualized language lessons that litter the cases in the first part of this book. At Art at The Mount, before launching into the how, participants were led through the catalyst portion of the class so they could engage with the project. Further, they knew there would be a product to share, thus enhancing the engagement even more; there was something to communicate and a reason for communicating it. Also significant was the fact that the media and the project subject were compatible – including for IG interaction. This was deliberate, as Bridget explained in an interview about how she planned for class:

Bridget: I think when I first started [at The Mount], I didn't always know the limitations ... I had mostly worked with Kindergarteners through sixth graders, all of whom can typically use scissors or glue things. And so, from experience now I find ... what kind of things most seniors or most preschoolers are able to do. There are always exceptions to that. There are some residents who can only move one hand. So what I do is I design projects, and I research [around that] ... and ... the media ... is one thing. There's also what kind of theme or subject can we put into it. There are some [subjects] ... kind of built into the project. For example, if we were doing collagraphs, which are paper prints there is subject matter that can work, and some works better than others. I am interested in the product in the sense that if you get a good product, people will come back, and they'll feel good. They have good self-esteem about completing it and pride. So, there is that. That's not always important, but it's important at least to have that sometimes. But then the subject matter too, I like to have things that they can talk about, especially things that spark memory in the residents. Because, if you can spark some memory and get them talking to the kids, then there's a conversation. And some good, valid subject matter just isn't conducive to having conversations. So I try to choose that kind of thing, like, for example, what do you think about when you think about home? And that's a subject that comes up often with the residents: they miss their houses, they miss their pets or their garden.

Rachel: And the kids resonate with that one as well?

Bridget: I think they do, especially because as a preschooler, you know, a lot of their [foci] are around home, and some of them have a hard time leaving home to come into a facility like [this]. So, you know, that's something they can talk about. Another thing might be a pet they really loved, both the kids and the residents. If the kids don't have a pet, the grandmother might have, or they might wish they did, or sometimes they see little kittens, so they both have a response to that. So I try to choose some things like that. Even sometimes things like weather. I did this one project once, where we talked about what kinds of lines describe weather. And we can talk about where people come from, what kind of weather they have there, because a lot of the residents come from different places. And you probably know this, but there's a lot of diversity in the kids and the staff, too – a lot of Asian or Hawaiian, Cambodian. So talking about the weather, where people come from is a part of having a frame that's not just the media; it's also what subject.

Bridget carefully balanced matter with media and modes so that participants had something valuable to express and equally valuable ways of expressing it. The curriculum also sought to create a cooperative spirit among participants; the facilitation required to capitalize on it is strikingly apparent in the completion component of the class.

Completion

In a typical class in the conference room, there would be sustained work for at least one hour, and then the number of participants would dwindle. Adult and child participants were encouraged to leave whenever they felt it necessary. There were other teachers in the ILC to care for anyone who returned. This end of class time when a handful of participants would be finishing their projects was often the ripest time for conversation and collaboration. This became obvious when Tim (cp) was encouraged by Marianne to assist Millie (age 80) to complete her project.

Crowns

The project is to create a multi-media crown representing an imaginary country by using kraft paper, cut-outs, glitter, markers, coloured pencils, coloured paper and a plastic garland. Tim is very interested in this project. Back in his classroom, Tim and his group have been learning about chickens. Tim thus decides that he will create a chicken country where he is king of the chickens. When he finishes his crown, Tim begins to dance spontaneously. When I ask him about this, he shows me how he has drawn dancing chickens on his crown. When he is finished dancing and showing his crown to other participants, Marianne invites Tim to assist her and Alma (age 92) in working on Millie's crown.

Millie is having trouble finishing her crown. She knows what she wants, but because of the effects of a stroke, she is physically unable to carry it out. She is also limited in terms of her speech. Nonetheless, she, Marianne, and Alma communicate through word and gesture what should go on the crown. After Tim decides he will help them, Marianne places the kraft paper for the crown between them and in front of Tim. This way they can all see the paper and each other.

Tim draws a chain of people across the paper while the group discusses what he is doing. 'I love watching him make people,' Marianne remarks of Tim.

Alma turns to Bridget who is walking by: 'We love watching him make people.' Alma then turns back to watch Tim.

As Tim draws, Alma asks as she points, 'Who's that there?'

Tim doesn't answer. He seems too engrossed in drawing. When he has finished drawing, he stands back and contemplates his work. Alma encourages him to take the drawing further: 'They'd look better with ears, though,' she suggests.

Tim smiles, is silent for a moment as if he's considering the suggestion, then walks back up to the paper and says, 'I'll make blue ears.' Tim struggles to make the ears. He discusses with the others that this difficulty might be because the heads he has made are small.

After minutes of drawing, the conversation turns to the weather in Millie's imaginary country. Millie can say only that she wants the weather to be nice. Alma decides: 'It should be partly hot and partly cold.'

Tim takes this to mean that all forms of weather should be represented on the crown. He lists the weather elements including sun, rain, snow, and wind, and draws each in a different point on the crown. While he draws, he discusses aloud what he is doing. He chooses to draw hale. As he draws, he explains, 'You need some darker white so that it will show up.' And he compliments himself on a well-crafted image: 'That's a nice shape.'

This episode is the epitome of a supportive learning environment. Surrounded by persons who valued and even depended on his skills and knowledge, Tim was encouraged to create signs that could communicate the group's ideas. Tim already demonstrated that he was a proficient user of multiple modes. In his own crown and performance of the crown, he created signs in two different visual modes (dance and multimedia construction) to communicate the concept of the country in which he would like to live, and he drew on texts of the classroom (oral and print) to inform his artwork. When he worked on Millie's crown, he drew on his knowledge of the media (e.g., how to use the colour white) as well as his knowledge of the subject matter (e.g., forms of weather) to create a piece that could please everyone. In this way, Tim used his sign-making proficiency to mediate Millie's disability and, in so doing, the product became, in Bakhtin's terms, quintessentially heteroglossic.

Respecting the 'What'

Although interaction was always at the forefront of the curricular objectives, for this to occur and for the program to create the best possible learning opportunities, all staff involved had to recognize the importance of the 'what.' This meant that all persons involved with *Art at The Mount* take art seriously. The staff commented during interviews that there was a difference between craft projects or free art time in the ILC and the projects in the art class. When I asked Marianne (a volunteer), for instance, what she thought the children were learning in art class, she told me, 'I think they're learning things they don't have the opportunity to be exposed to because we do do artwork, it's not arts and crafts. It's really artwork.' I questioned the difference between art and arts and crafts. Marianne answered: 'To me crafts is something that is set up, and you go through something step by step, and everybody comes out with the same product, the same final thing. To me art is being introduced to materials, given some samples and then you're let go on your own to see what you can create. And I think it's more creative than craft work, although I think craft work is also very valid and I enjoy myself, but I think artwork is much better creatively speaking.' I understood Marianne to mean that the art created in the art program is authentic in the sense that, because there is choice and openness in the projects, art can be connected to personal identities.

Authenticity also seemed to be related to the appreciation of art-making as a distinct set of skills and knowledge. Linda (an ILC teacher) recognized this when she explained why the art program was important and what it could offer that was different from, for example, the paint centre in the ILC: 'The kids are learning. They're learning about art up here. We do art downstairs, but none of us has an art degree so we don't know the terms and things like that. They're learning some of the terms of art. They're getting a richer experience in different textures and different types of ways of doing art, instead of just markers, paints, and crayons. They're able to share that with the residents. So the residents and kids are learning at the same thing the same time.'

Linda suggested that authenticity was allowed and enhanced by having quality tools, a diversity of media, as well as a teacher who was a practising artist. Bridget holds an advanced degree in sculpture and shows her work throughout North America. Rather than intimidating participants or other staff, Bridget's status as an artist was seen as something that could enrich the projects. Of this, Janice (a recreation therapist) said: '[Bridget] is an art teacher and really very skilled. She also stretches the people beyond what we all think they can really do. She really has ideas and ways to get them to do prints and things that are more complicated, because [she] has confidence in [the] materials.' Janice communicated that Bridget's knowledge and comfort with the materials gave the participants diverse experiences with media. Because Bridget pushed the participants to do what practising artists do, the programme rejected a deficit view of the participants and showcased their capabilities. To further showcase capabilities and to enhance the authentic nature of the art-making by connecting it to a purpose, Art at The Mount held a public show every June.

Conclusion

The adult participants in Art at The Mount were certainly conscious of how IG interaction benefited their communication skills. During an interview, adult participant Rebecca (age 90) said, '[The children] get me going.' On a number of occasions during class time she motioned to me to notice when a child was making a contribution to the conversation. She often said to me, 'Don't miss that!.' Frieda also stated numerous times how much she enjoyed what the children brought to the classes. After a class one day she shouted, 'This is *my* day! I love these children.' She later added, 'These children will be so smart – smarter than me, because they've been exposed.' I was never able to ascertain exactly what Frieda meant by 'exposed,' but it seemed she meant exposed to art and diversity. Like Rebecca, Frieda told me the children's talents allowed her to make art. As ILC director Jane commented, the benefits for the adult participants were more readily apparent; however, major learning opportunities were created for the children as well. Perhaps even more important is the phenomenon of children being valued and loved by the adult participants, not because of what they could bring to the future, but because of what they added to the community in the here and now. What then does it mean to children to be seen as competent and appreciated because of their knowledge and skills? What does it add to a child's life to live within diversity? Responses to these questions are the gift that the Art at the Mount curriculum gives to all who witness it.

For countries like Canada where the dominant discourse of what matters concerns a person's contribution to the global economy and where, consequently, children, older adults, and the disabled are viewed in deficit and pathological or potentially pathological terms, Art at The Mount is a refreshing lesson. This program allows some of society's most vulnerable people to come together to learn, communicate, and foster community. It is a program that focuses on participants' strengths and what participants can contribute to each other. Certain aspects of the program are noteworthy because of the ways in which they allowed this to happen. Specifically, these involve the use of authentic art and the means of dealing with diversity.

In terms of authentic art within the art classes

- participants were provided with quality materials and authentic projects that culminated in a public art show;
- participants were treated as important, contributing members of their community and seen as having ideas to convey and the capability of producing signs and communicating each in his or her own way;
- classes were run by a practising artist;
- classes were intentionally made up of diverse participants since diversity was viewed as something that increased learning opportunities;
- community was actively built by the facilitator's numerous strategies to foster IG interaction through seating arrangements and the content, and structure of the art activities;
- participants were encouraged to solve problems together; and
- art work was displayed communally and publicly (e.g., in hallways, bedrooms, eating areas, and at the annual public art show).

Building a program that accommodated diversity meant that a diversity of needs had to be met. This could be challenging, especially as many needs were not always consistent or predictable. Therefore, to foster community within the program

- classes were flexible in terms of who participated, when, where, how, and for how long;
- decisions related to participation were made by the participants themselves;
- classes alternated between being offered in a centrally located art room and within neighbourhoods in order to reduce barriers to participation;
- physical needs of participants were accommodated (e.g., keeping room temperatures up, providing lap blankets or shawls, providing easily held tools, and using low-tack tape to secure paper to the table, etc.);
- teachers and facilitators regardless of the population with whom they usually worked, attempted to demonstrate comfort with disability, aging, and young children;
- teachers and facilitators, attempted to pay attention to both generations during the planning and delivery of curricula;
- teachers and facilitators attempted to model cooperative behaviour by cooperating with each other; and
- participants were encouraged to help each other with the technical (e.g., cutting, gluing or drawing), procedural (e.g., what step comes next) and representational (e.g., what signifier can best relate the notion of 'home') demands of the tasks.

Stunningly, Art at The Mount is an example of a radical curriculum. It is radical because it

- focuses on what individuals contributed to the collective in non-economic terms;
- focuses on quality of life not necessarily readiness (although through the focus on quality of life, numerous learning opportunities that might help with preparedness were created);
- strives to create a community out of persons who did not normally come together;
- insists on meaningful interaction and thus better fostered community;

- insists that those who worked in the program confront their own biases; and
- makes good on the notion that learning is lifelong.

The above offers practical and theoretical starting points for thinking about asset-oriented practices. While there may be more opportunities for such practices outside rather than inside public schooling, classrooms can still be sites that decry pathologizing. The next chapter provides a look at how school spaces can be asset-oriented.

7

A Case Study of Asset-oriented Approaches to Cultural and Linguistic Diversity in Early Childhood Education

LUIGI IANNACCI

This chapter offers data and discussion developed from the study of CLD children in chapter 4 and provides reconceptualized understandings and approaches to pedagogy and assessment, linguistic incorporation, and community participation in order to further develop asset-oriented practices within classroom settings. Consistent with the critical orientations of *Early Childhood Curricula*, these understandings are commensurate with the theoretical and practical concerns of critical, multicultural education. Conventional notions of multicultural education have historically overemphasized curricular change and underemphasized the impact of socio-economic factors and socio-cultural power relations on student's lives (May, 1999). There are, however, no easy answers to the issues raised; resignation to structural rather than curricular concerns *and* inattentiveness toward what is possible within classrooms have both been inadequate in addressing the concerns this research explores. May (1999) articulates the dilemma:

> While rightly highlighting the theoretical naivety of early forms of multi-cultural education, critical educators have in turn been pilloried for an inability to relate the critical theory they espouse to actual multicultural policy and practice. Multicultural education may historically have been under-theorized, but at least it could be applied programmatically in schools. Too often, the concerns of critical educators have been largely ignored because they have presented as theory divorced from practice; a concern of radical academics with little immediate relevance to either policy makers or practitioners ... it is one thing to proclaim that the world needs to be changed, it is quite another to provide concrete ways by which we might begin the process. (pp. 4–5)

Thus what I suggest here is neither prescriptive nor all-encompassing: The curricular practices and policies outlined in this chapter are framed as *possibilities* intended to assist educators in developing asset-oriented practices within their classrooms that oppose and resist pathologizing processes identified as debilitating for CLD students in ECE. Further, the structural dynamics outlined in chapter 8 assist in making these curricular changes operational and are integral to creating conditions that foster an asset-oriented, transformative approach to CLD children's literacy and identity.

Pedagogy and Assessment

Some of the issues raised in chapter 4 were in part attributable to the fact that there is often no official curriculum for students learning ESL within school systems. As a result, CLD students are inappropriately evaluated in ways that do not recognize the development of their second language acquisition. Further, the standardized curricula CLD students are held accountable to facilitate models of curriculum that do not allow them or their teachers to negotiate their literacies and extend identity options beyond a deficit orientation. The tensions that exist as a result of a lack of official curriculum responsive to L2 acquisition are problematic for the CLD students I observed. There were, however, other events I noted that demonstrate the ways in which students and teachers negotiate and subvert deficit-driven assessment practices and narrow literacy curricula in ways that highlight students' resources and re-position them as competent.

Although Pat (JK/SK teacher at Norman Bethune Public School), for example, felt constrained by curricular and assessment mandates, generating curriculum was very important to her. In many instances Pat followed students' leads and organized instruction according to their needs, interests and assets. Pat noticed for example that Samina (a senior kindergarten student learning ESL) was engaging in various conventional print literacy activities and was very interested in animals. Pat organized a series of labelled pictures of animals and provided Samina opportunities to identify and learn about them. As Pat added more animals to the collection, Samina's interests in them and her ability to identify their names and characteristics grew. Pat's desire to facilitate personal connections with children that in turn, enabled them to develop links to literacy curricula was also evident throughout our interviews.

Pat: If they [students] stop to have a conversation and want to tell me about other things, I usually digress. I'll pick up on anything. Let's say we're reading this story *Lazy Mary*. OK, so Khaled starts talking: 'Ya, I had to lie in bed when I had my stitches' and yada, yada, yada, and if he goes on and on about it, we'll engage in that conversation.

This can go one of two ways: either he's really interested in telling me that story and he'll go back to the story of his own cueing and his own pulling back, or maybe he's not interested in this so he'll do anything to avoid it which of course you get students doing all the time and then it's my obligation to say: 'OK, right, yup, you've told me about that – in your bed with stitches. Did mommy come in the room just like this mommy in the book?' You just pull them back. To me it's be creative enough in your questions ...

A lot of times you try to make it as personally relevant as possible. If I'm reading a story with [child in her class], I'll say, 'Look at that bird – does it look like Sunshine?' Sunshine is her yellow canary. 'Does it sing like Sunshine?' That might get her interested, but I have to know that she's actually got a canary at home named Sunshine to ask that question in the first place.

Luigi: So based on who the child is, you are taking cues and improvising and providing lots of other contexts.

Pat: I would have to take this story and make it exciting for them. Why would you do it in a book [points to DRA book] when, I've got finger puppets that can be used all through this. Let's play with it.

Pat was also committed to protecting practices she believed important to her Kindergarten program despite pressure to remove them in order to make time and space for curriculum and assessment mandates. For example, during one of our interviews she discussed both the value and limitations of 'Show and Tell.' Although Pat was critical of the practice as it occurred in her classroom (e.g., items that were shared promoted violence, not everyone participated, it took a fair amount of time, etc.), she felt it was important to her students and therefore should not be eliminated in spite of the mandates she was reconciling: 'I wish I could cut out show and tell but then I think – no, they enjoy it so much and it does initiate all kinds of chatter that if I were to take that away, what is my value statement? Whatever you're bringing is not good enough? You must listen to me? Thou shalt DRA you? Like I can't justify it in that way.'

Pat also put a great deal of effort into trying to arrange her practice in ways that were commensurate with her pedagogical beliefs. She did not believe in following the sequential or instructional organization of the *Jolly Phonics* program, for example, but rather connected phonics instruction to the literature, themes, concepts and experiences her students were encountering at school and at home. The following story, an interview conducted with Pat and a conversation with Pat and Zafir's mother (mother of one of Pat's JK students learning ESL), demonstrate this organization of literacy practice.

Zafir and the Three Little Pigs

The children entered, and immediately began printing their names in their 'Name Book.' I sat next to a JK student named Zafir and noticed that his ability to write his own name with a broken line model was slowly improving.

Canadian-born, Zafir is the second-youngest child in his family. He has a younger brother and three older brothers. His mother told me that although she and her husband speak Arabic at home, her sons code switch in and out of both languages while they play. She wanted her children to learn Arabic so they could speak it when they visited Lebanon.

Zafir was extremely methodical about his work and finished tasks with a painstaking precision that often required extended periods of time. He was also fiercely independent and often rejected any assistance from adults or classmates. Pat told me he once slapped her hand away when she tried helping him cut some paper in hand-on-hand fashion. Zafir asserted his independence towards his classmates as well. Zafir was not very interested in conventional print literacy and for a good portion of the year preferred to print his name in his 'Name Book' using a broken-line model. He was however, very interested in drawing and his work was prolific.

On this day Zafir completed his work both by using a broken-line model and trying to print some of the letters himself. When satisfied with his work, he followed the class routine by putting it away then going to the carpet to flip through books as he waited for his classmates to finish and for Pat to begin circle time. Pat eventually sat on the rocking chair, welcomed the students and asked how they were. They chatted for a while before she named the student who would lead circle time. Each day a different student (chosen alphabetically) was asked to name the date, the days of the week and the months of the year while being permitted to ask classmates for help when he or she needed it. I watched Zafir as he looked around and followed everyone's lead by raising his hand when the circle leader asked for assistance.

Once this portion of circle time was over, Pat (as customary) began a literacy activity. This may be a shared reading of a picture book selected by Pat or the circle leader of the day. Alternatively, she may review environmental print (e.g., student's names). During this time, she reviewed initial letter/sound correspondences in words students were reading. 'Where's your name Samina? How do you know it's your name? What does it start with? What sound does it make?' In the middle of a fairytale unit, they reviewed the story of *The Three Little Pigs*. Since they had read several versions of *The Three Little Pigs*, she asked the children to retell the plot. Intermittently she also reviewed the 'P' sound. 'Where does it say Pig? How do you know? What sound does /p/ make? If you wanted to draw the three little pigs and write 'pigs,' what letter would you need to start? How do you write the letter?' Pat guided the students through her questions and allowed them to use the whiteboard to record their answers. Zafir was quiet and leaned forward to listen.

After the mini-lesson, students engaged in a variety of self-selected activities. Pat was conferencing with individual students during this time and asked them to read *The Three Little Pigs* using a book each of them had created as a guide. Students created these books by gluing sentences and their corresponding illustrations in the correct sequence. They then added various materials to the illustrations (e.g., spaghetti painted yellow for the house of straw, popsicles for the house made of sticks and square stickers for the house made of stone, etc.), to assist their recall. As I followed Zafir to his chosen activity, Pat called me aside and asked that I also sit with students and have them read to me. I agreed and Pat handed me a random pile of books belonging mostly to students who were not learning English as a second language.

I completed Pat's request then joined Zafir who was intensely engaged in sorting automobiles on the carpet. Pat then requested that I read with Zafir as well: 'I would just like to see what happens; it would be very interesting.' She handed me Zafir's *Three Little Pigs* book and, with some uneasiness about interrupting Zafir, I obliged. Since he was in his silent period, I questioned the appropriateness of asking him to verbalize responses. I was also apprehensive about pushing him because I had noticed he was irritated by adults trying to get him to speak.

I invited Zafir to sit with me and when he did I modified the activity and started reading the story aloud. Throughout I asked Zafir to respond to yes/no guided questions that required non-verbal responses.

> Luigi: Did he blow the house down?
> Zafir: (nods head to indicate 'yes')

Zafir occasionally quietly repeated key sentences from the story after I had read them.

> Luigi: I'll huff and I'll puff and I'll blow your house down!
> Zafir: Huff and puff and blow the house down.

I occasionally asked Zafir questions that required one-word answers in the form of closed or oral cloze questions

> Luigi: Who just blew the house down?
> Zafir: Wolf
> Luigi: Not by the hair on my Chinny, chin, _____?
> Zafir: Chin.

I continued this type of questioning through our collaborative reading. The ending of the story was inferred and read: 'The wolf didn't bother them anymore and they lived happily ever after.' The illustration showed the three little pigs standing around a boiling cauldron, stirring its contents. I ask Zafir who or what they were eating and he replied: 'The wolf.' Since conferencing required the entire activity time, students (with the aid of a parent volunteer) would complete the *Jolly Phonics* page Pat prepared to reinforce orthographic and sound-symbol concepts related to the letter 'P' on another day.

The following week Pat excitedly showed me an impressive illustration of a pig Zafir had drawn in his portfolio. She suggested that I talk with Zafir about the illustrations in his portfolio and label them. When I asked Zafir about his work, he named the illustrations he had drawn on the same page as the pig picture. When I asked whether we should write down what he had told me, he nodded in agreement, handed me a purple marker, then took it back and replaced it with a black one. About to label the illustration of the pig, I asked what letter I should start with. He uttered, 'P.' Zafir seemed interested in adding to his portfolio and eventually flipped the page and began drawing various illustrations. When finished, he again handed me the black marker to label his drawings.

The Maple Ridge school district scheduled parent-teacher interviews on the following day, Eid. Attendance among Muslim parents was very poor at both Elmwood and Norman Bethune. However, Zafir's mother had scheduled an appointment and Pat invited me to speak to her. Zafir's mother had questions and concerns about Zafir's silence at school and wondered if he had a speech problem. I told her about the silent period of language learning and let her know that this was something many students acquiring a second language experienced. She nodded as I spoke and added, 'My two other sons were the same way.' Pat and I reassured her and pointed out many instances that demonstrated his comprehension of classroom activity and routines. I told her about his penchant for the computer and the many sessions we had building things as well as our *Three Little Pigs* session. She recognized much of what Pat and I had described in terms of Zafir's competencies. She seemed reassured by the interview and added anecdotes about Zafir's similar interests at home.

Pat was conscious and critical of the fact that her students were constantly interrupted during play to be evaluated on their ability to perform discrete skills. Her commitment to scheduling extended periods of classroom time for play meant there were many occasions when her students could negotiate literacy curricula according to their own interests and assets. Although the following narrative demonstrates these interactions, it should be noted that the incident is not isolated and was shaped by events that occurred throughout the year that allowed for the enactment of a generative form of curriculum.

Khaled's Volcano

I sat next to Khaled who was busy at the Play-Doh centre. When I asked what he was doing, he replied, 'I'm making a Spider-Man Pizza.' When asked about toppings he answered 'Spiders, bad guys, webs.' I asked, 'Anything you can eat'? He responded 'No.' I asked him whether he had seen the Spider-Man movie and he replied, 'Ya.' I recognized that he was making a pizza that included only ingredients consistent with the Spider-Man movie. I added, 'Should we put in the Green Goblin?' He responded affirmatively and we began to mould a piece of Play-Doh in the shape of the villain and add it to the pizza. During our conversation it was clear that his expressive language was now far more developed than at the end of phase one of my research in January when he frequently uttered, 'No' to suggestions made during play by me and his peers.

With this in mind, I continued to make topping suggestions for Khaled's Spider-Man pizza. Eventually, fully satisfied with his creation, Khaled seemed ready to begin another activity. 'What should we do?' he asked.

I knew from Pat that Khaled was interested in dinosaurs (specifically *Tyrannosaurus rex* or 'T-Rex' as he referred to it) and volcanoes. She had shown me one of the vibrant paintings of a volcano he had made in September. Throughout the year, before circle began, Khaled asked me to read a book about dinosaurs several times. One picture in the book featured a large dinosaur with a volcano in the background. In late January, I was observing Khaled at the painting easel. When asked about his painting, he said it was a volcano. I pointed to the red painted area on the side and top of his volcano and asked him about it. He looked at me for a moment and I added: 'Is it lava?' He nodded and I asked, 'What's it doing?' He replied, 'Esploding, esploding.' He then painted a T-Rex; together we named the various parts on the body (the mouth, legs, the tiny arms, the claws, the scales) as he continued to paint. Khaled made many exploding sounds in unison with the strokes of his brush as he painted. It was the most engaged I had ever observed Khaled to be up that point.

In an effort to further explore his interest in volcanoes, I suggested he make a volcano after completing the Spider-man pizza. He jumped from his chair, picked up the Spider-man pizza and packed it back into its container. I asked, 'How are we going to make this? What do we do first?' He replied, 'Take out Play-Doh, put it in a ball with hands. Make it round.' Then he flattened it and tore off little pieces and said, 'Now take a little piece, put it on the table.' He layered the pieces in a clockwise fashion until they spiralled upwards. I remarked, 'It's like a cone,' and he repeated, 'Like a cone.' As Khaled continued to build and talk about his actions, a classmate wandered over to the table, looked and listened to what Khaled was doing and said, 'I want to make a volcano too.' Khaled handed him a chunk of Play-Doh and made a space for him. The student asked me, 'How do you make a volcano?' I replied, 'Maybe you should ask Khaled, he knows how to do it.' The student did so and Khaled immediately began demonstrating. 'Make a small ball and squish it and take small pieces and make a volcano going up-little piece by piece. Like a cone.' As the two worked on their volcanoes, I asked Khaled what the pieces he was placing on top and on the side of the volcano were called. He replied, 'Lava. When it esplodes, the lava comes.' I repeated, 'Ah, when the volcano explodes, the lava comes out of it.' Throughout the entire building process Khaled's peer asked him many questions about the volcano and offered suggestions. Khaled was able to answer his questions and guide him through the process as well as integrate the play cues he was offering. Khaled's progress throughout the year was palpable. Later in the day I asked Pat about his progress and she confirmed that both socially and academically Khaled had made tremendous strides since I left in late January.

When literacy curricula provides CLD students with opportunities for autonomous learning and the demonstration of their resources, evaluation practices have the potential to shift from pinpointing where students are in relation to a standardized curriculum to documenting the assets they possess and are acquiring. Assessment and evaluation therefore articulate growth and possibilities within a student's zone of proximal development as well as experiences that will facilitate their progress. As such, what learners can *do* with language and literacy rather than their lack of knowledge *about* language and literacy becomes a central focus of asset-oriented evaluation (Mendelsohn, 1989). Zafir and Khaled's ability to negotiate the curriculum in ways that took full advantage of both the second-language acquisition process and their own interests, facilitated assessments of their growth and progress that were far more revealing of their assets than any norm-referenced checklist. Further, revisiting the 'F Day' narrative in chapter 4 in relation to this understanding of assessment demonstrates how Ines' ability to name items in both Spanish and English should not be understood as an example of a student coping with difficulties completing a phonics worksheet, rather as a literacy event that demonstrates her ability to explore the differences between her first and second language in order to discover Spanish/English cognates and formulate cross-linguistic hypotheses regarding sound/symbol relationships. This is an accurate and asset-oriented depiction of Ines' abilities that resists understanding her behaviour as indicative of deficiency, and her literacy as at-risk. These depictions facilitate conditions that allow educators to reposition Ines, Zafir and Khaled as able students and become cognizant and responsive to their literacy development, literacy interests, learning history and 'cultural, intellectual, historical and political legacy' (Delpit, 2003, p. 14).

Asset-oriented approaches to assessment can also be reinforced by setting out curricular conditions that help foster *positive washback* that allows for 'bias for best' (Swain, 1984 in Mendelsohn, 1989). The approach encourages teachers to 'do everything possible to elicit [a] learner's best performance' (p. 104). This includes using various resources to aid the student (e.g., picture dictionaries, charts, or other reference materials), allotting sufficient time to learners to complete an evaluation, allowing students to review completed work relevant to the assessment or evaluation, offering suggestions on how to set about the task, cueing and prompting throughout the evaluation, and going 'off-script' when using packaged assessments in order to make the material relevant to students' background knowledge or to fill any gaps that may prevent them from demonstrating their assets (p. 104). Further, students' experience with the language of instruction and the cultural factors that may impact their performance (language and culture load) are fully considered *prior* to the administration of any assessment or development of curriculum. Fundamental questions that constantly inform *whether* these assessments are administered and the curriculum made available to CLD students are, 'Who are my students?'; 'What resources do they possess?'; 'Are these resources being accessed or ignored in lieu of experiences that may render them deficient?'

A generative approach to curriculum construction and development informed by these questions as well as positive washback may also potentially facilitate a repositioning of students as curriculum informants (Harste, Woodward, & Burke, 1984). As such, CLD students would no longer be recipients of knowledge deposits and pathologized for their inability to meet pre-established expectations. Through this shift, an emphasis on *who* rather than *what* the child is (or is not) is possible. Furthermore, the reciprocity between educators and students that must exist in order to develop curriculum responsive to CLD students' funds of knowledge has the potential to become realized as a result of this shift. The lived literacy curriculum creates a space where identities and literacies are honoured and flourish. An effective and official ESL curriculum document would aid and ensure that children's funds of knowledge are at the forefront of assessment and evaluation procedures. This curriculum must provide opportunities for CLD learners to access and cultivate their assets rather than transmit corporate values that colonize learning and learners.

Resisting and counteracting these pathologizing processes is also a matter of enacting culturally sensitive approaches to and understandings of assessment. These approaches are aware and critical of the tendency to construct and position cultural and linguistic assets as deficiencies that place CLD children at-risk. Brown and Barrera (1999) argue that understanding CLD children through multiple lenses such as cross-cultural developmental theory, socio-economics and cross-cultural understandings, can help educators perceive and interpret events and persons differently. 'The use of multiple lenses in screening and assessing allows us to access the richness of multiple possibilities and perspectives simultaneously' (p. 36). As such, constructions of dis/ability may be revised by an application of third-space thinking. This space fosters a move away from either/or polarities and binaries (able/disabled, normal/abnormal) into 'structures of symmetry that hold paradoxes together and reflect both poles [of the paradox]' (Bryner & Markova, 1996 in Brown & Barrera, 1999, p. 37). 'Third-space thinking challenges us to see, for example, that we cannot assess development apart from culture anymore than we can assess language apart from cognition or attachment' (p. 37). Unlike objectivist, functionalist stances embedded in subtractive orientations, 'third-space thinking is additive and inclusive, not subtractive and exclusive' (p. 37).

The use of multiple lenses and the cultivation of third-space thinking can help educators recognize forms of knowledge students bring to their classrooms. This shift may expand and ameliorate the identity options made available to students and forward ecological understandings of children that place them in the context of families, and families in the context of communities (Brown & Barrera, 1999). In so doing, constructions of CLD children as unfinished, intellectually incomplete, and defective are critically questioned and rendered impermissible. If the ways in which Pat constructed Khaled as immature, not ready for school, and inadequately parented (chapter 4) are reframed using third-space thinking for example, Khaled's interdependence (perceived as limited autonomy) may be understood as a strength from a family's cultural perspective. Unlike some children who require a great deal of time to develop trust relationships with adult caregivers, Khaled's interdependence meant that he had no difficulties developing trust with Pat or me. As a result, a variety of literacy and learning opportunities that resembled what occurred in 'Khaled's Volcano' were able to come to fruition, further suggesting that cross-cultural differences need to be re-examined within the context of assets. Assessing children using multiple lenses can ensure that 'what may be perceived as a weakness through one lens may be experienced as a significant strength from another' (p. 39).

Brown and Barrera's (1999) suggestion that there be a fusion of assessment and ethics is perhaps the most poignant point to consider concerning assessment and the present educational context. This necessitates asking to what extent assessment contributes to beneficial outcomes for a child and his or her family. Critically questioning the benefits of assessment and evaluation and asking whether children and their families benefit from these practices is essential. In becoming more conscious of the fact that assessments can cause harm as, for example, we demonstrate in chapter 3, we can critically address post-assessment practices and procedures in order to ensure that assessment and evaluation is *beneficial* to students. The time and resources afforded the administration of DRA in the schools and the subsequent deficit construction of CLD students mirrors the provincial standardized assessment occurring in all Grades 3, 6, and 9 classrooms as well as the national and international assessment and evaluation obsession presently fuelling the pathologizing of learners in minority world countries. We have to be critically aware that the focus on assessment is politically charged and not simply a natural part of schooling. Cannella (1997) points out that the very idea that evaluation must be conducted is a belief that is taken for granted and institutionalized. In light of the current assessment obsession, educators need to question and combat the ways in which practices have become technologies of contemporary colonization that are more about surveillance and monitoring than teaching and learning (Cannella & Viruru, 2004). In short, what must begin to inform the discourse of assessment and evaluation is a thorough consideration of ethics and an ethical commitment to enacting asset-oriented practices that honour CLD children.

Language use and literacy opportunities also have the potential to become reconceptualized within a context that values and systematically recognizes and responds to CLD children's assets. Central to this revisioning is the use of and focus on context-embedded communication to develop students' communicative competence defined as a language user's ability to function as a result of communicative settings that facilitate dynamic exchanges in which linguistic competence can adapt itself to all of the informational input (both linguistic and paralinguistic) occurring during interactions (Omaggio Hadley, 2001). In an asset-oriented classroom, CLD students would have access to communicative interaction but not be expected to have to participate directly in the interaction (Cummins, 1994). This would require students be provided 'access to language that is appropriately modified for them, and is issued in ways that allow learners to discover its formal and pragmatic properties' (Wong-Filmore, 1991, p. 64 in Cummins, 1994, p. 51). What is key here is 'discover its properties,' a notion that does not entail passivity or neglect on the teacher's part but rather the use of context-embedded communication that values purposeful and meaningful activity (e.g., focusing on and repeating a language structure such as 'under' and 'over' at the construction centre or the water table). Narratives such as 'Zafir and the Three Little Pigs' and 'Khaled's Volcano' demonstrate how necessary and effective context-embedded communication is in facilitating conditions that allow students' assets to be cultivated and rendered visible. Again, it is important to note that participation in the form of a response or a mimicking of a language structure should in no way be viewed as expected normal language acquisition behaviour since CLD students need to be given *time* to assimilate language structures as they experience their use. This requires teachers to become less focused on production and more attuned to the various ways CLD students communicate their needs and abilities through gesture, action, and verbal formulae (Ernst-Slavit et al., 2002). Teachers then become cognizant of and responsive to the linguistic and paralinguistic features of L2 acquisition as well as phenomena such as the silent period and English language anxiety. This is especially significant when we recall the 'selective mute' pathology inappropriately and problematically assigned to CLD students such as Khaled within chapter 4.

Fostering context-embedded communication should be a central aim in asset-oriented literacy curricula that would subsequently resist the fragmented and impoverished presentation and use of language. Instructional opportunities and approaches afforded CLD learners would be reflective of a whole-part-whole approach which necessitates beginning with the use of whole texts, deconstructing text features and applying and transferring learning into authentic reading and writing experiences (Hibbert & Iannacci, 2005). Phonics and phonemic awareness are therefore understood as essential skills taught through the use of environmental print, songs, rhymes, poems, books, and so forth. These skills are viewed as partial and incomplete in relation to the vast array of skills and strategies children require to further their literacy development. Skills are unpacked and made explicit for the purpose of enabling students to *use* them to communicate with others rather than demonstrate their knowledge about them. What fuels and is at the forefront of this approach is recognition that the 'central function of language use is meaningful communication' (Cummins, 1991, p. 170). This means rejecting the artificial 'letter of the week' approach deemed problematic and ineffective by researchers (Bell & Jarvis, 2002) yet employed by several commercial instructional programs used in many classrooms. In contrast, what informs literacy curricula is what occurs in children's homes, communities, and classrooms. What children are experiencing becomes the impetus for deciding what literacy opportunities are presented and organized for them. Skill-related instruction emerges as a result of these experiences as opposed to being set by a predetermined instructional scope and sequence, which exists outside the context of the classroom and distanced from children's literacies and lives.

Such an approach does not necessitate throwing out materials that isolate skills. Once the need for a skill has emerged from the context of the classroom and children's literacy lives, these materials may be used to support and/or reinforce skill acquisition. The fundamental difference is that these materials do not drive the literacy curriculum, but become an aid to children's literacy learning. Transfer of skills is imperative and therefore, what comes before and after the materials are used is far more important than what they actually do in and of themselves. Further, the use of these materials is tempered by a teacher's awareness of 'culture load' (Meyer, 2000) and the difficulties students may have understanding and using them. Above all, these notions destabilize the idea that CLD students' deficits require cures indicative of narrow conceptualizations of literacy curriculum that construct them as disabled.

Asset-oriented literacy curricula also provide opportunities for CLD students to engage with texts in ways beyond merely learning to crack the code. Rich (1998) and Comber (2003) stress the importance of understanding and instructionally responding to a model of reading that encompasses all the cueing systems or resources students have and need to develop literacy. These include graphophonic, syntactic, semantic, pragmatic, and critical resources. Thus, CLD students need to be provided with opportunities that draw and build on their graphophonic and syntactic resources, as well as their ability to explore the connections they make to and between texts (semantic). In addition, CLD students' engagement with and discovery of contextual dynamics within texts (pragmatic) and exploration of taken-for-granted notions and the non-neutrality of texts (critical) is also encouraged. In line with this mode of instruction is the importance of exposing CLD students to a variety of trade books in addition to the decodable texts that were by and large the bulk of reading material made available to them within the classrooms I researched.

Although exposure to books is clearly important, the instruction CLD students receive must also build on and exploit assets they have and need to develop reading comprehension. For example, the importance of making meaningful substitutions while reading in order to avoid being so tied to print that meaning gets lost, was almost entirely unaddressed as a result of the emphasis placed on phonics strategies. Considering the complexities of the English language and the importance of developing CLD students' pragmatic understandings of unfamiliar contexts and codes, sounding out is largely ineffective in aiding CLD students to read beyond controlled or levelled texts. As such, asset-oriented literacy curricula must consider the variety of resources CLD students have and must further develop in becoming readers. How these resources are rendered invisible and positioned as deficits in narrowly constructed reading assessments must also be considered in relation to the ways these contribute to CLD children's pathologizing. This is especially evident when we consider the links Sarah made in chapter 4 between CLD students' performance on reading assessments and their knowledge of culturally bound artifacts found in assessments such as DRA.

What I have outlined thus far is a crucial shift reflecting and responsive to an asset-oriented, meaning-focused approach to understanding CLD students' literacy development. Such an approach can also be developed through the ways in which a CLD student's L1 can be incorporated into literacy curricula.

Linguistic Incorporation

Although first languages were seldomly used as literacy curriculum resources, there were exceptions. Michelle, the ESL teacher at Elmwood, for example, often began her ESL sessions by taking the children from their classrooms and greeting them with a word she had learned in their languages or by drawing on their L1 knowledge. Beginning the sessions in this manner seemed to give the children permission to code switch into their L1 when they needed or wanted to. The following story from my second visit to Elmwood depicts the environment fostered by Michelle.

Uno, Dos, Tres, Cuatro

Michelle came to the door to pick up the ESL students. She greeted all of them and then looked directly at Ines who was standing at the front of the line and said, 'hola.' Ines smileed back at her and cheerfully responded, 'hola.' Michelle asked Ines if she would like to count all the children in Spanish to make sure everyone was present. Ines agreed and counted, 'Uno, Dos, Tres, Cuatro' as we made our way to the ESL room. Michelle echoed Ines, told her she was taking Spanish lessons, and asked for her help in learning the language. She then asked Janna if she would like to count in Albanian and Janna obliged. This continued with Kamwi and Nomali until we entered the ESL room.

On 'E' day Michelle delivered a phonics lesson similar to that described in the 'F Day' and 'R Day' narratives described in chapter 4. At the end of the lesson Michelle asked the students to think of words that began with 'E' and opened a picture dictionary to the 'E' page to aid them. Ines looked at the pictures carefully, but did not respond. Michelle pointed to a picture of an egg and said: 'What's this?' Ines paused thoughtfully and said, 'huevo.' Michelle affirmed her answer and added, 'Oh, in Spanish this is a huevo. In English it's called an egg.' Ines repeated 'egg.' Michelle asked her what letter it started with and Ines replied 'E.' Michelle then took a piece of paper and drew a picture of an egg and wrote the letter E under it. She then asked the students what letters should follow, and with their collective help, continued to label her egg illustration. She then told the students they would also be drawing and labeling pictures of things that began with 'E.' She provided each of them a picture dictionary to help with the task.

As I began working with Ines and Janna, Ines pointed to an elephant and said, 'elefante.' I repeated what she had taught me and pointed out how similar the word was in English. She drew a picture of an elephant and as she finished its ears, Michelle pointed to her picture and said, 'This begins with 'E' as well and you have two of them.' Michelle tugged on her own ear lobe to give Ines a clue. Ines said, 'oreja' and we both affirmed her response. Michelle added, 'In English it's called an ear.' She then wrote the word 'ear' on Ines' sheet with an arrow pointing towards the ears on Ines's elephant. Ines then pointed to the tusk in the elephant picture and said, 'colmillo.' Once again, I greeted her response positively and repeated the word in English for her. Janna was seated next to Ines listening intently as she drew and labelled 'E' items from the picture dictionary. Eventually she too began to name items in Albanian and then English. Occasionally she thought of other 'E' words in English on her own and then named them in Albanian.

Once the session was over, we escorted the students back to the Grade 1 classroom. I had a brief discussion with Michelle about what occurred and her willingness to let students code switch into their first languages. Michelle believed it is 'fair enough' to do so because they were learning English. She also recognizeed that some of them have fairly well developed skills in both languages and wanted to draw on that.

I entered the classroom as the students were preparing for snack and then recess. I opened my notebook and began recording what had just transpired. Ines wandered over to me and asked what I was writing. She asked me whether she could write in my notebook. I handed it to her and she drew a picture of a man. I asked her who it was and she replied, 'you.' Underneath the picture she wrote, 'man' and 'ombra' and demonstrated her conventional and phonetic spelling prowess in English and Spanish. Her text also reflected the structure of the bilingual books she had enjoyed co-reading during one-on-one and whole class interactions.

I responded to the benefits students gained when their L1 was accessed and to the extensive monolingualism I observed, by planning experiences that attempted to access students' L1 knowledge. I did this when teachers voluntarily gave me instructional time to do so. Bilingual books as well as chimes and songs that drew on students' L1 were used as recources that facilitated L1 use in the classroom and helped CLD students negotiate the literacy curriculum. Sarah (the Grade 1 teacher at Norman Bethune) provided me with the most instructional time to respond to students' cultural and linguistic diversity; eventually she scheduled a portion of the day for me to work with the class during my visits.

By January, I felt comfortable enough to ask Sarah whether she would think about using multilingual environmental print in her classroom. She agreed and I made colour-coded multilingual labels in Spanish, Arabic, English, and Polish for objects and concepts that featured prevalently in her classroom (the chalkboard, windows, numbers, colours etc.). I showed the multilingual environmental print to the students and asked them whether they could identify the words. When students found a familiar word they read it out loud and their class-mates repeated it. When the students could not read the label I told them what it said in English and asked for volunteers to pronounce the word in their L1 and teach it to the class. Students noticed when the pronunciation of words matched how they were spelled. We discussed the orthography of Arabic and how phonetic pronunciations of the Arabic words were also provided on the labels. I then explained that the labels would be placed on the item or concept and that the students could continue to teach each other how to pronounce the words.

I kept in touch with Sarah. Before I returned for phase two of the study, she told me that she observed CLD students trying to teach their classmates how to pronounce the various words featured around the classroom. She also mentioned that CLD students seemed more com-fortable talking about and using their first languages than they had been previously. When I returned to her classroom in June, I had similar observations and additionally noted that code switching was no longer just occurring during unofficial and transitional class times as it had been at the beginning of the year. Although these changes to the lin-guistic classroom space were affirming and hopeful, I knew it was impossible and overly optimistic to believe they could combat the lin-guistic and cultural hegemony I had observed throughout my study. I wondered whether my actions meant anything and whether they would be dismissed by critical multiculturalists as window dressing no different from the multilingual welcome signs present in the halls of the schools. I thought about the effects the deficit and pathological con-structions of CLD students, unmodified expectations, and taken-for-granted dominance of English had on CLD children. Were multilingual literacy practices significant in challenging deficit approaches to or understandings of CLD students? An interview with Nomali's mother [mother of a Grade 1 student at Elmwood discussed in chapter 4] fur-ther impelled my questioning. Her suggestions made me think some of the practices I had put in place were not in vain. 'It cannot be overem-phasized that Nomali can feel whether other children appreciate her language and her background because the other thing which I noticed was, my children were kind of embarrassed to be who they are. Because it wasn't cool to be different. It's never cool to be different. But defi-nitely it will help having Nomali share something in her language and somebody remember that word and when they say it to her, I think it will be just great.'

Supporting multilingualism and literacy events that make the most of students' linguistic resources is vitally important to educational contexts that foster asset-oriented practices. There are several ways that multilingual literacy can be fostered in classrooms operating within a multiliteracies framework. First, it is essential to accurately identify languages spoken by students. I encountered many errors pertaining to L1 spoken at home in documents pertaining to the students in this study. Information found in student records is fallible. The processes by which schools gather data and the conditions parents encounter during an initial information-gathering meeting can create conditions that ensure inaccuracies. Teachers should ask the students themselves, their older sisters or brothers and parents about a first language spoken at home.

Once students' first languages have been identified, teachers can create multilingual environmental print consisting of common items (e.g., blackboard, window, etc.) and concepts (e.g., colours, numbers) found in the classroom. Websites can be found to translate English words into various languages. Whenever possible, involve students in writing and placing multilingual environmental print in the classroom and provide opportunities for them to speak words in their first languages (Herrell & Jordan, 2004). During this process it is also valuable to make cognates explicit while asking students to do the same. Multilingual posters, alphabets of the languages spoken by class members, the names of children in their own language and in English, product packaging with various languages written on it, common phrases in various languages and work done by students in their L1 can also be posted and brought into the classroom to create a multilingual print environment (Schwarzer, Haywood, & Lorenzen, 2003).

Teachers can also provide students with texts written in both English and first languages for use in read-aloud, independent, and home-reading programs. When using bilingual books during shared reading sessions, students who speak the language of the book can sit beside the teacher and either read the first-language text or translate what the teacher has read in English into their first language. If they translate, the teacher can follow the text written in their L1 and look for words that resemble what they have read while pointing these words out to the student and the rest of the class. Most of the students in my study were eager to participate in this shared oral reading aloud. In fact, this configuration of practice arose as a result of Ines' desire to demonstrate her knowledge of Spanish to her classmates. She asked to sit next to me and showed me how to incorporate her into the shared reading of the bilingual text. I repeated the practice with other students who also became my co-teachers and consequently were viewed as classmates possessing valuable assets that became explicit and instructionally relevant.

Students can also create their own bilingual books or texts. Although none of my participants had an opportunity to create a complete bilingual narrative, some of them wrote and drew various 'identity texts' (i.e., texts in which CLD students have invested their identities and reflect who they are) (Cummins, 2005). Ines' Man/Ombra offering is an example of such a text. These texts mirrored the structure of the bilingual books to which CLD students were being exposed and could have been extended into a complete book with the help of parents or classroom volunteers with the same L1.

In order to cultivate 'heteroglossia' (Bakhtin, 1981), and foster classroom conditions that create the 'third space' (Wilson, 2003), acceptance of code-switching must be made explicit and its usefulness as a pedagogic resource recognized. Montague and Meza-Zaragosa (1999) have demonstrated the benefits of eliciting responses in children's first languages. Teachers who did this created conditions that allowed ESL students to renegotiate their 'less than' school identities by showcasing their linguistic resources. Within these classrooms, English L1 children began to understand that their often quiet ESL classmates had fully developed thoughts expressible in their L1 but not in the privileged code.

Fránquiz and De La Luz Reyes (1998) have also advocated the recognition of code switching as a pedagogic resource and demonstrated its benefits for CLD children in English language classrooms that often make 'English a prerequisite for learning ... [and] limit students' opportunities to use their store of cultural and linguistic knowledge and experiences as resources' (p. 211). The authors describe various 'acts of inclusion' that address the 'burning question' many teachers have: 'If I am not fluent in the languages my students speak, how can I effectively teach English language arts to a linguistically diverse class?' (p. 212). Acts of inclusion showcased teachers who elicited responses in the students' first languages that ultimately 'provided an opportunity for a linguistically diverse learner to be a competent member and more 'expert other' within an English lesson' (Fránquiz & De La Luz Reyes, 1998, p. 213). What is central to these acts of inclusion is the negotiation of literacy curricula. When code switching is allowed, English teachers also interactively code switch in order to draw on their students' L1.

Improvisation and situated decision-making may allow them to engage and include CLD students by using L1 to support L2 learning. More importantly, students' linguistic assets and identities may become valued and pronounced within the classroom as opposed to being hidden and silenced. Delpit (2002) believes that code switching can lower socio-affective filters that impede L2 learning (p. 40) and argues, 'Since language is one of the most important expressions of identity, indeed, "the skin that we speak," then to reject a person's language can only feel as if we are rejecting him [or her]' (p. 47). Informed understandings and practices that explicitly encourage code switching can therefore perhaps improve conditions for L2 learning while creating 'curriculum that apprises the students of their intellectual legacy' (p. 41).

There are many other practices teachers can develop that access and make use of CLD students' L1. Cummins (2001) suggests that, 'each day, one student can be invited to bring in a word that is particularly meaningful to him or her and all students in the class can learn this word and talk (in English) about its meaning and cultural connotations' (p. 212). Nomali's mother's experiences and her suggestions corroborate the need for this practice in schools. Teachers can also generate a list of words that are commonly used and important to classroom life (e.g., bathroom, coats, lunch, etc.) and keep the list in an accessible place. The Internet can serve as a translation resource. When CLD parents volunteer to work in classrooms or come in for an interview, teachers can make explicit how acceptable code switching is and encourage them to code switch or engage in prolonged conversations with students who share their L1 or their own children. Parent volunteers can also be instructed to help students who share their L1 and C1 create dual language books and other identity texts. These suggestions are by no means all encompassing. Ultimately, multilingual literacy practices should continue to evolve and be recognized as sound pedagogy that lowers classroom language barriers, increases the status of students' L1 by capitalizing on their assets, and ultimately, opens up identity options available to CLD students within schools.

Community Participation

Consistent with the teachings of critical theory that inform this book, what became increasingly apparent throughout my research was the need for schools to be more aware of how power operates within and informs interactions between CLD parents and teachers, and CLD parents and their children. The sacrifices immigrant parents make to come to Canada, in part to provide their children (and sometimes their future children) with a better life, informs why they *have* to believe that schools are good and filled with highly capable professionals who know what is right for their children. The ways in which political climates and consequent policies create barriers for schools to achieve this ideal is distressing and difficult to confront. Those who work within schools need to be sensitive to the weight of their authority and cognizant of how CLD parents often defer to them believing they know what is best. The impact of expertism on family dynamics needs to be fully considered before parents are alerted to problems their children are having in school and remedial attention and identification processes are recommended. Educators need to be wary and more self-critical of what they say to CLD parents about their children and a great deal more suspicious and intolerant of scientific and efficiency discourses that have colonized school literacy curricula and pathologized CLD students. This is especially significant when we consider how school-assigned pathologies can impact the relationships and interactions of CLD parents with their children. This was especially well demonstrated by Farah's mother's concern about her daughter's progress and the subsequent ways she too blamed her for deficiencies documented in her report card.

A lack of attention to power was also evident in the expectations schools had of CLD parents. Home reading programs, homework, and important information was sent home with little regard for CLD parents' English proficiency. This often reinforced teachers' understandings of CLD parents as unable and unwilling to be involved with school matters. What needs to be questioned is the utility of sending materials home written in English with the expectation that they will be understood, completed, and returned. Although literacy practices such as dual-language book-based home reading programs and homework that capitalizes on students L1 are options that address this issue, what needs serious consideration is the allocation of resources to translation services. As previously mentioned, schools in North America and internationally are and will continue to be progressively more diverse. School district central offices can forge positive and productive relationships with parents when important information that affects parental interaction with schools is sent home in first languages. Additionally, the scheduling of interviews to avoid conflict with major religious holidays such as Eid is not only respectful to CLD parents but also helps forge the links educators want between schools and parents.

What also needs to be more fully appreciated are the impediments to CLD parents' participation. When CLD parents are involved in schools, whether it be on committees or in volunteering their time in their child's classroom, their participation needs to be negotiated and the funds of knowledge they posses need to be recognized and accessed. To this end, it would be advantageous to tap into parents' linguistic and cultural resources and involve them more in the biliteracy of the children who speak their language. Opportunities for co-creation of the various types of identity texts mentioned earlier become vast within a classroom that makes CLD parents valuable resources rather than just more hands to carry out menial or pedagogically impoverished tasks. This recognition and accessing of assets was most apparent in Pat's classroom. Zafir's mother was pleased that Pat had asked her to teach both her and her students about Ramadan and Eid. She was thrilled to offer Pat her assistance. Zafir's mother explained:

> We worked together to make a story about the Eid and Ramadan. We told everybody that Ramadan is a fast and explained what we do when fasting and that at the end of the month of Ramada there is the Eid. We explained that we prepare special food and some of the kids asked for recipes. We gave the children things we make for gifts at the Eid. It was very nice. Pat told me once (and I really remember this) that she told them about Christmas. She didn't know how to talk about the Eid even though half the class was Muslim students. I made up the balance by explaining Eid to the Christian students. I am happy that my children are going to a school that cares about everything.

Conclusion

Despite the moments of suffering I witnessed at Elmwood and Norman Bethune, this chapter demonstrates there is reason for hope that asset-oriented practices are possible, even in the face of schools dedicated to the cult of efficiency and monolingualism. There are, indeed, spaces where caring, courageous, and informed adults can help children transcend deficit discourses. If we decide as educators to be these adults, we must defy and combat discourses that negatively impact CLD children and, ultimately, *all* children in ECE settings. We must develop and

experiment with asset-oriented approaches to curricula that understand children as at-promise rather than as pathologies. Chapter 8
offers further insight into the theorizing that can underpin these
approaches.

8
Conclusion Talking-Points to Foster Asset-Oriented Practices in Childhood and Early Childhood Education

RACHEL HEYDON AND LUIGI IANNACCI

The Language of Us and Them

We like things.
   They fixate on objects.
We try to make friends.
   They display attention-seeking behaviors.
We take a break.
   They display off-task behavior.
We stand up for ourselves.
   They are non-compliant.
We have hobbies.
   They self-stim.
We choose our friends wisely.
   They display poor peer socialization.
We persevere.
   They perseverate.
We love people.
   They have dependencies on people.
We go for walks.
   They run away.
We insist.
   They tantrum.
We change our minds.
   They are disoriented and have short attention spans.
We are talented.
   They have splinter skills.
We are human.
   They are.......?   (Shevin, 2003)

Deficit-oriented discourses that dominate the minority world have divided the world into 'us' and 'them': those who are able, those who are disabled, those who are young, those who are old, those who speak English as a first language, those who do not, those who are valuable, and those who are dispensable. On and on the binaries persist, fuelled by people's fears of losing privilege in these 'more dangerous times' (Lubeck, 2000, p. 278), an era when the bottom line is what matters most and in some cases is all that matters. Binaries are made and maintained through various institutions of which education is a major one. Sadly, as outlined in chapter 2, education's ability to live out a 'discourse of social justice' (Shields et al., 2005) or an ethics of doing no harm to the other (Cornell, 1992) has been critically injured by education's perceived importance in the fight against deficient workers. Having been largely co-opted by governments who want to 'ensure schools play their part in rectifying economic stagnation and ensuring global competitiveness' (McLaren, 2005, p. 28), the lives young children live within early childhood education settings are today greatly controlled by an administration enraptured by a 'cult of efficiency' (Stein, 2001). This cult sidesteps democratic debate about public aims in a diverse society by putting the accumulation of capital before anything else. It denies childhood as a time important in itself and unlike the respect for children's work depicted in chapters 6 and 7, it belies its contributions to society. Many other devastating effects of early childhood curricula designed for efficiency and as the corrective for these dangerous times are illustrated throughout *Early Childhood Curricula*.

What many of these effects have in common is the creation and protection of the 'normate' (Thomson, 1997, p. 8). What is this normate? Ironically, as demonstrated through chapter 1's description of who gets pathologized it is unfixed and to varying degrees, situational. There are, however, some constants in its application: children living in poverty, children whose L1 is a language other than English, persons of colour, persons whose bodies are not like most others' bodies. Such groups are positioned as 'them' and their every move is perceived through the lens of pathology or potential pathology. The position of 'them' is dehumanizing; one has to fight an uphill battle for agency and for an identity built on one's 'funds of knowledge' (Moll, 1992). Moreover, education premised on functionalist psychology's deficit-driven discourses constructs difference as a pathology within the child (or parent) and does not acknowledge the role and responsibilities of social structures or institutions themselves in children's struggles. For example, what are the effects of culturally inappropriate curricula? Returning to the cases of the Navajo, Maori, and Bedouin youth in Shields et al.'s (2005) *Pathologizing Practices*, there is a sad sameness in the studies even though the people are diverse and geographically remote from each other. In looking at schools in the United States, Israel, and New Zealand, the researchers found, just as we have in Canada, that within these settings 'agency–the purposeful engagement of actors in any particular context–was largely eroded' (pp. 127–128) for the people who were 'minoritized' (Shields et al., 2005, p. 26) or in Shevin's (2003) terms, those minoritized were rendered a 'them.'

Our Responsibility to Others

What has plagued us throughout our research, the actual writing of this book, and our daily interactions with children and their families has been the breathtaking acknowledgement that while we were once both a 'them,' today as educators we are now an 'us.' This move has meant a shift in power, privilege, and (perhaps most difficult to negotiate) in identity. In trying to grapple with these changes, Rachel (2002) wrote the following narrative:

PRACTICE-TEACHING

'... bite your tongue'
'... I'm going to wash your mouth out with soap'
'... be still before the Lord'
   But God gave me a mouth, a tongue, a throat, and eyes that see the wrong in the world, so I can't stay quiet. I am never staying quiet (in my own house anyway) – a curse or a blessing, depending on how you see it. This is a curse from my butt's point of view, for as a child, it was always getting a lickin' from my nonna: 'You just never know when to shut your mouth young lady.'
   I am practice teaching. (Don't worry, it's not the real thing as the name seems to suggest.) There is a student in the classroom called C, and she thinks she has a lovely name. Everyone else knows that it isn't: everyone else knows that it's a white trash name. In countless neighbourhoods like the ones I've lived in there must be dozens of Cs: the outcome of too many poor, bloated-bellied women watching soap operas and believing, hoping, praying, that there is magic in a name and justice in the world.
   Coming into Mr. X's classroom for my first placement, I am forewarned

about C. She is a problem for all of her teachers, and everyone knows about her family, since various siblings are scattered throughout the school. No one need have mentioned anything; I recognize her almost instantly.

It is my first division meeting. I had often wondered what teachers did when they congregated behind closed doors. I had certain fantasies. I tried to believe that they were not true.

The teachers' conversation continually reverts back to C and her family.

'She doesn't do any work in my class. Am I supposed to just accept this?'

'She doesn't do any work in anyone's class. Forget about it.'

'It's kind of sad, but you know, there are too many others to worry about. She's too far gone. Put your energy someplace else.'

'She's not the only one, poor things, none of those kids have a chance'

'I know C has it rough, but she doesn't help things either. '

'She has a really bad attitude.'

'I hate to be mean, but sometimes she deserves what she gets.'

They say these things. These adults decide that if you are poor, raised by your mother, and that mother doesn't spend every minute of every day doing penance for her mistakes, then you aren't worth the time.

I sit there, listen, and I nod my head in agreement, because the needle of shame has sewn the thread of humiliation tightly through my lips. Once it was me they used to speak about this way.

I'm in the alcove of the hallway, and I see them. It's snowing outside, and I hear the violence of the wind, despite the noise of the children from the playground. Mr. X, who's on hall duty has C up against the wall. She is small, and he is big.

'I said, what are you doing in here, C? You know the rules, you're not allowed inside until the bell rings.'

'They took my boots. They took my tights offa me. I'm cold, so I had to come in.' Her legs are bone-bare, transparent. She clutches a pair of white plastic cowboy boots, and her naked feet are painful to look at.

'For God's sake C, why did you let them do that? Uh? I want an answer. Why do you let people push you around like that?' He hunches over her little body. She sobs now. She sobs, and her body shakes.

Between gulps for air she manages, 'I don't let them. Why is everyone so mean to me? Everyone picks on me.'

'You let them, C.' If you didn't let them, they couldn't do it. You got that? You need to toughen up. Stop being such a baby. Now put your boots on.' Putting on her boots is an ordeal. Hands and feet are numb; the plastic of the boots is unforgiving. 'Get them on, C. Come on now, I don't have all day.'

She tries. It is hard. And I know, as I watch – wanting to throw up – that having that man looking at you, hunched over you, so close, is the hardest thing of all. So I oversee and do nothing.

Having privilege means bearing responsibility not *for* but *to* the other. Our teaching, research, and personal lives have become joined in the response to the 'face' of the suffering other (Levinas & Kearney, 1986). *Early Childhood Curricula* is one attempt to unsew our lips and to say 'No' to Mr. X. We are painfully aware, however, that our representations of the children in this book may themselves be violative because, with all representations, there is the risk of essentializing the living, breathing, changing people whom one is representing:

When writing of the other, there is the potential for injury. When [one] pretends that the representation can totalise the subject, one's prose can imitate synchrony and give the impression that ... reader, writer and subject, are walking side-by-side experiencing a shared reality. Cornell (1992) says through her interpretation of Derrida that the nature of language as a system can do this. Consider that, 'the very power to name is for Derrida 'the originary violence of language which consists in inscribing within a difference, in classifying ... To think the unique *within* the system, to inscribe it there, such is the gesture of arche-writing: arch-violence' (p. 51) ... In such a view, within every act of writing, [one] is – to a greater or lesser extent – pinning some things down, transforming supple and generative memories and imaginations into words, sentences, and paragraphs that are heavy as stones. This heaviness stems from the fact that what was once able to defy permanence, is now locked into a complex code. This code is a construct that obscures the original and draws the eyes to a type of false stand-in or stand-for. (Heydon, 2004, n.p.)

Philosopher Emmanuel Levinas who informs the ethical sensibility of much of the book is also worried about the implications of representing another. Within his insistence that ethics must be predicated on respecting the alterity, that is, the absolute uniqueness of the other, Levinas refers to certain types of fixed representations as being constructed through a 'said.' He explains that a said can 'reduce [the other] to a fixed identity or synchronised presence – it is an ontological closure to the other' (Levinas & Kearney, 1986, p. 29). This closure is a position of power over the other; it is a false claim of a complete knowledge of that other. The representation of the other that can ensue is a *de*formed one. As chapter 2 mentions through Fine (1995), this representation can maintain the status quo of helping institutions such as schools where social inequalities are born and raised under the guise of saving children. This can happen when a curriculum is built on that deformed representation. Throughout the cases in *Early Childhood Curricula* and in Shields et al. (2005), we have detected an incredible hubris in governments and individuals in positions of power (e.g., school administrators and psychologists as shown in chapter 6) with regard to children and the parents of children who live in poverty or hold some other minoritized status. There is the sense that the privileged adult person knows best what the other needs and the will of the privileged adult is to be done. We have already shown that children and other minoritized individuals such as the older adults depicted in chapter 7, can be supportive of each other. This in no way negates, however, that structural inequities must still be recognized and amended by society in general and the educational milieu specifically. This necessitates that those with privilege must be willing to distribute more equitably that privilege and be ready to learn *from* the other (Todd, 2003).

In our new-found positions of power, we hope to present an alternative to the authoritative, fixed, hierarchical, objective, and hegemonic discourses and practices of early childhood education curricula found in our current era. We have endeavoured to express within the very fabric of our writing the desire for a humble, plastic, and adhocratic (Skrtic, 2005) curriculum that is generated from children's funds of knowledge. This attempt is manifest in the hesitations in our writing, our inclusions of gaps, elisions, and our open narratives. As mentioned in the opening chapter, these strategies are part of what Levinas (1991) refers to as 'saying.' With Levinas, the hope for representation is in the saying. 'Language as saying is an ethical openness to the other' (Levinas & Kearney, 1986, p. 29). Saying can undo the threads of the said and motion to what resides outside the said. Saying is a means through which one may surrender to the other, declare one's peace and undo the temptation to conquer. In the minority world where children have been colonized by adults as evidenced in the accounts in these chapters and other studies (e.g., Cannella & Viruru, 2004), saying is an ethical imperative. Levinas (1991) calls saying a type of 'passivity.' 'Saying is this passivity of passivity and this dedication to the other, this sincerity. Not the communication of a said, which would immediately cover over and extinguish or absorb the said, but saying holding open its openness without excuses, evasions or alibis, delivering itself without saying anything said' (p. 143). To submit in this way is to expose one's ways of seeing and being in the world, to announce how one is apprehending and treating the other. This is Levinas's (1991) 'pre-reflexive iteration,' a complete revealing of 'the "here I am" which is identified with nothing but the very voice that states and delivers itself, the voice that signifies' (p. 143). Thus, as in the ethical praxis's refusal to replace one authoritative discourse with another, we offer talking points for ECE curricula to de-pathologize children rather than prescribe solutions. We encourage other educators to use these talking points to make informed judg-ments about the transferability and significance of the findings to their own situations (Donmoyer, 2001).

For 'Working Teachers'

Recently in response to a published version of chapter 3 (Heydon & Iannacci, 2005) a woman signing herself 'a working teacher' wrote us a harsh critique. The teacher expressed what appeared to be anger and frustration over the article's insistence on opening up definitions of literacy. We read the letter to mean that our views made things more difficult for teachers who, in the words of the letter, were 'making every effort to *actually* help kids.' The implication was that our work was of no help and served only to widen the ivory tower/front lines divide. Shortly after sending this email, the woman then sent us another. She apologized for the harsh tone of the first and said her working life was very difficult and it was easier to direct her anger at us than at education officials in the government as to do so would be 'dangerous.'

The correspondence with this teacher brought to the fore tensions that underlie our 'everyday/everynight' (Smith, 1999, p. 4) working lives. When educators choose to complicate or to use theories that deconstruct (Lather, 1991), whom do they assist, if anyone? Are the projects of formulating problems and deconstructing ethically bankrupt endeavours? These are not new questions in the context of the 'practitioner/academic' divide. For instance, Lather and Smithies (1997) play with these ideas in their investigation into women living with HIV/AIDS. In their book *Troubling the Angels*, the authors move back and forth between Smithies' role as a counsellor (or practitioner) of whom the popular expectation is that she is to simplify, smooth over, mend what is broken, and Lather's role as the academic which is to complicate, make messy, and to shatter what is taken for granted. We understand the frustration of educators such as 'a working teacher' who witness the suffering of children and who want to ease that suffering, but who find themselves in situations where help is scarce. Yet, we believe that deconstructing hegemonic discourses, formulating problems and excavating the roots of practices that feel like second nature are not counterproductive. Instead, we see, as Spivak (1993), Cornell (1992), and Skrtic (1995) do, that deconstruction is an ethical imperative. Deconstruction can show educators the limits of their practices, make apparent their blind spots, and help them to make connections between the micro and the macro; as with unsaying the said (Levinas, 1991), deconstruction rejects authoritarian theories. This is precisely why Cornell (1992) calls deconstruction 'the philosophy of the limit.' Such a philosophy can therefore help educators to perceive children as individuals and to acknowledge the importance of the particularities of their teaching and learning situations, most notably the specifics of the living, breathing children who stand before them. It is only through this process that we are able to reconstruct practices such as those in chapters 6 and 7 where beautiful, positive learning opportunities can be created for children.

While our identities are strongly linked with being teachers, we know that we are no longer teachers in the sense that classroom teachers would recognize. We therefore stand alongside working teachers and strive to develop collegial, supportive dialogue that is informed by the common purpose, but also by the different contributions that each of us can make. We hope that our respect for the work of teaching is palpable in *Early Childhood Curricula*. We understand that sometimes when we teach children, we act with the best of intentions and see the worst of consequences. There are moments in the book when teacher readers might recognize their acts and feel disheartened. Yet, like Shields et al. (2005) we do not blame individual teachers for the processes of pathologizing, but recognize that all educators, as citizens of the minority world, are implicated in a web of deficit-driven discourses and curricula that pathologize children and can rob people of their sense of agency; being blinded by dominant ways of doing and being is what makes hegemony *hegemony*. Deconstruction, however, can help one see that a lack of agency or responsibility is a chimera. Indeed, teachers are not without power to make positive changes in children's lives. Cummins (2001), for example, argues that 'inter-group power relations in the broader society are reflected in the organization of schooling (curriculum, language of instruction, assessment practices, tracking, degree of parental participation, etc.) and in the mindset that educators bring to the teaching of [in this instance] culturally diverse students' (pp. 197–198). Yet he goes on to say that these relations do not have to determine the micro-relations between teaching, children, and families. The very fact that 'coercive relations of power' (p. 203) can operate through the interactions between teachers and children means that teachers and children can challenge them. On the part of educators, this first means that they must feel their own responsibility. 'When educators see the problems as being outside of their own control, their positioning has paralyzed them, preventing them from even acting in their own classrooms, where they are extremely powerful people. Therefore, as Bruner (1996) suggests, unless these positionings, these theorizings, by teachers and others involved in the education of minoritized children are addressed first, little change can occur' (Shields et al., 2005, p. 151). Readers of this book can see how, despite the ties that bind in the case of, for example, Craig (chapter 5), there were many moments where an asset-oriented disposition could create real opportunities for positive learning in children. This was also the case in chapter 7, for example, where ESL teacher Michelle capitalized on Ines's first language and where Pat's classroom fostered the creation of Khaled's volcano.

Our respect for the work of teaching means that we see teachers not as technicians who deliver a pre-determined curriculum, rather as intellectuals who are in the best position to make curricular decisions. The theorizing we next present works towards the development of asset-oriented curricula and flies in the face of efficiency-driven curricula in order to position teachers in the very way we have just described.

Thoughts towards Ethical, Asset-Oriented Curricula

Recently Rachel and her graduate student Ping Wang conducted an analysis of a Kindergarten curriculum (Heydon & Wang, 2006). Aspects of this analysis may be helpful in understanding asset-oriented curricula. The ethical framework of the analysis drew on work by educational policy researchers Kumar and Mitchell (2004), who found that responding ethically in contemporary education presents a number of challenges. In their discussion of ethics in educational administration,

Kumar and Mitchell (2004) identify three 'managerial strategies' (p. 130) that forward efficiency over ethics. First is the 'denial of proximity' (p. 130), where persons in power keep a distance between themselves and those whom they administer. Second is the 'effacement of face' (p. 132), where relationships are rendered asymmetrical through the creation and maintenance of hierarchy. Third is the 'reduction to traits,' where as a result of the first two strategies, persons in an organization are reduced 'to a collection of traits or attributes that define the expected and accepted location of the individual within the organization' (p. 133). The Kindergarten analysis (Heydon & Wang, 2006) was based on the understanding that each of these strategies could be considered in relation to curricular models with their corollaries suggesting some preconditions for building ethical curricula.

1 'Proximity serves as a precondition of [ethics][1] as 'distance eliminates or reduces the [ethical] impulse because it is easier to dismiss, discount, or discard people when they are out of sight' (Kumar & Mitchell, 2004, p. 130). Therefore, persons in direct contact with children (e.g., classroom teachers and parents) are perhaps in the best position to make ethical curricular decisions.
2 Reciprocal, symmetrical relationships where both parties give and receive are humanizing relationships. Perceiving the other's humanity helps one to respond ethically to him/her. This in turn can create a climate where reciprocity is expected and fostered. To enact reciprocal relationships in classrooms means that teachers *and* children must contribute to the formation of the curriculum.
3 All members of an organization need to be seen in their 'totality' (p. 133) as ethical human beings not just in terms of their 'roles' (e.g., the role of the student or teacher) (p. 134). Curricula should therefore support teachers and children to exercise their individual responsibilities to others. This may mean that 'compliance' with orders 'from above' (p. 134) needs to be replaced with cooperation and sometimes even dissent (p. 32).

As explained in the Kindergarten analysis, the form a curriculum takes can expand or limit educators' abilities to respond ethically to students. While there are myriad forms curricula can take, they generally

---

1 The authors use the term morality, but the way they use it is suggestive of Cornell's (1992) definition of ethics.

fall within one of three main categories: 'Schwab (1971) indicates that there are three eclectic arts for solving practical (i.e., teaching and learning) problems by using theories. One is the ability to match prescribed theories with problems, which often do not match well. The other is to tailor or adapt theories to fit a situation; however, there may be no appropriate theories for many situational problems. The third is to invent new solutions that fit situations' (Heydon & Wang, 2006, pp. 32–33). The analysis expressed each of these approaches as a particular curricular paradigm called the 'prescriptive,' 'adaptable,' and 'emergent' paradigms (p. 33). Using Schubert (1986), the analysis claims that each paradigm is a 'loosely connected set of ideas, values, and rules that governs the conduct of inquiry, the ways in which data are interpreted, and the way the world may be viewed' (p. 170). As an aggregate these paradigms 'create a continuum of opportunities for efficiency through to ethics (see Figure 1). No paradigm is devoid of opportunities for efficiency or ethics, yet the ways in which the paradigms configure teachers, children, and the teaching and learning environment can limit or expand the possibilities for each. Though efficiency may be important, curricula that are on the far end of the efficiency side are more likely to be cult-like in Stein's (2001) sense, because they do not ask critical, ethical questions about the purpose(s) of efficiency' (p. 33).

The Prescriptive Paradigm

As per the analysis, 'the prescriptive paradigm takes a static and mechanical view of curriculum. In this paradigm, curriculum designers work outside of the classroom. Designers perceive theory as preceding practice and thus able to direct practice. The environment and the behaviour of teachers and children tend to be highly controlled. Prakash and Waks (1985) describe this paradigm as the "technical conception" which is "the image of education as rational production, as the efficient adjustment of productive means to determinate, measurable ends" (pp. 81)' (Heydon & Wang, 2006, p. 33).

Tyler's (1949) backwards design continues to inform curricula within the prescriptive paradigm, although today this type of curriculum is usually referred to as 'design-down.' This is, of course, the type of curricula that ruled the educational universes of the schools in this book just as they dominate most early childhood education in the minority world. As the cases demonstrate, curricula within the prescriptive paradigm limit ethical discussions because they are out of line with all

Figure 1. Continuum of Curricular Paradigms and Opportunities for Efficiency and Ethics

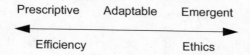

three corollaries. Specifically, this paradigm places curriculum development away from those with proximity to the children affected by the curriculum; it denies the contributions children and families can make to curriculum design, and it configures teachers as technicians. The teacher role then becomes a fill-in for teachers as whole ethical beings.

The Emergent Paradigm

The analysis argues that 'the emergent paradigm' takes a dynamic and critical view of curriculum. In this paradigm, practice is inseparable from theory; they inform and promote each other. The emergent curriculum envisions children as contributing participants of a community and society-at-large (Goffin & Wilson, 2001). Therefore, children are viewed as an important source of the curriculum. Teachers are viewed as both practitioners and researchers; thus, the curriculum supports teachers in exercising their professional judgment. In this paradigm, the curriculum is more a culture than a model or an approach. Empowering children and teachers and encouraging harmonious collaborations in schools and communities are dominant values and norms. From another perspective, the emergent paradigm is an ecological system in which every curricular commonplace connects closely and supports each other (Bronfenbrenner, 1989, pp. 34–35). The Kindergarten analysis places such curricula at the ethical end of the curricular continuum, as it meets the terms of all three ethical corollaries. The curricular examples in chapters 6 and 7 that address the curricular questions what, who, and by whom, all show the power of curriculum that privileges the assets, the funds of knowledge, and the personhood of the learners.

'Working teachers' may question how they can enact the curriculum of the emergent paradigm when they exist in a world that suffers from what we have referred to in a tongue-in-cheek manner as 'design-down disorder' (Heydon, Hibbert, & Iannacci, 2004/2005, p. 317). Strickland

(1994) has cleverly provided a response in the form of curriculum 'cross-checking.' Cross-checking, she says, 'allows students' needs and interests to guide instruction and then uses curriculum documents to reference particular goals, expectations, or standards that have been met. The documents are no longer primary in organizing planning; instead, planning is guided by teachers' professional and informed responses to the students themselves within a specific context' (p. 317). Cross-checking re-positions curriculum as something co-created and negotiated between students and teachers rather than rendered 'stereo-typed and dead' (Dewey, 1938). Curriculum emerges from relation-ships rather than from requirements and becomes a 'dialogue rather than a document' (Routman, 2000, p. xxxviii) and a 'multistoried pro-cess' responsive to the 'dynamic interplay of multiple, ongoing, experi-ential narratives that are continually reconstructed over time through interactive situations' (Olson, 2000, p. 169).

When curriculum shifts to an emergent paradigm, assessment and evaluation must also shift. They move from pinpointing where stu-dents are in relation to a document (e.g., state mandated curricular out-comes), to becoming a record of the assets children bring to a learning situation. The purposes of assessment and evaluation are no longer to classify children against the ideal of the normate, but to be used as an articulation of growth and possibilities within children's zone of proxi-mal development. They can also be used in charting the kinds of expe-riences that can facilitate children's progress. As such, what learners can *do* in the world rather than their lack of knowledge *about* the world becomes a central focus of asset-oriented evaluation (Mendelsohn, 1989). In concrete terms, this process could be used to reorient an observer of Ines in the 'F Day' narrative of chapter 4. For instance, one could now see her naming and comparing items in both Spanish and English as a bilingual capability, rather than as a deficiency for which she is compensating in response to difficulties with phonics instruction. This asset-oriented depiction of Ines's abilities is something that could never be captured by standardized assessments such as the Develop-mental Reading Assessment (Beaver, 2001a). The shift to seeing what Ines can do repositions her as an able student who, with a responsive curriculum, can learn through her 'cultural, intellectual, historical and political legacy' (Delpit, 2003, p. 14).

Assessment can still be an important tool in an asset-oriented approach. As demonstrated in chapter 7, it can be oriented to allow for *positive washback* and 'bias for best.' These approaches attempt to elicit students' best performances through the use of resources, accommodations, teacher cueing, and prompting as well as by providing students with as much context as possible so they can fill in gaps that may exist between their background knowledge and the requirements of an assessment. Asset-oriented assessment practices recognize students' first language as a resource that may impact performance when testing occurs in the language being acquired. For educators to develop asset-oriented practices, they must keep questions such as, 'Who are my students?'; 'What resources do they possess?'; and 'Are these resources being accessed or ignored in lieu of experiences that may render them deficient?' at the forefront of their planning for and thinking about assessment.

Curriculum construction and development informed by these questions, positive washback, and cross-checking may also potentially facilitate a repositioning of students as curricular informants rather than recipients of knowledge deposits who are pathologized for their inability to meet pre-established expectations. Through this change, an emphasis on *who* rather than *what* the child is (or is not) is possible. This shift may allow reciprocity to grow between educators and students or even, as seen in Art at The Mount, amongst learners themselves. The lived curriculum creates a space where identities and people's semiotic resources are honoured and nurtured. This perspective is soundly respected in the work of educators who have taken the time to learn about children and their families outside the boundaries of school-sanctioned learning. It is here that 'contrary to the deficit perspective that defines some children and their families by their so-called 'deficiencies,' the funds of knowledge perspective defines them as skillful and resourceful teachers and learners. In their ordinary lives they facilitate their own learning and that of others and, as a consequence, they have much to teach classroom teachers' (Gregory et al., 2004, p. 11).

Asset-Oriented Curricula in Practice

The Kindergarten analysis (Heydon & Wang, 2006) offers some beginning examples of such curricula, for example, the 'Reggio Emilia form of ECE founded in the Emilia region of Italy' (p. 35). Reggio Emilia 'uses no formal curriculum document and teachers co-construct curriculum with other teachers, children, and parents. Rather than being consumers of curricula, children are considered "creator(s) and producer(s) of values and culture"' (Rodari, 1996, p. 116) (p. 35). Children, rather than being curtailed by the reductionistic semiotic opportunities this book has illustrated through, for example, the biomedical approach to literacy, are encouraged to use many symbolic languages, such as music, drawing, painting, clay, block construction, dramatic play, dance, writing, and so on, to represent their thoughts and feelings. Moreover, the environment is seen as a third teacher to children and as such, educators play particular attention to its ability to enhance children's quality of life including their aesthetic pleasure. Of course this emphasis on expanding children's semiotic resources and providing what might be called authentic or purposeful learning opportunities within a community is just what is documented in chapters 6 and 7 of this book. Moreover, these examples show curricula that do not centre on print as the privileged form of semiosis, but instead enable children to use and refine multiple sign systems as well as develop literacies in content knowledge (e.g., social studies and history) so they can make all of the semiotic decisions outlined by Jewitt and Kress (2003): (1) decide what one wants to signify (which requires content knowledge); (2) choose the apt signifier (which requires knowledge of semiotic systems and tools); (3) decide 'how the sign is made most suitable on the occasion of its communication' (p. 11). Emergent curricula based on this multimodal and social semiotic theoretical framework reject the notion that literacy as reading should be the focus of a curriculum with its corollary that skill attainment is sequential and predictable.

Bucking the trend of curricula in the minority world in favour of a living, vibrant curriculum from the emergent paradigm is the Te Whariki (New Zealand Ministry of Education, 1996), or 'woven mat' ECE curriculum. Concerned about the failure of a deficit-oriented educational system and wanting to capitalize on the cultural diversity of its population, the New Zealand government committed itself to operationalizing a socio-cultural curriculum (Carr, 2003), and as such created Te Whariki. This is another example of a curriculum that offers vision and support to ECE but allows for teacher, child, and community discretion in the co-creation of their enacted curricula.

Te Whariki takes a holistic and integrative approach. In Te Whariki, principles and strands are woven together (see Figure 2) to make the fabric of the curriculum. It is organized by four major principles: empowerment, holistic development, family and community, and relationships. Five strands and goals arise and are *woven* from these principles. These strands and goals are well-being, belonging, contribution, communication and exploration (pp. 15–16). Within this organizing structure, skills, knowledge and attitudes that support the principles and strands are articulated not as expectations that students will demonstrate by the end of a specified grade as is the case with outcomes-based curricula governed by developmental psychology, but rather as a set of organizing principles that help adults conceptualize the intent of a goal and their responsibilities in organizing and managing learning experiences for children. Te Whariki provides critical questions for educator's reflection that constantly re-assert the positioning of adults and children in relation to one another. The curriculum focuses on *who* children are rather than *what* they must become. The funds of knowledge they bring to school are acknowledged and systematically fostered as 'identity-referenced curriculum practice' (Carr, 2003, n.p.).

Assessment is connected to 'developing actual and possible selves (identities)' (Carr, 2004, n.p.). Similar to Reggio Emilia's famed process of 'documentation,' where educators carefully record what happens in the program to inform the next stage of the curriculum, Te Whariki employs 'Learning Stories.' These stories are used as powerful research tools that 'position the learner at the leading edge of his or her competence and confidence' (Carr, 2004, n.p.) and consequently construct and position learners as 'at-promise' (Swadener & Lubeck, 1995a) rather than at-risk; capable rather than deficient. Reggio Emilia with its practice of documentation and insistence that educators go through critical cycles of reflection is considered by many educators to promote 'thinking and practice of the greatest rigour' (Dahlberg, Moss, & Pence, 1999, p. 13). Similarly, Te Whariki creates a shining example of a curriculum and an ethics towards children that protects their individual integrity. What all the asset-oriented approaches to early childhood curriculum we present also have in common is a disavowal of a particularly narrow, instrumental form of science that Coles (2000) calls 'bad science.' This is the science that splintered curriculum into isolated bits of nonsense at Elmwood and that relegated Craig to the status of a pathology that needed to be segregated and cured. And with instrumental science's mechanistic view of learning and pathologizing of difference, this form of theory and its curricula is also what denied children in these pages the right to forge complex identities of *becoming*, because instead, they were only supported into *becoming like* (the dominant culture).

The de-pathologizing, asset-oriented practices presented in this book, including the aforementioned examples of Reggio Emilia and Te Whariki, cannot, of course, be transplanted from one locale to another.

Figure 2. Te Whariki

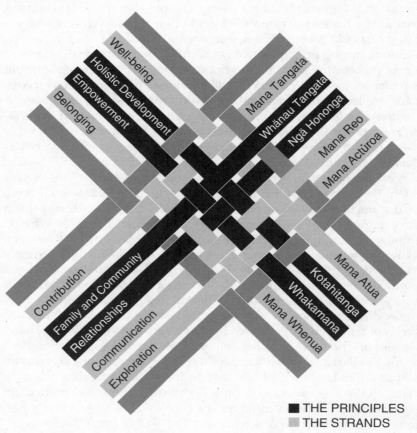

THE PRINCIPLES
THE STRANDS

Ethical, asset-oriented curricula in an emergent paradigm must be developed *within context* in response to what the children themselves and their communities of difference find meaningful. In considering how such a curriculum can be negotiated, we return to Skrtic's notion of the adhocracy (2005) but add that the panel of people who make curricular decisions in the adhocracy must include, as we have already mentioned, children, as well as parents. Moreover, the adhocracy in communities of difference must include deep conversations about diverse goals and values. This means theoretical diversity as opposed to any one group of children being seen as the sole domain of a particular group of professionals (e.g., disabled children belong to special education).

This chapter has been structured to help educators participate in adhocratic discussions to foster asset-oriented curricula. For the ease of educators, we provide a synopsis in the form of a table of the major characteristics of the conditions that foster pathologizing of children and those that foster asset-oriented approaches to children (see Figure 3).

Figure 3. Summary of Conditions That Can Create Curricula that De/Pathologize

Conditions That Can Create Curricula That Pathologize	Conditions That Can Foster Asset-Oriented Curricula
• Cult of efficiency • Childhood as a time of preparation for the workforce • Us & them posturing	• Ethics • Childhood as an important time in and of itself • Respect for the other's alterity • Acceptance of responsibility for responding to the 'face' in a nonviolative manner • Communities of difference
• Children's contributions to society are belied • Abnormal/normal binaries	• Children's contributions are recognized and supported • Deconstruction of binaries by understanding they are socially created and perpetuate inequalities
• Early identification of needs • Fixed • Childhood as grossly manipulated by adults • Needs discourses regulate policies for children (colonizing) • 'Saving' the at-risk (charity)	• Identification of funds of knowledge • Mutable (unsaying the said) • Children as curricular informants • Children's personhood and agency are respected and fostered (de-colonizing) • Minoritized support each other • Structural inequities are recognized and addressed • Includes the recognition and relinquishing of privilege
• Empathy (e.g., I know how the other feels) • Authoritative • Objectivity and hegemony • Teacher as disempowered • Teacher as 'agent of the state'	• Learning from the other • Humble, open to critique • Pre-reflexive iteration and deconstruction • Teacher as able to ameliorate children's lives • Teacher as critically mediating the space between child and state

- Teacher as technician and curriculum produced far away from teaching and learning site
- Education ruled by bureaucracy and top-down management style
- Prescriptive curricula
- Teachers' first responsibility is the curriculum
- Curriculum allows narrow semiotic opportunities (e.g., literacy is equated with decoding) and therefore creates minimal options for self-expression and the reading of others' signs
- Learning as mechanical

- Early childhood education focuses on readiness (e.g., emergent literacy)
- Fear of the other and pathologizing of disability
- Parent a barrier to school's learning agenda
- Students who struggle belong to special education
- Theoretical hegemony
- Monolingual habitus
- Children as segregated

- Teacher as action-oriented intellectual and curriculum created in situ.
- Education created and sustained by a grass-roots adhocracy
- Emergent curricula
- Teachers' first responsibility is the child
- Curriculum is built on social semiotics and multimodality and therefore offers expansive options for self-expression and the reading of others' signs.
- Learning as complex orchestration of cognitive, physical, affective, and discursive factors located in a particular time and place
- ECE focuses on expanding children's practices (e.g., early literacy)
- Diversity as asset and identity
- Parent as curricular informant
- Communal responsibility for every student's education
- Theoretical diversity
- Multilingual communities
- Intergenerational communities

Conclusion

In the end, what we have found through our formal research, our lived experiences as teachers, and our experiences as pathologized children is that educators must recognize the limits in their understandings of others, particularly those understandings that see those others in deficit terms. As educators we must all keep our senses attuned to what children know, value, and do. Those of us who have taught children have all experienced the joyous surprise of catching them doing something we did not think they could do: the new word, the new insight, or the new action. What if we rejoiced in children's accomplishments and also came to see children as 'children at-promise' (Swadener & Lubeck, 1995a) so much so that our surprise was replaced with a joyful expectation that the accomplishment was surely something imminently possible?

When educators are assessing whether their own curricular practices are asset-oriented or deficit-driven, they might consider asking themselves the following: How does the discourse they are using construct the object of the curriculum, that is, the child? Is the child recognized for what s/he knows, values, and is able to do? Is a notion of normal, be it a normal child or a normal pattern of learning, promoted in this curriculum? Educators might also investigate whether they see themselves in the following:

Criteria for Staff Personality Disorder Personality Disorders: Staff Personality Disorder 601.83

A pervasive pattern of condescension, degradation of others, and controlling behaviour beginning by early adulthood and present in a variety of contexts, as indicated by five (or more) of the following:

1. Condescending or degrading use of body language, vocal inflection, and behavior.
2. Presentation of two or more markedly different personality styles based entirely on context.
3. Persistent protection of people in positions of power even if such people have done something unethical or illegal.
4. Employment in one of the 'helping professions', or other situations in which a person has or can secure power over others.
5. Rigidity in application of rules and explanations to other people.
6. Persistent or stereotyped use of euphemisms, jargon, deceptive language, and double standards in language.
7. Persistent use of degradation, ridicule, and violence, either gratuitously or grossly out of proportion to the situation.

These diagnostic criteria for 'Staff Personality Disorder' are available on the website humorously named the Institute for the Study of the Neurologically Typical. This website opens with the quote 'The common belief that (persons) with pervasive developmental disorders are humourless is frequently mistaken (Stephen Bauer M.D. M.P.H.)' (n.p.). Bauer's quote is obviously true when one considers that Baggs, the author of the website, is a person who was diagnosed with autism. Indeed, through the use of satire, Baggs inverts the deficit-oriented, instrumental discourse that was applied to him/her to demonstrate the absurdity of the medical model and the way in which it is premised on ableism. We found this use of humour an apt way to end this chapter and book that asks for educators to deconstruct their discourses and biases in order to see the limits of their understandings (and expectations of) others.

As to our own blind-spots, there are undoubtedly many. As such, we renounce the (re)inscription of any dominant discourse and offer our work as a movement towards curricula that do as little harm as possible to children. This work is flawed, but perhaps this is the only ethical route, for as Chanter (1997) says of Levinas: 'Levinas does not see his work as definitive, but as provoking new interpretations, as taking up a position only to be deposed, displaced, dislocated, by other philosophers who are thereby charged with not letting his saying rest in the said, or allowing it to become a static, fixed, lifeless statement – reduced to a thesis or proposition that bears no relation to the other to which it was addressed, and by whom it was inspired. As Levinas says, books "call for other books"' (p. 70). We present then, the words of this book as an invitation to the other's response.

References

Albers, P., & Murphy, S. (2000). *Telling pieces: Art as literacy in middle school classes*. Mahwah, NJ: Lawrence Erlbaum Associates, Publishers.

Alldred, P. (1998). Ethnography and discourse analysis: Dilemmas in representing the voices of children. In J. Ribbens & R. Edwards (Eds.), *Feminist dilemmas in qualitative research: Public knowledge and private lives* (pp. 148–170). London: Sage.

Allington, R. (2001). *What really matters to struggling readers: Designing research-based programs*. New York: Longman.

American Psychiatric Association. (1995). *Diagnostic and Statistical Manual of mental disorders*. (4th ed.). Washington, DC. Author.

Apple, M. (2000). Between neo-liberalism and neoconservatism: Education and conservatism in a global context. In N.C. Burbules & C.A. Torres (Eds.), *Globalization and education: Critical perspectives* (pp. 57–77). New York: Routledge.

Andrews, J.E., Carnine, D.W., Coutinho, M.J., Edgar, E.B., Forness, S.R., Fuchs, L.S., Jordan, D., Kauffman, J.M., Patton, J.M., Paul, J., Rosell, J., Rueda, R., Schiller, E, Skrtic, T.M., & Wong, J. (2000). Bridging the special education divide. *Remedial and Special Education, 21*(5), 258–267.

Arnove, R.F. (2005). To what ends: Educational reform around the world. *Indiana Journal of Global Legal Studies, 12*(1), 79–95.

Ashworth, M. (1975). *Immigrant children and Canadian schools*. British Columbia: McClelland and Stewart.

Baker, B. (2002a). The hunt for disability: The new eugenics and the normalization of school children. *Teachers College Record, 104*, 663–703.

Baker, B. (2002b). Disorganizing educational tropes: Conceptions of dis/ability and curriculum. *Journal of Curriculum Theorizing, 19*(2), 47–80.

Bakhtin, M.M. (1981). *The dialogic imagination*. (C. Emerson & M. Holquist, Trans.). Austin, TX: University of Texas Press.

Bakhtin M.M. (1986). The problem of speech genres. (V.W. Mcgee, Trans.). In C. Emerson C. & M. Holquist (Eds.), *Speech Genres & Other Late Essays* (pp. 60–102). Austin, TX: University of Texas Press.

Barone, D. (2002). Literacy teaching in two kindergarten classrooms in a school labeled at-risk. *The Elementary School Journal, 102*(5), 415–441.

Beaver, J. (2001a). *Developmental reading assessment*. Parsippany, NJ: Celebration Press.

Beaver, J. (2001b). *Developmental reading assessment: K-3 teacher resource guide* (Rev. ed.). Parsippany, NJ: Celebration Press.

Bell, D., & Jarvis, D. (2002). Letting go of 'letter of the week.' *Primary Voices K-6, 11*(2), 10–25.

Bernhard, K., Lefebvre, M.L., Chud, G., & Lange, R. (1995). *Paths to equity: Cultural, linguistic and racial diversity in Canadian early childhood education*. Toronto, ON: York Lanes Press.

Bertram, T., & Pascal, C. (2002). *Early years education: An international perspective*. London: Qualifications and Curriculum Authority. Retrieved 27 April 2006 from http://www.inca.org.uk/pdf/early_years.pdf

Bhabba, H.K. (1994). *Location of culture*. London: Routledge.

Books, S. (2002). Making poverty pay: Children and the 1996 Welfare Law. In G.S. Canella & J.L. Kincheloe (Eds.), *Kidworld: Childhood studies, global perspectives, and education* (pp. 21–38). New York: Peter Lang.

Bourne, J. (2001). Discourses and identities in a multi–lingual primary classroom. *Oxford Review of Education, 27* (1), 103–114.

Boyd, F.B., & Brock, C.H. (2004). Constructing pedagogies of empowerment in multicultural and multilingual classrooms: Implications for theory and practice. In F.B. Boyd, C.H. Brock, & M.S. Rozendal (Eds.), *Multicultural and multilingual literacy and language* (pp. 1–11). New York: Guilford Press.

Bronfenbrenner, U. (1989). Ecological systems theory. In R. Vasta (Ed.), *Six theories of child development: Vol. 6. Revised formulations and current issues. Annuals of child development: A research annual* (pp. 187–249). Greenwich, CT: JAI Press.

Brookes, A-L., & Kelly, U.A. (1989). Writing pedagogy: A dialogue of hope. *Journal of Education, 171*(2), 117–131.

Brown, W., & Barrera, I. (1999). Enduring problems in assessment: The persistent challenges of cultural dynamics and family issues. *Journal of Infants and Young Children, 12*(1), 34–42.

Bruner, J. (1996). *The Culture of Education*. Cambridge, MA: Harvard University Press.

Brynjolson, R. (1998). *Art and illustration for the classroom: A guide for teachers and parents*. Winnipeg, MB: Peguis Publishers.

Burbules, N.C., & Torres, C.A. (2000). Globalization and education: An intro-

duction. In *Globalization and education: Critical perspectives* (pp. 1–26). New York: Routledge.

Cameron, D. (Ed.). (1998). *Dancing at the Louvre: Faith Ringgold's French collection and other story quilts.* Berkeley, CA: University of California Press.

Cannella, G.S. (1997). *Deconstructing early childhood education: Social justice and revolution.* New York: Peter Lang.

Cannella, G.S. (2002). Global perspectives, cultural studies, and the construction of a postmodern childhood studies. In G.S. Canella & J.L. Kincheloe (Eds.), *Kidworld: Childhood studies, global perspectives, and education* (pp. 3–20). New York: Peter Lang.

Cannella, G.S., & Viruru, R. (2004). *Childhood and post-colonization: Power, education, and contemporary practice.* London: Falmer Press.

Carr, M. (2003, April). *Wisnieski award for teacher education: Progressive ideals and accountability in teacher education.* Paper presented at the annual meeting of the American Educational Research Association, Chicago, Illinois.

Carr, M. (2004, September). *Actual and possible selves.* Keynote address to EECERAQ 14th annual conference, Malta. Retrieved 10 May 2005 from http://www.educ.um.edv.mt/computing/Eph/Presentations/ Margaret%20Carr.pdf.

Chamberlain, S.P. (2005). Alfredo Artiles and Beth Harry: Issues of overrepresentation and educational equity for culturally and linguistically diverse students. *Intervention in School and Clinic, 41*(2), 110–113.

Chanter, T. (1997). The betrayal of philosophy: Emmanuel Levinas's otherwise than being. *Philosophy and Social Criticism, 23*(6), 65–79.

Cisneros, S. (1994). *Hairs/Pelitos.* New York: Drangonfly Books.

Citizenship and Immigration Canada. (2003). *Facts and figures: Immigration overview.* Retrieved 2 May 2005 from http://www.cic.gc.ca/english/pdf/ pub/facts2002.pdf

Clandinin, J., & Connelly, M. (2000) *Narrative inquiry: Experience and story in qualitative research.* San Francisco: Jossey-Bass.

Coles, G. (2000). *Misreading reading: The bad science that hurts children.* Portsmouth, NH: Heinemann.

Coles, G. (2003). Brain activity, genetics and learning to read. In N. Hall, J. Larson, & J. Marsh (Eds.), *Handbook of early childhood literacy* (pp. 167–177). London: Sage.

Comber, B. (2003). Critical literacy: What does it look like in the early years? In N. Hall, J., Larson & J. Marsh (Eds.), *Handbook of early childhood literacy* (pp. 355–368). London: Sage.

Coppock, V., & Hopton, J. (2000). *Critical perspectives on mental health.* London: Routledge.

Cornell, D. (1992). *The philosophy of the limit*. New York: Routledge.

Cummins, J. (1991). Language development and academic learning. In L. Malave & G. Duquette (Eds.), *Language, culture and cognition: A collection of studies in first and second language acquisition*, (pp. 161–175). Philadelphia: Multilingual Matters.

Cummins, J. (1994). *Cultural diversity in schools*. New York: State University of New York Press.

Cummins, J. (2001). *Negotiating identities: Education for empowerment in a diverse society*. Los Angeles: California Association for Bilingual Education.

Cummins, J. (2003). Challenging the construction of difference as deficit: Where are identity, intellect, imagination, and power in the new regime of truth? In P.P. Trifonas (Ed.), *Pedagogies of difference: Rethinking education for social change*, (pp. 41–60). New York and London: RoutledgeFalmer.

Cummins, J. (2005, April). *Diverse futures: Rethinking the image of the child in Canadian schools*. Presented at the Joan Pederson Distinguished Lecture Series, University of Western Ontario.

Dahlberg, D., Moss, P., & Pence, A. (1999). *Beyond quality in early childhood education and care: Postmodern perspectives*. London: Falmer Press.

Danko-McGhee, K., & Slutsky, R. (2003). Preparing early childhood teachers to use art in the classroom: Inspirations from Reggio Emilia. *Journal of Art Education, 56*(4), 12–18.

David, T., Raban, B., Ure, C., Goouch, K., Jago, M., & Barriere, I. (2000). *Making sense of early literacy: A practitioner's perspective*. Stoke on Trent: Trentham.

Dei, G.S., & Karumanchery, L.L. (2001). School reform in Ontario: The 'Marketization of education' and the resulting silence on equity. In J.P. Portelli & R.P. Solomon (Eds), *The erosion of democracy in education: Critique to possibilities* (pp.189–215). Calgary, AB: Detselig Enterprises Ltd.

Delpit, L. (1995). *Other people's children: Cultural conflict in the classroom*. New York: New Press.

Delpit, L. (2002). No kinda sense. In L. Delpit & J.K. Dowdy (Eds.), *The skin that we speak: Thoughts on language and culture in the classroom* (pp. 32–48). New York: New Press.

Delpit, L. (2003). Educators as 'Seed People': Growing a new future. *Educational Researcher, 32* (7), 14–21.

Delpit, L., & Dowdy, J.K. (Eds.). (2002). *The skin that we speak: Thoughts on language and culture in the classroom*. New York: New Press.

Derrida, J. (2002). *Deconstruction in a nutshell: A conversation with Jacques Derrida*. New York: Fordham University Press.

Derrida, J. (2000). Intellectual courage: An interview by Thomas Assheuer.

Culture Machine 2: The university culture machine, Retrieved 8 December 2003 from http://culturemachine.tees.ac.uk/frm_f1.htm.

Devine, D. (2003). *Children, power and schooling: How childhood is structured in the primary school.* Staffordshire: Trentham.

Dewey, J. (1938). *Experience and education.* New York: Macmillan.

Dinero, S.C. (2002). Special education use among Negev Bedouin Arabs of Israel. *Race, Ethnicity and Education, 5*(4), 377–396.

Donmoyer, R. (2001). Paradigm talk reconsidered. In V. Richardson (Ed.), *Handbook of research on teaching* (4th ed.) (pp. 174–197). Washington, DC: American Educational Research Association.

Duffy, A. (2004a). Why are ESL students left behind? *Toronto Star.* Retrieved 2 May 2005 from http://www.thestar.com/NASApp/cs/ContentSe... d'1095966966261.

Duffy, A. (2004b). Fears of an underclass: Newcomers to Canada struggle to close wage gap. *Toronto Star.* Retrieved 2 May 2005 from http://www.the-star.com/NASApp/cs/ContentServer?pagename =thestar/Layout/ Article_Type1&c=Article&cid=1096280571875&ca ll_pageid=1096063291893&col=1096063291594

Easthope, C., & Easthope, G. (2000). Intensification, extension, and complexity of teachers' workload. *British Journal of Sociology of Education, 21*(1), 43–59.

Egan, K. (1978). What is curriculum? *Curriculum Inquiry, 8,* 65–72.

Egan, K. (2003). Retrospective on 'what is curriculum?' *Journal of the Canadian Association for Curriculum Studies, 1,* 17–24.

Elkind, D. (2001). *The hurried child: Growing up too fast too soon* (3rd ed.). Cambridge, MA: Perseus Publishing.

Emberley, R. (1990). *Taking a walk: A book in two languages/Caminando: Un libro en dos lenguas.* Boston: Little, Brown.

Ernst-Slavit, G., Moore, M., & Maloney, C. (2002). Changing lives: Teaching English and literature to ESL students. *Journal of Adolescent & Adult Literacy, 46,* (2) 116–128.

European Roma Rights Centre. (2003). *The ERRC legal strategy to challenge racial segregation and discrimination in Czech schools.* Retrieved 31 July 2006 from http://www.errc.org/cikk.php?cikk=601.

Fagot, B. I., & Leve, L. D. (1998). Teacher ratings of externalizing behavior at school entry for boys and girls: Similar early predictors and different corre-lates. *Journal of Child Psychology and Psychiatry, 39*(4), 555–566.

Falconer, R.C., & Byrnes. D.A. (2003). When good intentions are not enough: A response to increasing diversity in an early childhood setting. *Journal of Research in Childhood Education, 17*(2), 188–200.

Fantuzzo, J.W., Weiss, A.D., Atkins, M., Meyers, R., & Noone, M. (1998). A contextually relevant assessment of the impact of child maltreatment on the social competencies of low-income urban children. *Journal of the American Academy of Child and Adolescent Psychiatry, 37*(11), 1201–1208.

Farrington, D.P., & Loeber, R. (1999). Risk factors for delinquency over time and place. *Youth Update, 17*(2), 4–5.

Fedoruk, G.M. (1989). Kindergarten screening for 1st-grade learning problems: The conceptual inadequacy of a child-deficit model. *Childhood Education, 66*(1), 40–42.

Fine, M. (1995). The politics of who's 'at risk.' In B.B. Swadener & S. Lubeck (Eds.), *Children and families 'at promise': Deconstructing the discourse of risk* (pp. 76–96). Albany, NY: Albany State University of New York Press.

Flippo, R. (2001a). The study, findings, and experts' points of view. In R. Flippo (Ed.), *Reading researchers in search of common ground* (pp. 1–6). Newark, NJ: International Reading Association.

Flippo, R. (2001b). The 'real' common ground: Pulling the threads together. In R. Flippo (Ed.), *Reading researchers in search of common ground* (pp. 178–184). Newark, NJ: International Reading Association.

Ford, M.A., Sladeczek, I.E., Carlson, J., & Kratochwill, T.R. (1998). Selective mutism: Phenomenological characteristics. *School Psychology Quarterly, 13*(3), 192–227.

Ford-Smith, H. (1995). Making white ladies: Race, gender and the production of identities in late colonial Jamaica. *Resources for Feminist Research, 23*(4), 55–66.

Foucault, M. (1977). *Discipline and punish: The birth of the prison* (A. Sheridan, Trans.). New York: Pantheon.

Fránquiz, M.E, & De la Luz Reyes, M. (1998). Creating inclusive learning communities through English language arts: From Chanclas to Canicas. *Language Arts, 75*(3), 211–220.

Freire, P. (1970). *Pedagogy of the oppressed* (M.B. Ramos, Trans.). New York: Seabury Press.

Friedman, B. (1997). The integration of proactive aging education into existing educational curricula. In K. Brabazon & R. Disch (Eds.), *Intergenerational approaches in aging: Implications for education, policy and practice* (pp. 103–110). New York: Haworth.

Gallagher, D.J. (2004). The importance of constructivism and constructivist pedagogy for disability studies in education [Electronic Version]. *Disability Studies Quarterly, 24*(2). Retrieved 1 May 2006 from http://www.dsq-ds.org/_articles_html/2004/spring/dsq_spr04_gallagher.html.

Garan, E.M. (2002). *Resisting reading mandates: How to triumph with the truth.* Portsmouth, NH: Heinemann.

Garan, E.M., Shanahan, T., & Henkin, R. (2001). What does the report of the National Reading Panel really tell us about teaching phonics? Responses. *Language Arts, 79*, 61–71.

Gee, J.P. (1990). *Social linguistics and literacies: Ideology in discourses*. London: Falmer Press.

Gee, J.P. (2001). A sociocultural perspective on early literacy development. In S.B. Newman, D.K. Dickinson (Eds.), *Handbook of early literacy research* (pp. 30–42). New York: Guilford Press.

Geva, E., Yaghoub-Zadeh, Z., & Shuster, B. (2000). Understanding individual differ-ences in word recognition skills of ESL children. *Annals of Dyslexia, 50*, 123–154.

Gillen, J., & Hall, N. (2003). The emergence of early childhood literacy. In N. Hall, J. Larson, & J. Marsh (Eds.), *Handbook of Early Childhood Literacy* (pp. 3–12). London: Sage.

Giroux, H. (2002a). Neo-liberalism, corporate culture, and the promise of higher education: The university as a democratic public sphere. *Harvard Educational Review, 72*(4), 425–464.

Giroux, H. (2002b). Rethinking cultural politics and radical pedagogy. In C. Borg, J. Buttigieg, P. Mayo (Eds.). *Gramsci and Education* (pp. 41–66). Boston: Rowman & Littlefield.

Giroux, H. (2006). Public pedagogy and the politics of neoliberalism: Making the political more pedagogical. In A. Dirlik (Ed.), *Pedagogies of the global* (pp. 59–75). Boulder, CO: Paradigm.

Gittins, D. (2004). The historical construction of childhood. In M.J. Kehily (Ed.), *An introduction to childhood studies* (pp. 25–38). New York: Open University Press.

Goffin, S. G., & Wilson, C. S. (2001). *Curriculum models and early childhood educa-tion* (2nd ed.). Columbus, OH: Merrill.

Goodnow, J. (1995). Parents' knowledge and expectations. In M.H. Bornstein (Ed.), *Handbook of parenting, Vol. 3: Status and social conditions of parenting* (pp. 305–332). Mahway, NJ: Lawrence Erlbaum.

Government of Canada. (1999a). *Federal, provincial and territorial governments launch dialogue process for national children's agenda* [Electronic version]. Retrieved 27 February 2004 from http://socialunion.gc.ca/news/99may7e.html.

Government of Canada. (1999b). *Notes for an address by the honourable Pierre Pet-tigrew, Minister of Human Resources Development Canada: A national children's agenda: Developing a shared vision measuring child well-being and monitoring progress* [Electronic version]. Retrieved 27 February, 2004 from http://socialunion.gc.ca/nca/may7–speech_e.html.

Government of Canada. (2004). *Supporting families and children: Government of*

Canada initiatives [Electronic Version]. Retrieved 1 May 2006, from http://
socialunion.gc.ca/nca/supporting_e.html.

Government of Ontario. (2005). *About Ontario.* Toronto: Author. Retrieved 31
March 2006 from http://www.gov.on.ca/ont/portal/!ut/p/.cmd/cs/.ce/
7_0_A/.s/7_0_252/_s.7_0_A/7_0_252/_l/en?docid=004172

Granger, C. (2004). *Silence in second language learning: A psychoanalytic reading.*
Great Britain: Multilingual Matters Ltd.

Gregory, E., Long, S., & Volk, D. (2004). Introduction: Syncretic literacy studies:
Starting points. In E. Gregory, S. Long, & D. Volk (Eds.), *Many pathways to literacy: Young children learning with siblings, grandparents, peers, and communities*
(pp. 1–6). New York and London: RoutledgeFalmer.

Habermas, J. (1972). *Knowledge and human interests* (J.J. Shapiro, Trans.). Boston:
Beacon Press.

Halliday, M.A.K. (1978). *Language as social semiotic: The social interpretation of
language and meaning.* London: Edward Arnold.

Harris, R.M. (1992). *Librarianship: The erosion of a woman's profession.* Norwood,
NJ: Ablex.

Harris, R.M., & Dewdney, P. (1994). *Barriers to information: How formal help systems fail battered women.* Westport, CT: Greenwood Press.

Harste, J.C., Woodward, V.A., & Burke, C.L. (1984). *Language stories and literacy
lessons.* Portsmouth, NH: Heinemann.

Heath, S.B. (1983). *Ways with words: Language, life, and work in communities and
classrooms.* Cambridge, UK: Cambridge University Press.

Herrell, A., & Jordan, M. (2004). *Fifty strategies for teaching English language
learners* (2nd ed.). Upper Saddle River, Pearson, NJ: Merrill Prentice Hall.

Herrera, S.G., & Murry, K.G. (2005). *Mastering ESL and bilingual methods: Differ-
entiated instruction for culturally and linguistically diverse (CLD) students.* Boston: Allyn and Bacon.

Heydon, R. (2002). *Which way to insight? A special educator's search for an ethical
praxis in an era of liminality.* Unpublished doctoral dissertation, University of
Toronto.

Heydon, R. (2004). Writing nonna: A consideration of ethical representation in
narrative research. *Language & Literacy, 6*(1). Retrieved 21 August 2006, from
http://www.langandlit.ualberta.ca/archivesDate.html.

Heydon, R. (2005). The theory and practice of pedagogical ethics: Features for
an ethical praxis in/out of special education. *Journal of Curriculum Studies,
37*(4), 381–394.

Heydon, R., & Iannacci, L. (2005). Biomedical literacy: Two curriculum teachers challenge the treatment of dis/ability in contemporary literacy education. *Language & Literacy, 7*(2). Retrieved 21 August 2006, from http://
www.langandlit.ualberta.ca/archivesDate.html.

Heydon, R., Hibbert, K., & Iannacci, L. (2004/2005). Strategies to support balanced literacy approaches in pre-and inservice teacher education. *Journal of Adolescent and Adult Literacy, 48*(4), 312–319.

Heydon, R., & Wang, P. (2006). Curricular ethics in early childhood education programming: A challenge to the Ontario kindergarten program. *McGill Journal of Education, 41*(1), 29–49.

Hibbert, K., & Iannacci, L. (2005). From dissemination to discernment: The commodification of literacy instruction and the fostering of 'good teacher consumerism.' *The Reading Teacher, 58* (8), 716–727.

Hicks, D. (2002). *Reading lives: Working-class children and literacy learning.* New York: Teachers College Press.

Hunniford, B. (2004). *Early identification procedures in Ontario school boards: A descriptive analysis.* Unpublished master's thesis, University of Western Ontario.

Iannacci, L. (2005). *Othered among others: A critical narrative of culturally and linguistically diverse (CLD) learners' literacy and identity in early childhood education (ECE).* Unpublished doctoral dissertation, University of Western Ontario.

Institute for the Study of the Neurologically Typical. (n.d.). *Criteria for staff personality Disorder.* Retrieved 8 August 2006 from http://isnt.autistics.org/dsn-staff.html.

Jenks, C. (2004). Constructing childhood sociologically. In M.J. Kehily (Ed.), *An introduction to childhood studies* (pp. 77–95). New York: Open University Press.

Jewitt, C., & Kress, G. (2003). Introduction. In C. Jewitt & G. Kress (Eds.), *Multimodal literacy* (pp. 1–18). New York: Peter Lang.

Kalyanpur, M., Harry, B., & Skrtic, T. (2000). Equity and advocacy expectations of culturally diverse families' participation in special education. *International Journal of Disability, Development and Education, 47*(2), 119–136.

Kehily, M.J. (Ed.). (2004). *An introduction to childhood studies.* Maidenhead, UK: Open University Press.

Kendrick, M. (2003). *Converging worlds: Play, literacy, and culture in early childhood.* Bern and New York: Peter Lang.

Killbridge, K.M. (1997). *Include me too! Human diversity in early childhood education.* Toronto: Harcourt Brace.

Kincheloe, J., & Steinburg, S. (1997). *Changing multiculturalism.* Philadelphia: Open University Press.

Kress, G. (1997). *Before writing: Rethinking the paths to literacy.* London and New York: Routledge.

Kumar, R., & Mitchell, C. (2004). What happens to educational administration when organization trumps ethics? *McGill Journal of Education, 39*(2), 127–144.

Ladson-Billings, G. (2004). New directions in multicultural education. In J. Banks & C. Banks (Eds.), *Handbook at research or multicultural education* (2nd ed.) (pp. 50–65). San Francisco Jossey-Bass.

Lankshear, C., & Knobel, M. (2003). *New literacies: Changing knowledge and classroom learning*. Buckingham, UK: Open University Press.

Lather, P.A. (1991). *Getting smart: Feminist research and pedagogy with/in the postmodern*. New York: Routledge.

Lather, P.A., & Smithies, C. (1997). *Troubling the angels: Women living with HIV/AIDS*. Boulder, CO: Westview Press.

Lavigne, J.V., Arend, R., Rosenbaum, D., Binns, H. J., Christoffel, K.K., & Gibbons, R.D. (1998). Psychiatric disorders with onset in the preschool years I: Stability of diagnosis. *Journal of the American Academy of Child and Adolescent Psychiatry, 37*(12), 1246–1254.

Learning Disabilities Association of Ontario. (n.d.). *Promoting early intervention* [electronic version]. Retrieved 1 May 2006 from http://ldao.ca/resources/education/pei/index.php.

Lemann, N. (2002, 28 March). The president's big test. *Frontline*. Retrieved 10 May 2004 from http://www.pbs.org/wgbh/pages/frontline/shows/schools/nochil d/lemann.html.

Levinas, E. (1991). *Otherwise than being or beyond essence*. (A. Lingis, Trans.). Boston: Kluwer Academic Publishers.

Levinas, E., & Kearney, R. (1986). Dialogue with Emmanuel Levinas. In R. Cohen (Ed.), *Face to face with Levinas* (pp. 13–33). Albany: State University of New York Press.

Lewison, M., Seely Flint, A., & Van Sluys, K. (2002). Taking on critical literacy: The journey of newcomers and novices. *Language Arts, 79*(5), 382–392.

Lipson, M.Y., & Wixson, K.K. (2003). *Assessment and instruction of reading and writing difficulty: An interactive approach* (3rd ed.). Boston: Allyn & Bacon.

Lloyd, S. (1992). *The jolly phonics handbook*. Chigwell, UK: Jolly Learning.

Lubeck, S. (2000). On reassessing the relevance of the child development knowledge base to education: A response. *Human Development, 43*(4/5), 273–278.

Luke, A. (1998). Getting over method: Literacy teaching as work in 'new times.' *Language Arts, 74*, 305–313.

MacMillan, D.L., & Hendrick, I.G. (1993). Evolution and legacies. In J.I. Goodlad and T.C. Lovitt (Eds.), *Integrating general and special education* (pp. 23–48). New York: Merill.

Majhanovich, S. (2005). Immigrant students and Canadian education: Compromised hopes. In S. Majhanovich (Ed.), *Comparative and global equity access and*

democracy in education: Globalization, comparative education and policy research. Dordrecht, The Netherlands: Springer.

Marsh, C. (2004). *Key concepts for understanding curriculum* (3rd ed.). London: RoutledgeFalmer.

Martin, A. (1988). Screening, early intervention, and remediation: Obscuring children's potential. *Harvard Educational Review, 58*(4), 488–501.

May, S. (1999). Introduction: Towards critical multiculturalism. In S. May (Ed.), *Critical multiculturalism* (pp. 1–41). London: Falmer Press.

McCain, M., & Mustard, F. (1999). *Reversing the real brain drain: Early years study, final report.* Toronto: Canadian Institute for Advanced Research.

McCain, M., & Mustard, F. (2002). *The early years study: Three years later. From early child development to human development: Enabling communities.* Toronto: Canadian Institute for Advanced Research.

McGuinness, D. (1999). *Why our children can't read and what we can do about it: A scientific revolution in reading.* New York: Touchstone.

McLaren, P. (1993). *Schooling as a ritual performance: Towards a political economy of educational symbols and gestures.* New York: Routledge.

McLaren, P. (1994). White terror and oppositional agency: Towards a critical multiculturalism. In D.T. Goldberg (Ed.), *Multiculturalism: A critical reader* (pp. 45–74). Cambridge, MA: Blackwell.

McLaren, P. (2005). *Capitalists and conquerors: A critical pedagogy against empire.* Lanham, MD: Rowman & Littlefield.

McLaren, P. (2006). Some reflections on critical pedagogy in the age of global empire. In C.A. Rossatto, R.L. Allen, & M. Pruyn (Ed.), *Reinventing critical pedagogy: Widening the circle of anti-oppression education* (pp. 79–98). Lanham, MD: Rowman & Littlefield.

Mendelsohn, D.J. (1989). Testing should reflect teaching. *TESL Canada Journal, 7* (1), 95–108.

Meyer, L. M. (2000). Barriers to meaningful instruction for English learners. *Theory into Practice. 39*(4), 228–236.

Meyer, R.J. (2002). Captives of the script: Killing us softy with phonics. *Language Arts, 79,* 452–461.

Mickelson, J.-R. (2000). *Our sons were labeled behavior disordered: Here are the stories of our lives.* Troy, NY: Educator's International Press.

Minami, M., & Ovando, C. (2004). Language issues in multicultural contexts. In J. Banks & C. Banks (Eds.), *Handbook of research on multicultural education* (2nd ed.) (pp. 567–588). San Francisco: Jossey-Bass.

Moll, L. (1992). Funds of knowledge for teaching: Using a qualitative approach to connect homes and classrooms. *Theory into Practice, 31*(2), 132–41.

Montague, S., & Meza-Zaragosa, E. (1999). Elicited response in the pre-kinder-

garten setting with a dual language program: Good or bad idea? *Bilingual Research Journal, 23*(2/3), 289–296.

Murphy, S. (2006). Assessment allegories: A reflective essay. *Language & Literacy, 8*(1). Retrieved 10 July 2006 from http://www.langandlit.ualberta.ca/Winter2006/Muphy.pdf.

New Zealand Ministry of Education. (1996). *Te Whariki: Early childhood curriculum.* Wellington: Author. Retrieved 25 March 2005 from http://www.min-edu.govt.nz/web/downloadable/dl3567_v1/whariki .pdf.

Nichols, W.D., Rupley, W.H., Webb-Johnson, G., & Tlusty, G. (2000). Teachers role in providing culturally responsive literacy instruction. *Reading Horizons, 41*(1), 1–18.

Obiakor, F.E. (2001). Research on culturally and linguistically diverse populations. *Multicultural Perspectives, 3*(4), 5–10.

OECD (Organisation for Economic Co-operation and Development). (2001). *Starting strong: Early childhood education and care.* Paris: Author. Retrieved 27 April 2006 from http://www1.oecd.org/publications/e-book/9101011e.pdf.

Ogle, D.M., & Farstrup, A.E. (2002, 15 April). Letter to Dr. Rod Paige, Secretary of Education, U.S. Department of Education. International Reading Association. Retrieved 11 May 2004 from http://www.reading.org/media/press/paige_letter.html.

Olson, M. (2000). Curriculum as multistoried process. *Canadian Journal of Education, 25*(2), 169–179.

Omaggio Hadley, A. (2001). *Teaching language in context* (3rd edition). Boston: Heinle & Heinle.

Ontario Human Rights Commision. (2003). *The opportunity to succeed: Achieving barrier-free education for students with disabilities consultation report.* Toronto: Ontario Human Rights Commission.

Ontario Ministry of Education and Training. (1982). *Policy/program memorandum no. 11: Early identification of children's learning needs.* Toronto: Queen's Printer for Ontario.

Ontario Ministry of Education. (1997). *The Ontario curriculum grades 1–8: Language.* Toronto: Queen's Printer for Ontario.

Ontario Ministry of Education. (1998). *The kindergarten program.* Toronto: Queen's Printer for Ontario.

Ontario Ministry of Education. (1999). *Resource manual for the special education grant Intensive Support Amount (ISA): Guidelines for school boards, 1999–2000.* Toronto: Ontario Ministry of Education.

Ontario Ministry of Education. (2001). *The Ontario curriculum grades 1–8: English as a second language and English literacy development: A Resource Guide.* Toronto: Queen's Printer for Ontario.

Ontario Ministry of Education and Training. (2003). *Early reading strategy: The report of the expert panel on early reading in Ontario*. Toronto: Queen's Printer for Ontario.

Ontario Ministry of Education. (2006a). *The Kindergarten program*. Toronto: Author.

Ontario Ministry of Education. (2006b). *The Ontario curriculum grades 1–8: Language*. Toronto: Author.

O'Shea, D.J., O'Shea, L.J., Algozzine, R., & Hammitte, D.J. (2001). *Families and teachers of individuals with disabilities: Collaborative orientations and responsive practices*. Boston: Allyn & Bacon.

Pahl, K. (1999). *Transformations: Children's meaning making in a nursery*. Stoke on Trent: Trentham.

Pappamihiel, N.E. (2002). English as a second language students and English language anxiety: Issues in the mainstream classroom. *Research in the Teaching of English, 36*, 327–355.

Patton, J.M. (1998). The disproportionate representation of African Americans in special education: Looking behind the curtain for understanding and solutions. *Journal of Special Education, 32* (1), 25–35.

Pearson, P.D. (2001). Life in the radical middle: A personal apology for a balanced view of reading. In R. Flippo (Ed.), *Reading researchers in search of common ground* (pp. 78–83). Newark, NJ: International Reading Association.

Pellicano, R.R. (1987). At risk: A view of 'social advantage.' *Educational Leadership, 44*(6), 47–49.

People for Education. (2005). *Annual report on elementary schools*, 36. Retrieved 2 August 2006 from http://www.peopleforeducation.com/tracking/summrpts/elem/200 5/elem_2005. pdf.

Perrone, V. (1992). The position of the ACEI: Stop standardized testing in early grades. *Education Digest, 57* (5), 42–46.

Pitri, E. (2001). The role of artistic play in problem-solving. *Art Education, 54* (3), 46–51.

Polakow, V. (1993). *Lives on the edge: Single mothers and their children in the other America*. Chicago: University of Chicago Press.

Polakow, V. (1995). Naming and blaming: Beyond a pedagogy of the poor. In B.B. Swadener & S. Lubeck (Eds.), *Children and families 'at promise': Deconstructing the discourse of risk* (pp. 263–270). Albany, NY: Albany State University of New York Press.

Prakash, M.S., & Waks, L.J. (1985). Four conceptions of excellence. *Teachers College Record, 89*, 79–101.

Quantz, R.A. (1992). On critical ethnography (with some postmodern considerations). In M.D. LeCompte, W.L. Millroy, & J. Preissle (Eds.), *The Handbook of Qualitative Research in Education* (pp. 447–505). San Diego: Academic Press.

Rich, S.J. (1998). *Reading for meaning in the elementary school*. Toronto: ITP Nelson.

Richmond, S. (1998). In praise of practice: A defense of art making in education. *Journal of Aesthetic Education, 32*(2), 11–20.

Rodari, G. (1996). *The grammar of fantasy: An introduction to the art of inventing stories*. New York: Teachers and Writers Collaborate.

Rodriguez, E. (1999). Intelligence, special education, and post-formal thinking: constructing an alternative to educational psychology. In J.L. Kincheloe, S. Steinberg, & P.H. Hinchey (Eds.), *The post-formal reader: Cognition and education* (pp. 391–408). New York: Falmer Press.

Rogers, W.S. (2004). Promoting better childhoods: Constructions of child concern. In M.J. Kehily (Ed.), *An introduction to childhood studies* (pp. 125–144). New York: Open University Press.

Rose, N. (1992). Of madness itself: *Histoire de la folie* and the object of psychiatric history. In A. Still & I. Velody (Eds.), *Rewriting the history of madness: Studies in Foucault's histoire de la folie* (pp. 142–149). London: Routledge.

Rosenblatt, L.M. (1978). *The reader, the text, the poem*. Carbondale: Southern Illinois University Press.

Routman, R. (2000). *Conversations: Strategies for teaching, learning and evaluating*. Portsmouth, NH: Heinemann.

Rozanski, M. (2002). *Investing in public education: Advancing the goal of continuous improvement in Student learning and achievement* (Report on the Education Equality Task Force). Retrieved 4 June 2007 from http://www.edu.gov.on.ca/eng/document/reports/task02/.

Rueda, R., & Windmueller, M.P. (2006). English language learners, LD, an overrepresentation: A multiple-level analysis. *Journal of Learning Disabilities, 39*(2), 99–107.

Sandow, S. (1994). Whose special need? In S. Sandow (Ed.), *Whose special need? Some perceptions of special educational needs* (pp. 153–159). London: Paul Chapman.

Schubert, W.H. (1986). *Curriculum: Perspective, paradigm, and possibility*. New York: Macmillan.

Schwab, J.J. (1971). The practical: Arts of eclectic. *School Review, 79*, 493–542.

Schwab, J.J. (1973). The practical 3: Translation into curriculum. *School Review, 81*, 501–522.

Schwarzer, D., Haywood, A., & Lorenzen, C. (2003). Fostering multiliteracy in linguistically diverse classroom. *Language Arts, 80* (6), 453–460.

Segall, W.E. (2006). *School reform in a global society*. Oxford: Rowman & Littlefield.

Shevin, M. (2003). Us and them. *Shevin Consulting.* Retrieved 21 August 2006, from http://www.shevin.org/articles-harmonica.html.

Shields, C.M., Bishop, R., & Mazawi, A.E. (2005). *Pathologizing practices: The impact of deficit thinking on education.* New York: Peter Lang.

Short, K.G., Kauffman, G., & Kahn, L.H. (2000). 'I just *need* to draw': Responding to literature across multiple sign systems. *The Reading Teacher, 54*(2), 160–171.

Simon, R.I. (1992). *Teaching against the grain: Texts for a pedagogy of possibility.* Toronto: OISE Press.

Siraj-Blatchford, I., & Clarke, P. (2000). *Supporting identity, diversity and language in the early years.* Buckingham: Open University Press.

Skrtic, T.M. (1991). *Behind special education: A critical analysis of professional culture and school organization.* Denver: Love Publishing.

Skrtic, T.M. (1995). *Disability and democracy: Reconstructing (special) education for Postmodernity.* New York: Teachers College Press.

Skrtic, T.M. (2005). A political economy of learning disabilities. *Learning Disability Quarterly, 28*(2), 149–156.

Skutnabb-Kangas, T. (2000). *Linguistic genocide in education or worldwide diversity and human rights?* London: Lawrence Erlbaum Associates.

Sleeter, C. (1987). Why is there a learning disability? A critical analysis of the birth of the field in its social context. In T.S. Popkewitz (Ed.), *The formation of school subjects: The struggle for creating an American institution* (pp. 210–237). New York: Falmer.

Sleeter, C.E., & Bernal, D.D. (2004). Critical pedagogy, critical race theory, and antiracist education. In J. Banks & C. Banks (Eds.), *Handbook of research on multicultural education* (2nd ed.) (pp. 240–258). San Francisco: Jossey-Bass.

Smith, D.E. (1987). *The everyday world as problematic: A feminist sociology.* Boston: Northeastern University Press.

Smith, D.E. (1999). *Writing the social: Critique, theory, and investigations.* Toronto: University of Toronto Press.

Smith, F. (2003). *Understanding reading: A psycholinguistic analysis of reading and learning to read* (6th ed.). Mahwah, NJ: Lawrence Erlbaum Associates.

Smyth, J., Dow, A., Hattam, R., Reid, A., & Shacklock, G. (2000). Deindustrialization, global capital and the crisis in teachers' work. In *Teachers' work in a globalizing economy* (pp. 1–14): London: Falmer Press.

Spivak, G.C. (1993). *Outside in the teaching machine.* New York: Routledge.

Stanovich, K.E. (1986). Matthew effects in reading: Some consequences of individual differences in the acquisition of literacy. *Reading Research Quarterly, 21* (4), 360–406.

Stanovich, K.E. (1994). Romance and reality. *The Reading Teacher, 47* (4), 280–291.

Statistics Canada. (2001). *Population by mother tongue (2001 Census)*. Retrieved 31 March 2006 from http://www40.statcan.ca/l01/cst01/demo11b.htm.

Stein, J. G. (2001). *The cult of efficiency.* Toronto: Anansi.

Stooke, R. (2003). (Re)Visioning the Ontario early years study: Almost a fairy tale – but not quite. *Journal of Curriculum Theorizing, 19* (2), 91–101.

Stooke, R. (2004). *Healthy, wealthy and ready for school: Supporting young children's education and development in the era of the national children's agenda.* Unpublished doctoral dissertation, University of Western Ontario.

Strickland, D.S. (1994). Reinventing our literacy programs: Books, basics, balance. *The Reading Teacher, 48,* 294–302.

Street, B. (1984). *Literacy in theory and practice*. Cambridge, UK: Cambridge University Press.

Suárez-Orozco, C. (2001). Afterword: Understanding and serving the children of immigrants. *Harvard Educational Review, 71* (3), 579–589.

Swadener, B. B. (1995). Children and families 'at promise': Deconstructing the discourse of risk. In B. B. Swadener & S. Lubeck (Eds.), *Children and families 'at promise': Deconstructing the discourse of risk* (pp. 17–49). Albany: State University of New York Press.

Swadener, B.B., & Lubeck, S. (1995a). (Eds.). *Children and families 'at promise': Deconstructing the discourse of risk*. Albany: State University of New York Press.

Swadener, B.B., & Lubeck, S. (1995b). The social construction of children and families 'at risk': An introduction. In B.B. Swadener & S. Lubeck (Eds.), *Children and families 'at promise': Deconstructing the discourse of risk* (pp. 1–16). Albany: State University of New York Press.

Taylor, D. (1998). *Beginning to read and the spin doctors of science: The political campaign to change America's mind about how children learn to read*. Urbana, IL: National Council of Teachers of English.

Thew, N. (2000). Race, class and gender. In J. Mills & R. Mills (Eds.), *Childhood studies: A reader in perspectives of childhood* (pp. 131–144). London: Routledge.

Thomson, G.R. (1997). *Extraordinary bodies: Figuring physical disability in American culture and literature*. New York: Columbia University Press.

Todd, S. (2003). *Learning from the other: Levinas, psychoanalysis, and ethical possibilities in education*. Albany: State University of New York Press.

Toohey, K. (2000). *Learning English at school: Identity, social relations and classroom* Clevedon, UK: Multilingual Matters.

Tyler, R.W. (1949). *Basic principles of curriculum and instruction*. Chicago: University of Chicago Press.

United Nations. (2002). Number of world's migrants reaches 175 million mark. Retrieved 31 July 2006 from http://www.un.org/esa/population/publications/ittmig2002/pre ss-release-eng.htm.

Valenzuela, A. (1999). *Subtractive schooling: U.S.-Mexican youth and the politics of caring*. Albany: State University of New York Press.

Walkerdine, V. (1994). Femininity as performance. In L. Stone & G.M. Boldt (Eds.), *The education feminism reader* (pp. 57–69). New York: Routledge.

Weber, K., & Bennett, S. (1999). *Special education in Ontario schools* (4th ed.). Thornhill, ON: Highland Press.

Weiner, E.J. (2005). *Private learning, public needs: The neo-liberal assault on democratic education*. New York: Peter Lang.

Wertsch, J.V. (1991). *Voices of the mind: A sociocultural approach to mediated action*. Cambridge, MA.: Harvard University Press.

Wertsch, J.V. (1998). *Mind as action*. New York: Oxford University Press.

Wilson, A. (2003). Researching in the third space: Locating, claiming and valuing the research domain. In S. Goodman, T. Lillis, J. Maybin, & N. Mercer (Eds.), *Language, literacy and education: A reader* (pp. 293–308). Staffordshire, UK: Trentham.

Wink, J. (2005). *Critical pedagogy: Notes from the real world* (3rd ed.). Boston: Pearson/Allyn & Bacon.

Wolfe, D., Wekerle, C., Reitzel-Jaffe, D., & Lefebvre, L. (1998). Factors associated with abusive relationships among maltreated and nonmaltreated youth. *Development and Psychopathology, 10*(1), 61–85.

Wright, S. (1997). Learning how to learn: The arts as core in an emergent curriculum. *Childhood Education, 73*, 361–365.

Index